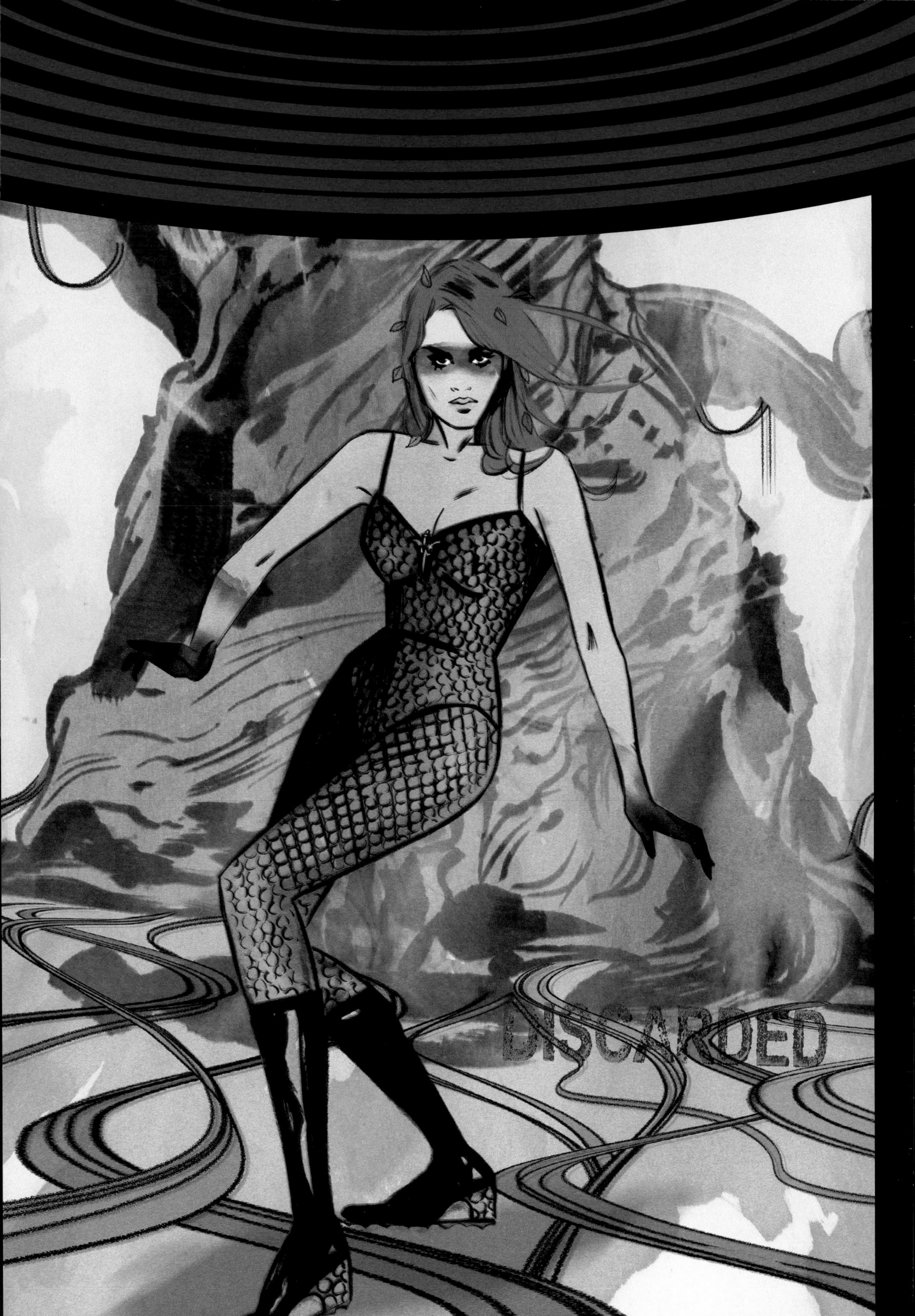



# ALL-STAR BATMAN

## VOL.2 ENDS OF THE EARTH

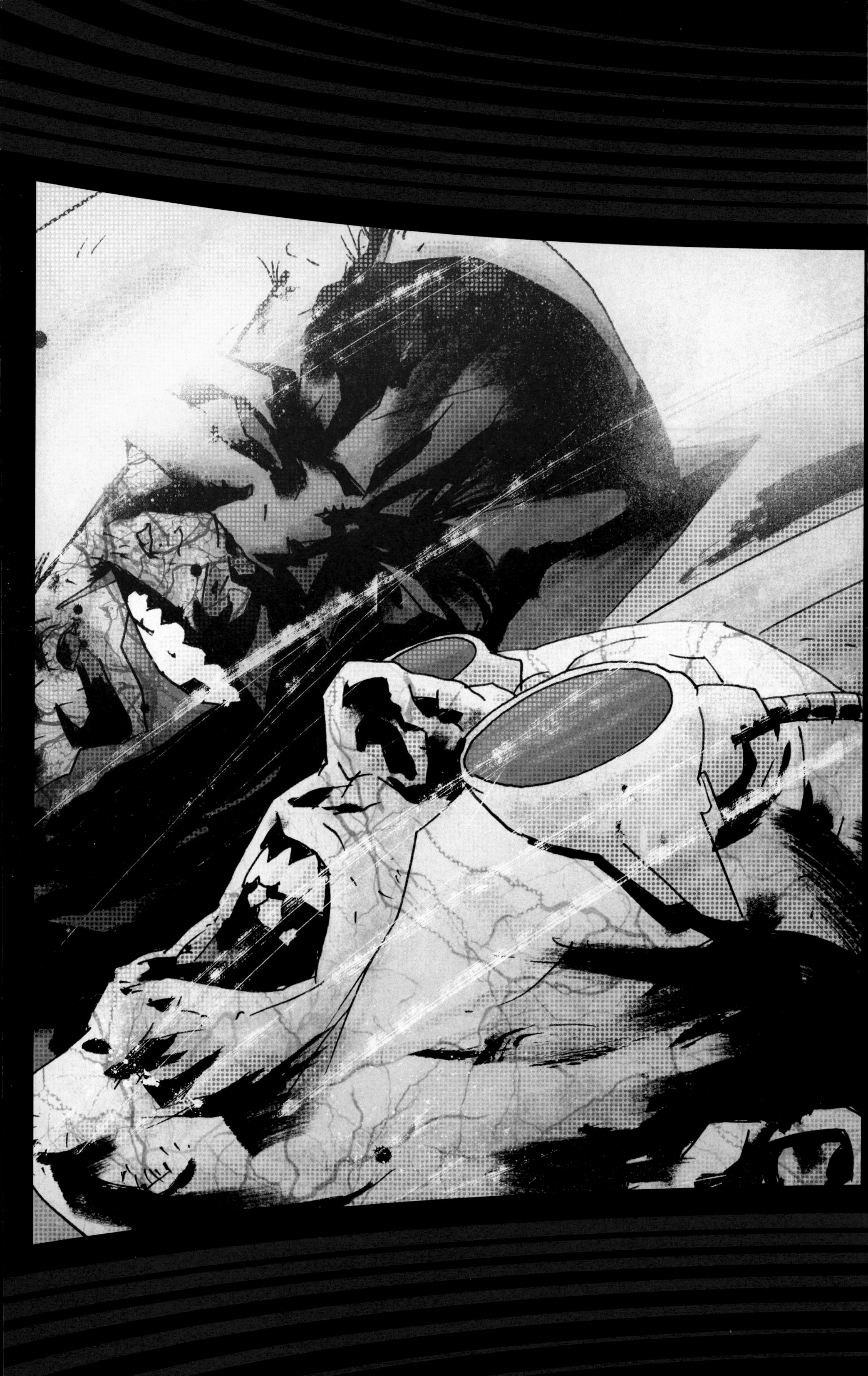

# ALL-STAR BATMAN

## VOL.2 ENDS OF THE EARTH

**SCOTT SNYDER**
writer

**JOCK**
**FRANCESCO FRANCAVILLA**
**TULA LOTAY**
**GIUSEPPE CAMUNCOLI**
**MARK MORALES**
artists

**FRANCESCO FRANCAVILLA**
**MATT HOLLINGSWORTH**
**TULA LOTAY**
**DEAN WHITE**
**LEE LOUGHRIDGE**
colorists

**STEVE WANDS**
letterer

**JOCK**
collection cover artist

BATMAN created by BOB KANE with BILL FINGER

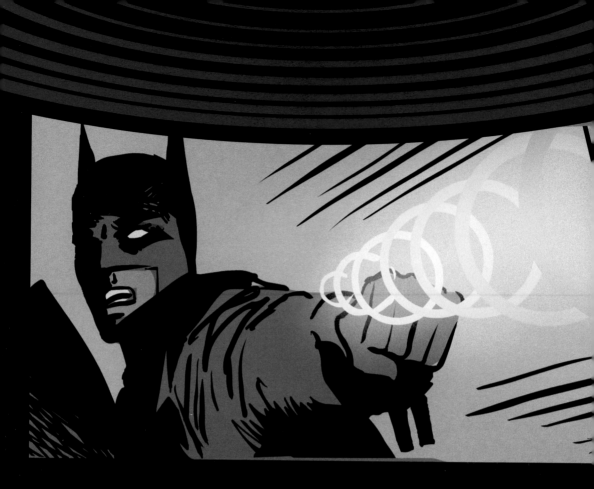

**MARK DOYLE** Editor - Original Series * **REBECCA TAYLOR** Associate Editor - Original Series * **DAVE WIELGOSZ** Assistant Editor - Original Series
**JEB WOODARD** Group Editor - Collected Editions * **ROBIN WILDMAN** Editor - Collected Edition
**STEVE COOK** Design Director - Books * **DAMIAN RYLAND** Publication Design

**BOB HARRAS** Senior VP - Editor-in-Chief, DC Comics

**DIANE NELSON** President * **DAN DiDIO** Publisher * **JIM LEE** Publisher * **GEOFF JOHNS** President & Chief Creative Officer
**AMIT DESAI** Executive VP - Business & Marketing Strategy, Direct to Consumer & Global Franchise Management * **SAM ADES** Senior VP - Direct to Consumer
**BOBBIE CHASE** VP - Talent Development * **MARK CHIARELLO** Senior VP - Art, Design & Collected Editions
**JOHN CUNNINGHAM** Senior VP - Sales & Trade Marketing * **ANNE DePIES** Senior VP - Business Strategy, Finance & Administration
**DON FALLETTI** VP - Manufacturing Operations * **LAWRENCE GANEM** VP - Editorial Administration & Talent Relations
**ALISON GILL** Senior VP - Manufacturing & Operations * **HANK KANALZ** Senior VP - Editorial Strategy & Administration
**JAY KOGAN** VP - Legal Affairs * **THOMAS LOFTUS** VP - Business Affairs
**JACK MAHAN** VP - Business Affairs * **NICK J. NAPOLITANO** VP - Manufacturing Administration
**EDDIE SCANNELL** VP - Consumer Marketing * **COURTNEY SIMMONS** Senior VP - Publicity & Communications
**JIM (SKI) SOKOLOWSKI** VP - Comic Book Specialty Sales & Trade Marketing * **NANCY SPEARS** VP - Mass, Book, Digital Sales & Trade Marketing

ALL-STAR BATMAN VOL. 2: ENDS OF THE EARTH



DC Comics, 2900 West Alameda Ave., Burbank, CA 91505. Printed by LSC Communications, Kendallville, IN, USA. 8/4/17. First Printing.
ISBN: 978-1-4012-7443-6

Library of Congress Cataloging-in-Publication Data is available.



PEFC Certified
Printed on paper from sustainably managed forests, controlled sources
PEFC
PEFC/29-31-337
www.pefc.org

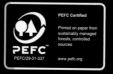

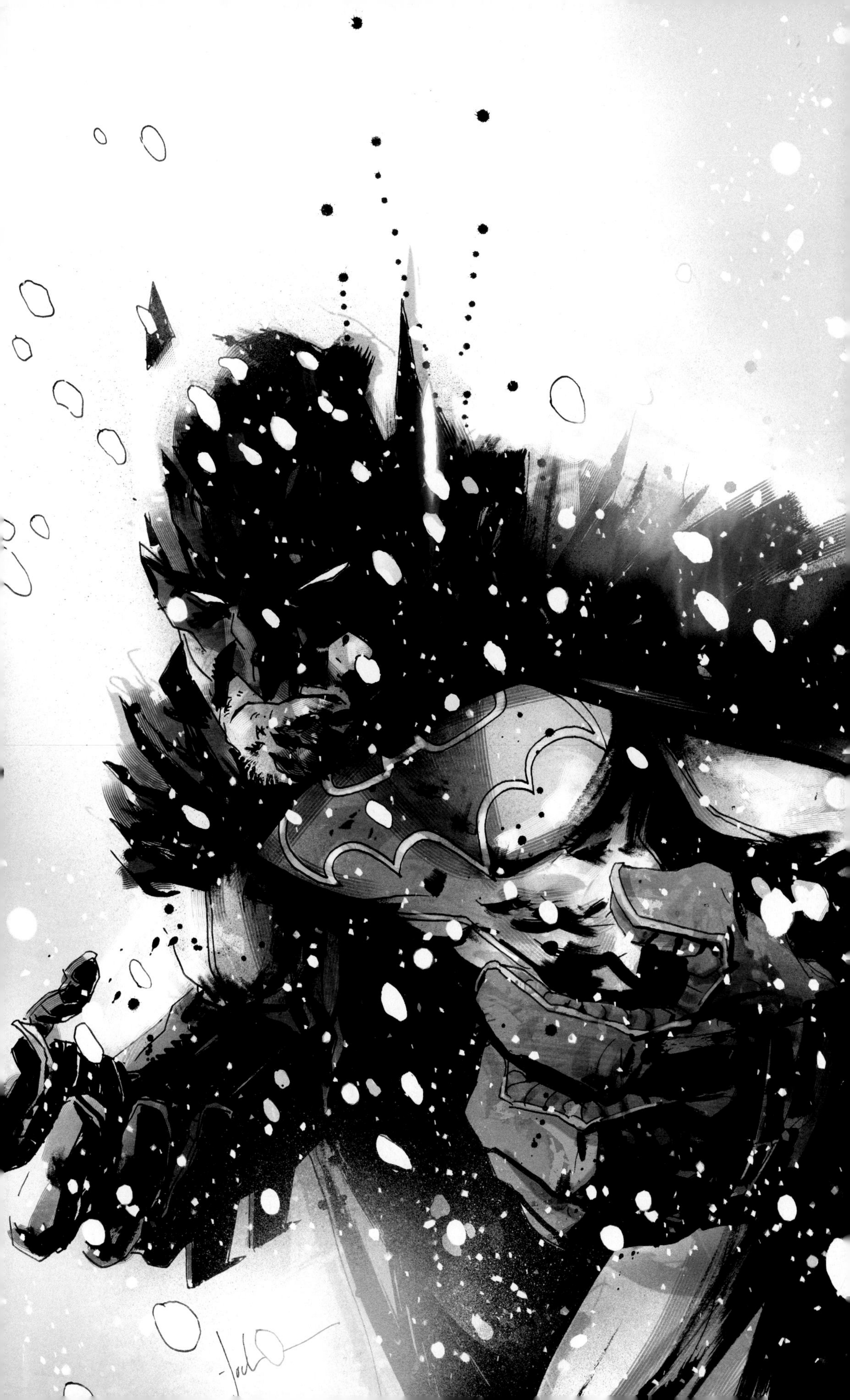

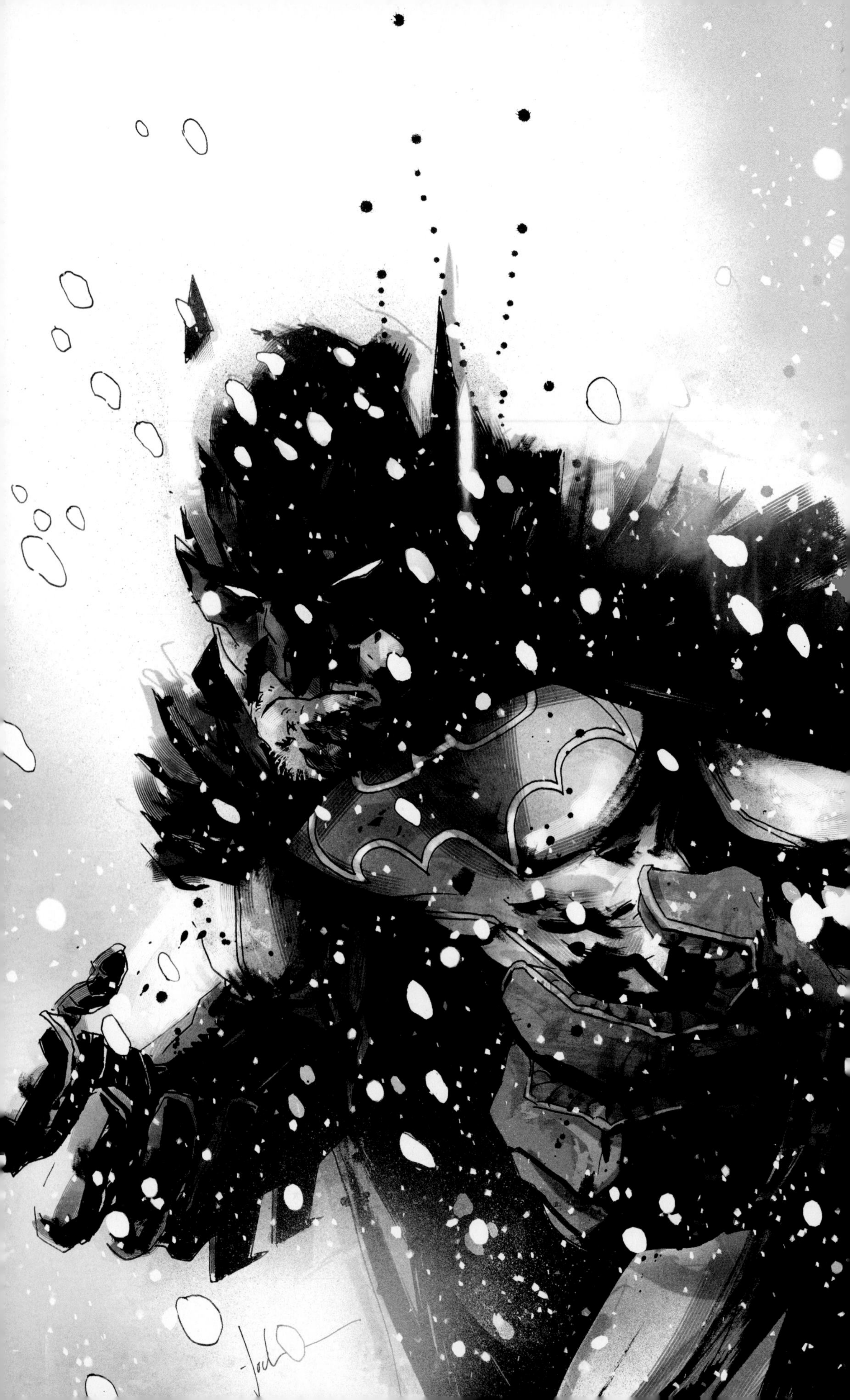

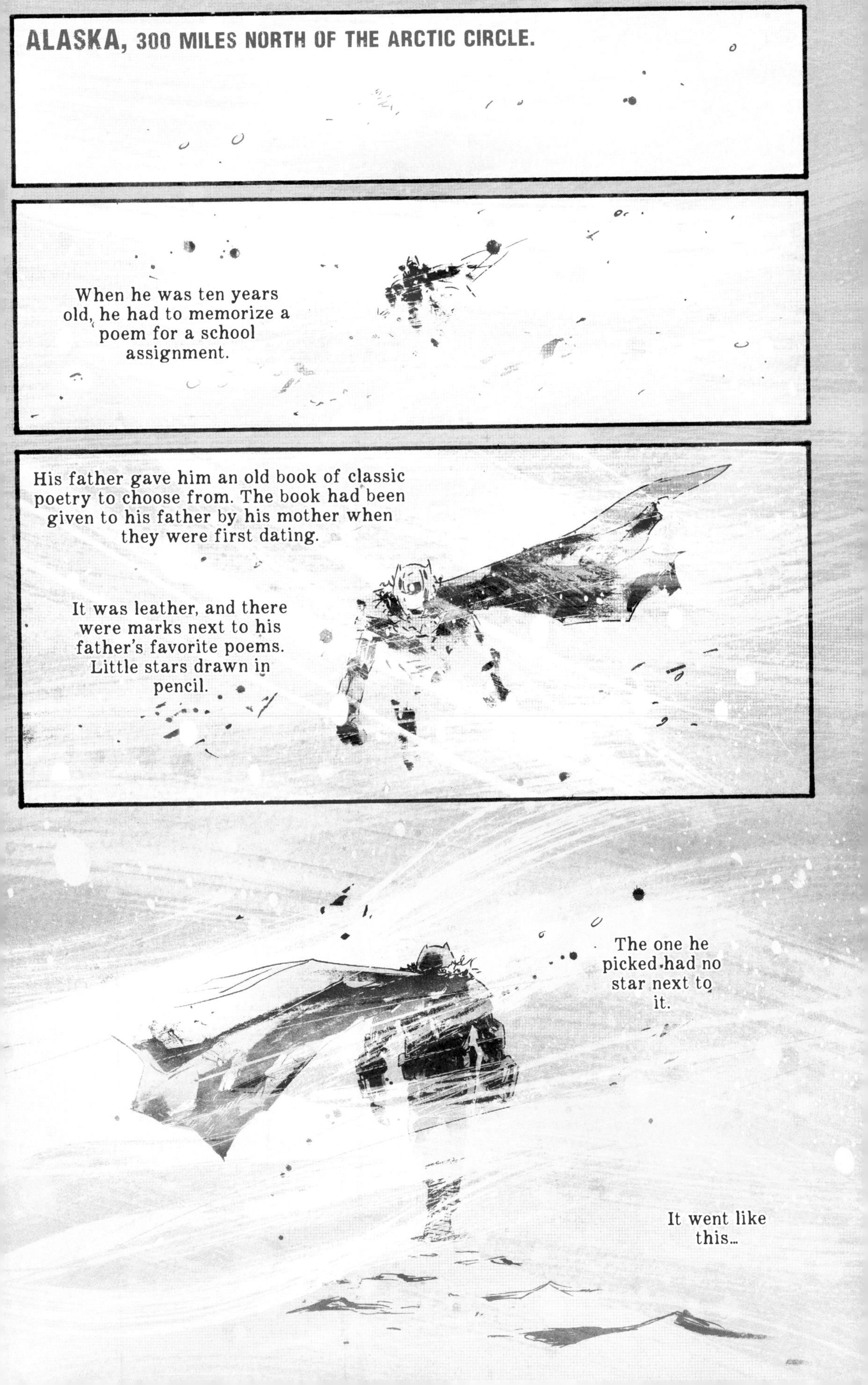
ALASKA, 300 MILES NORTH OF THE ARCTIC CIRCLE.
When he was ten years old, he had to memorize a poem for a school assignment.
His father gave him an old book of classic poetry to choose from. The book had been given to his father by his mother when they were first dating.
It was leather, and there were marks next to his father's favorite poems. Little stars drawn in pencil.
The one he picked had no star next to it.
It went like this...

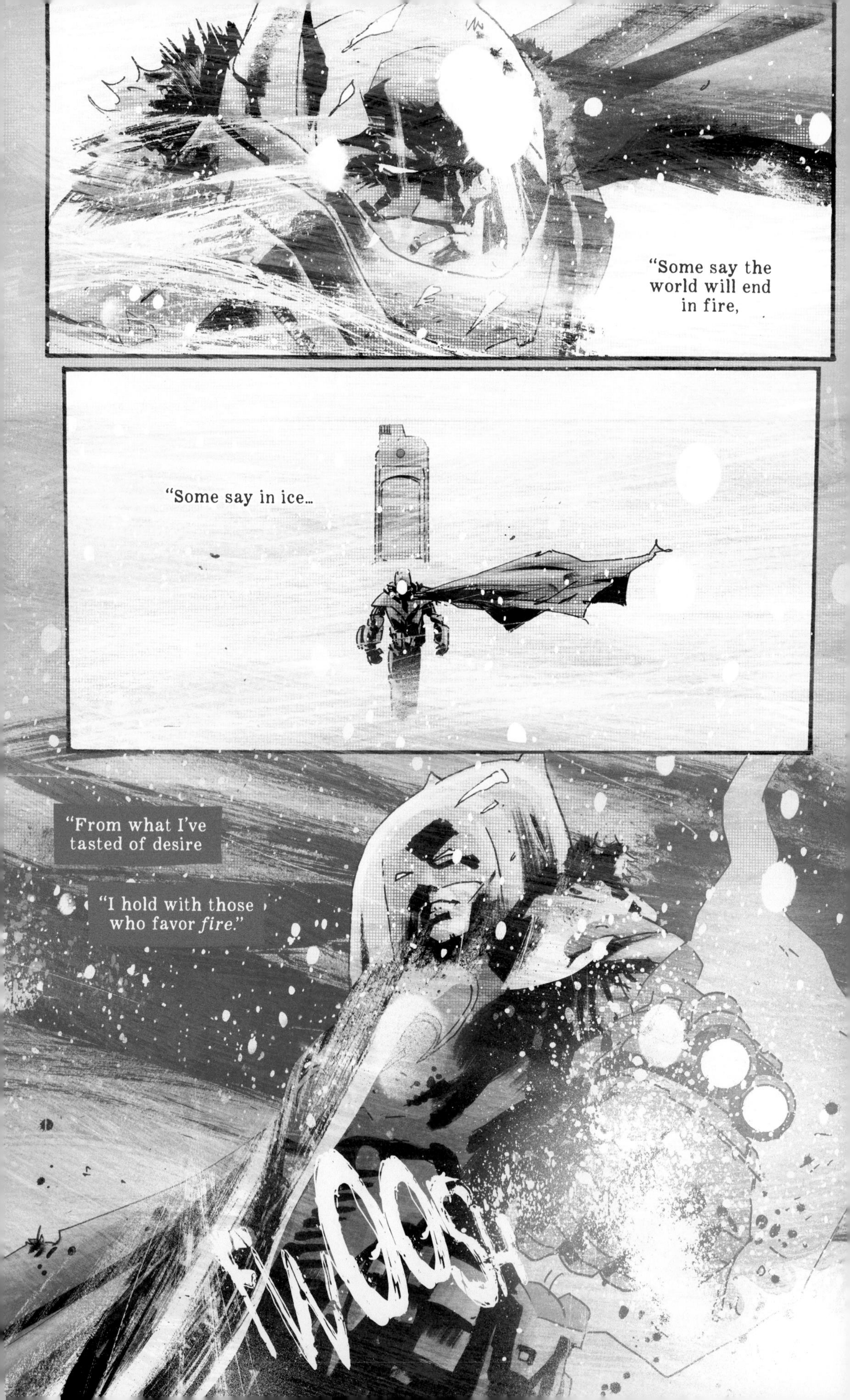
"Some say the world will end in fire,
"Some say in ice...
"From what I've tasted of desire
"I hold with those who favor *fire*."
WOOSH

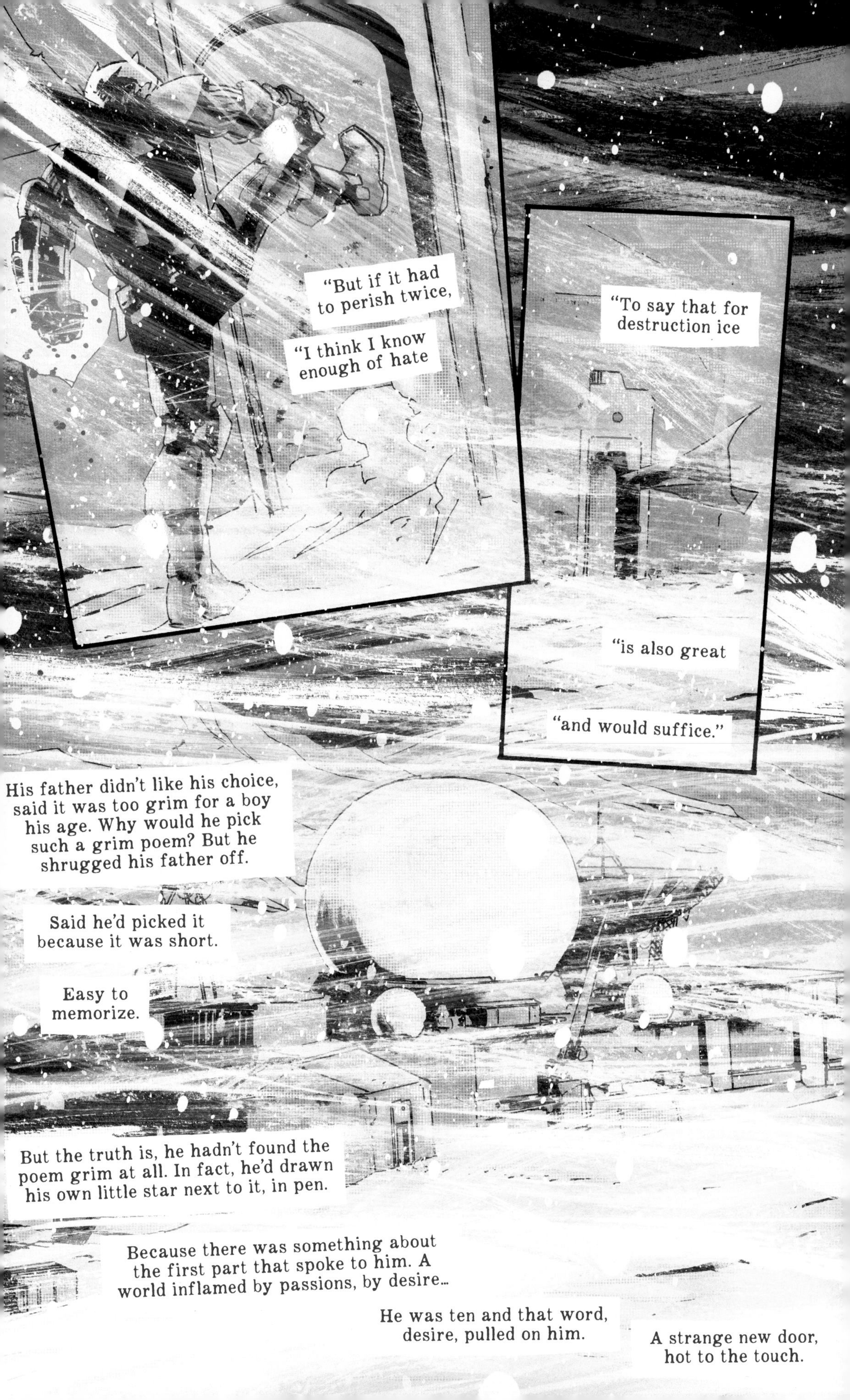
"But if it had to perish twice,
"I think I know enough of hate
"To say that for destruction ice
"is also great
"and would suffice."
His father didn't like his choice, said it was too grim for a boy his age. Why would he pick such a grim poem? But he shrugged his father off.
Said he'd picked it because it was short.
Easy to memorize.
But the truth is, he hadn't found the poem grim at all. In fact, he'd drawn his own little star next to it, in pen.
Because there was something about the first part that spoke to him. A world inflamed by passions, by desire...
He was ten and that word, desire, pulled on him.
A strange new door, hot to the touch.

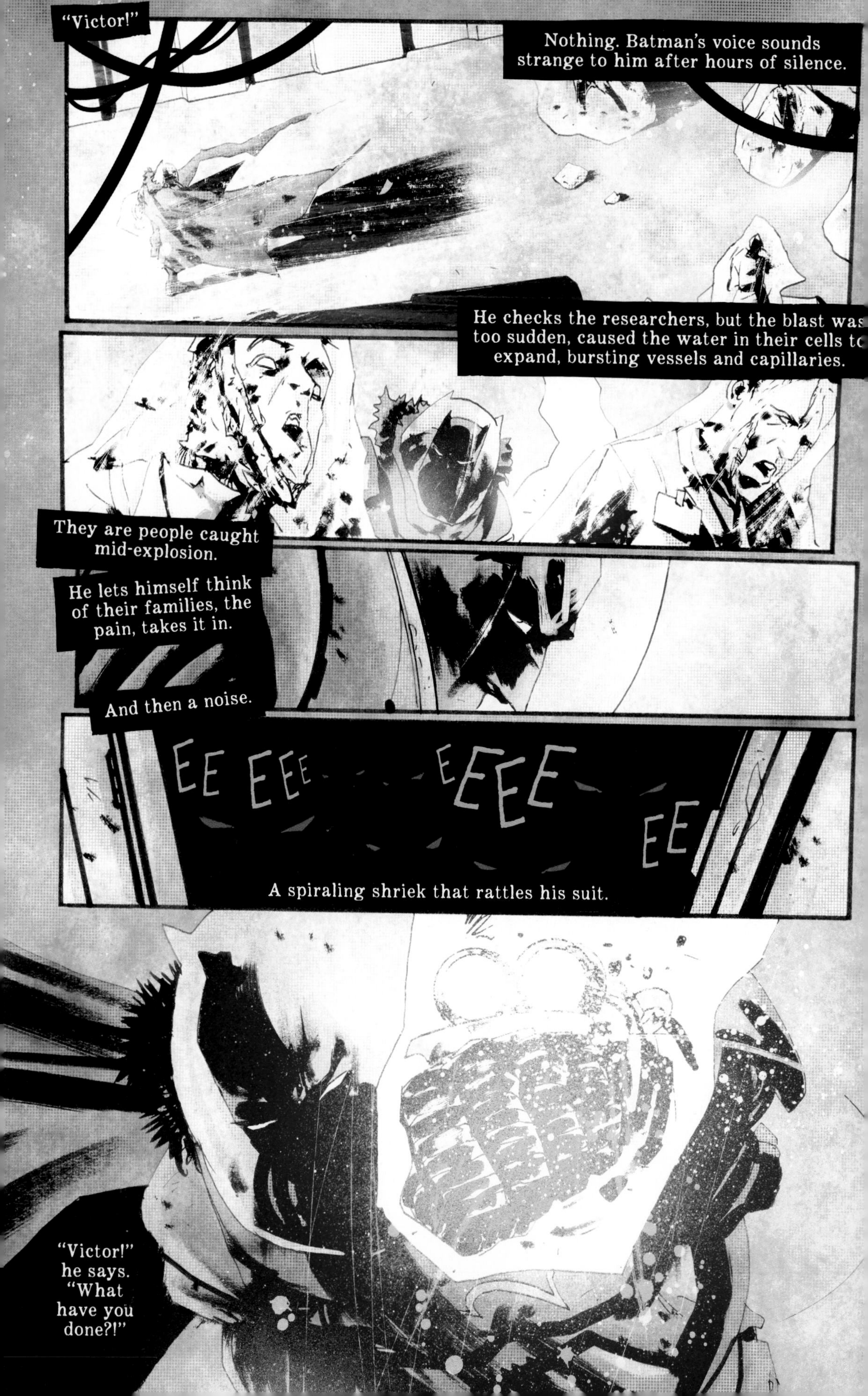
"Victor!"
Nothing. Batman's voice sounds strange to him after hours of silence.
He checks the researchers, but the blast was too sudden, caused the water in their cells to expand, bursting vessels and capillaries.
They are people caught mid-explosion.
He lets himself think of their families, the pain, takes it in.
And then a noise.
EE EEE EEEE EE
A spiraling shriek that rattles his suit.
"Victor!" he says. "What have you done?!"

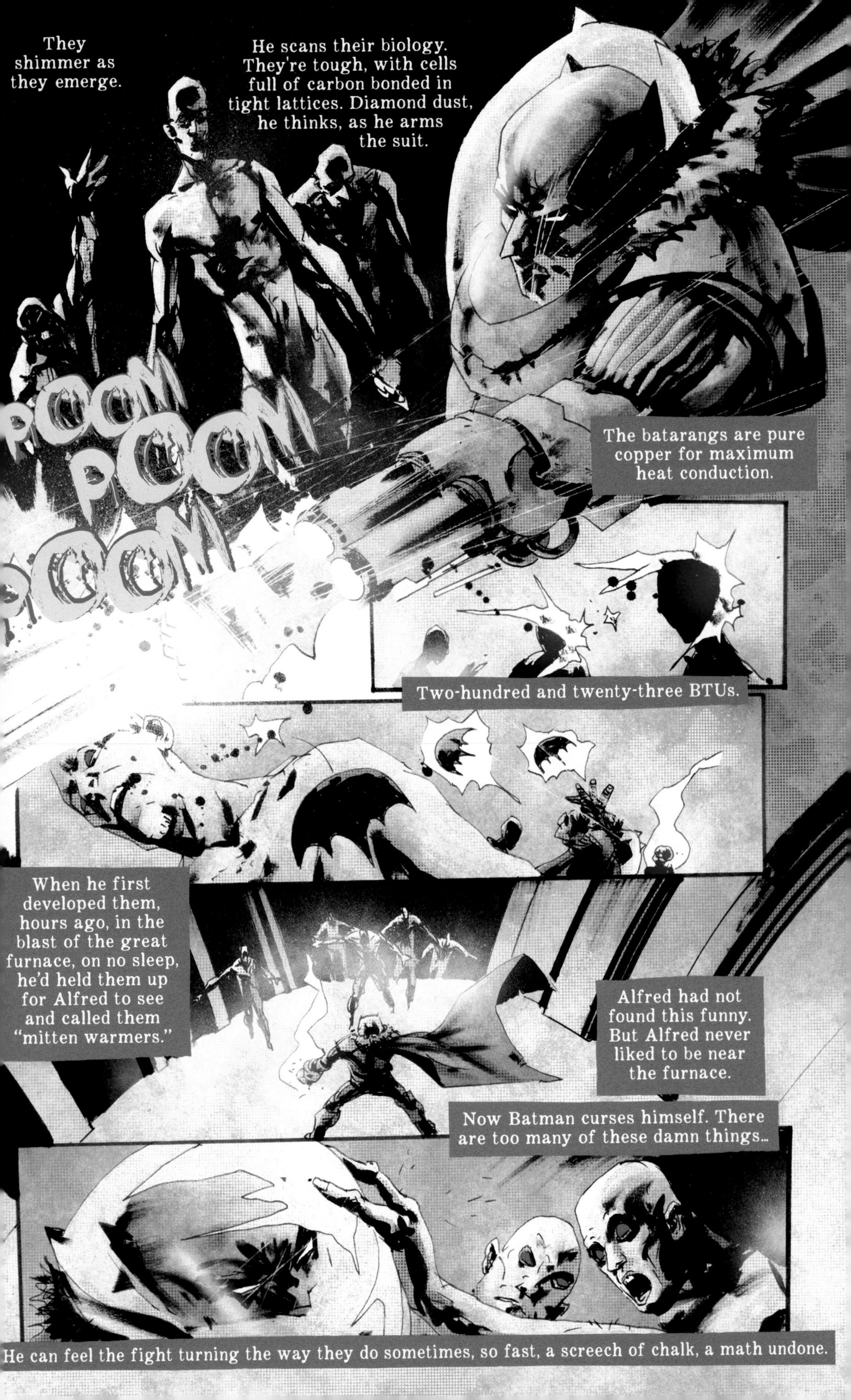
They shimmer as they emerge.
He scans their biology. They're tough, with cells full of carbon bonded in tight lattices. Diamond dust, he thinks, as he arms the suit.
POOM POOM POOM POOM
The batarangs are pure copper for maximum heat conduction.
Two-hundred and twenty-three BTUs.
When he first developed them, hours ago, in the blast of the great furnace, on no sleep, he'd held them up for Alfred to see and called them "mitten warmers."
Alfred had not found this funny. But Alfred never liked to be near the furnace.
Now Batman curses himself. There are too many of these damn things...
He can feel the fight turning the way they do sometimes, so fast, a screech of chalk, a math undone.

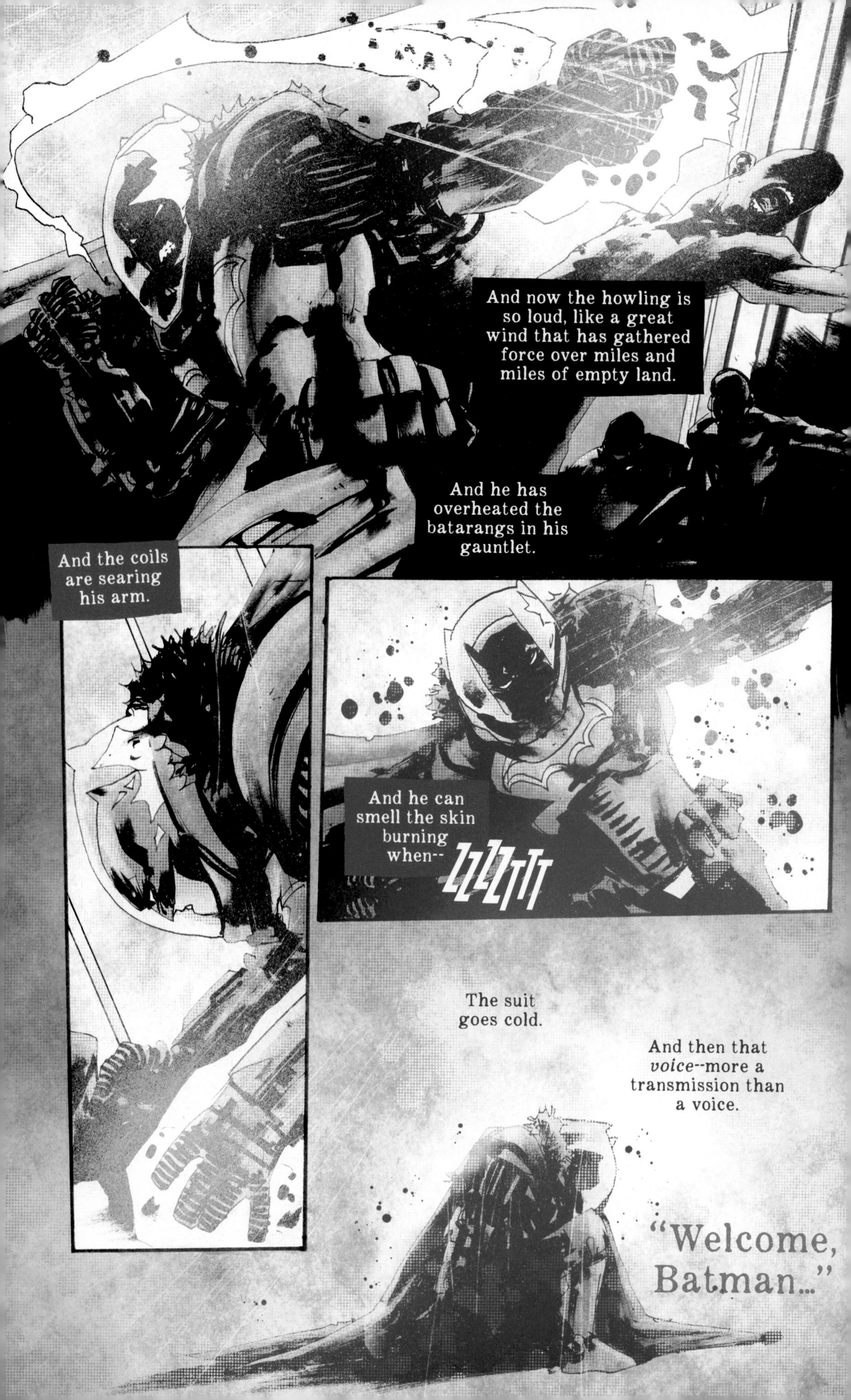
And now the howling is so loud, like a great wind that has gathered force over miles and miles of empty land.
And he has overheated the batarangs in his gauntlet.
And the coils are searing his arm.
And he can smell the skin burning when--
ZZZZTTT
The suit goes cold.
And then that *voice*--more a transmission than a voice.
"Welcome, Batman..."

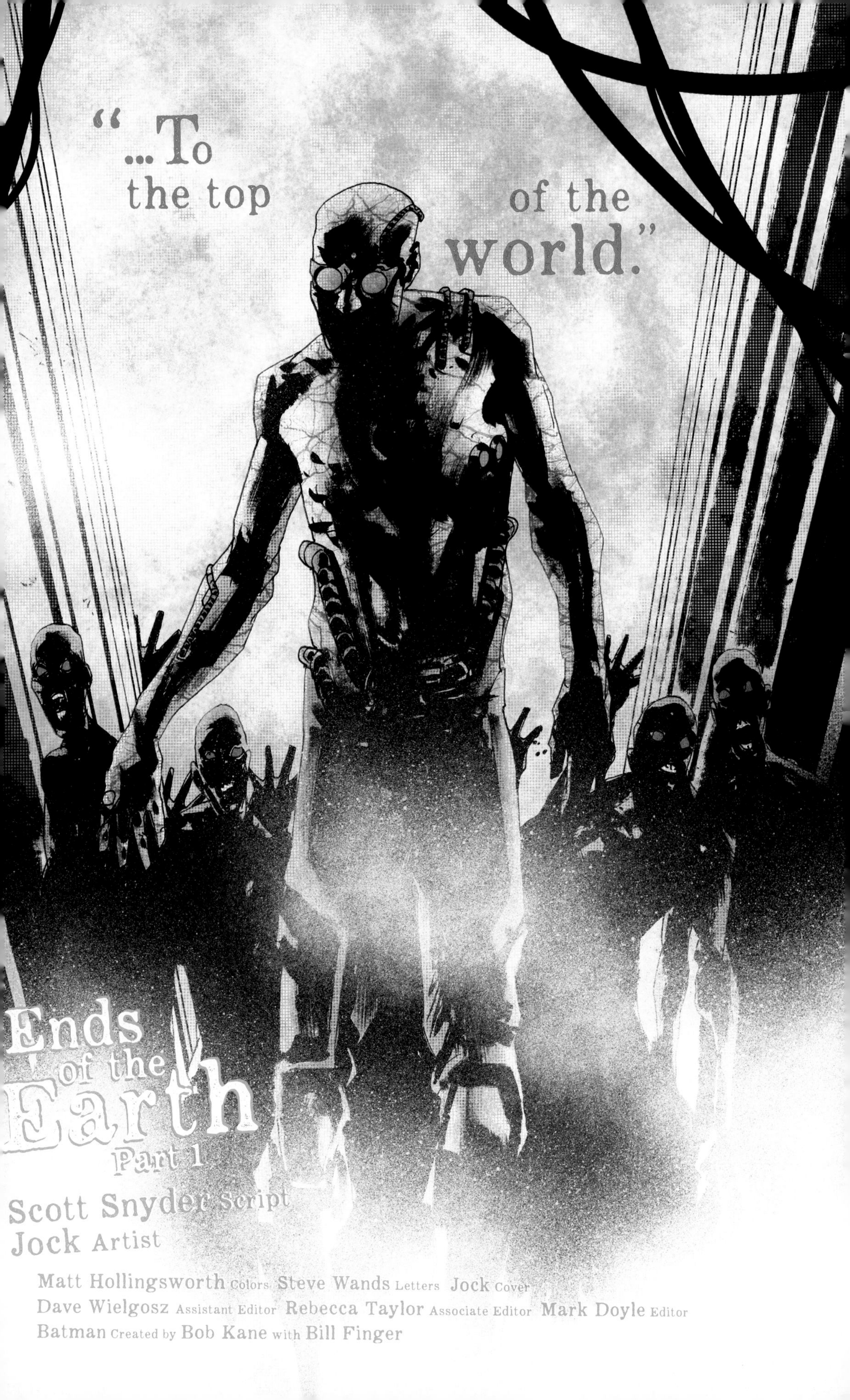
"...To the top of the world."
Ends of the Earth
Part 1
Scott Snyder Script
Jock Artist
Matt Hollingsworth Colors Steve Wands Letters Jock Cover
Dave Wielgosz Assistant Editor Rebecca Taylor Associate Editor Mark Doyle Editor
Batman Created by Bob Kane with Bill Finger

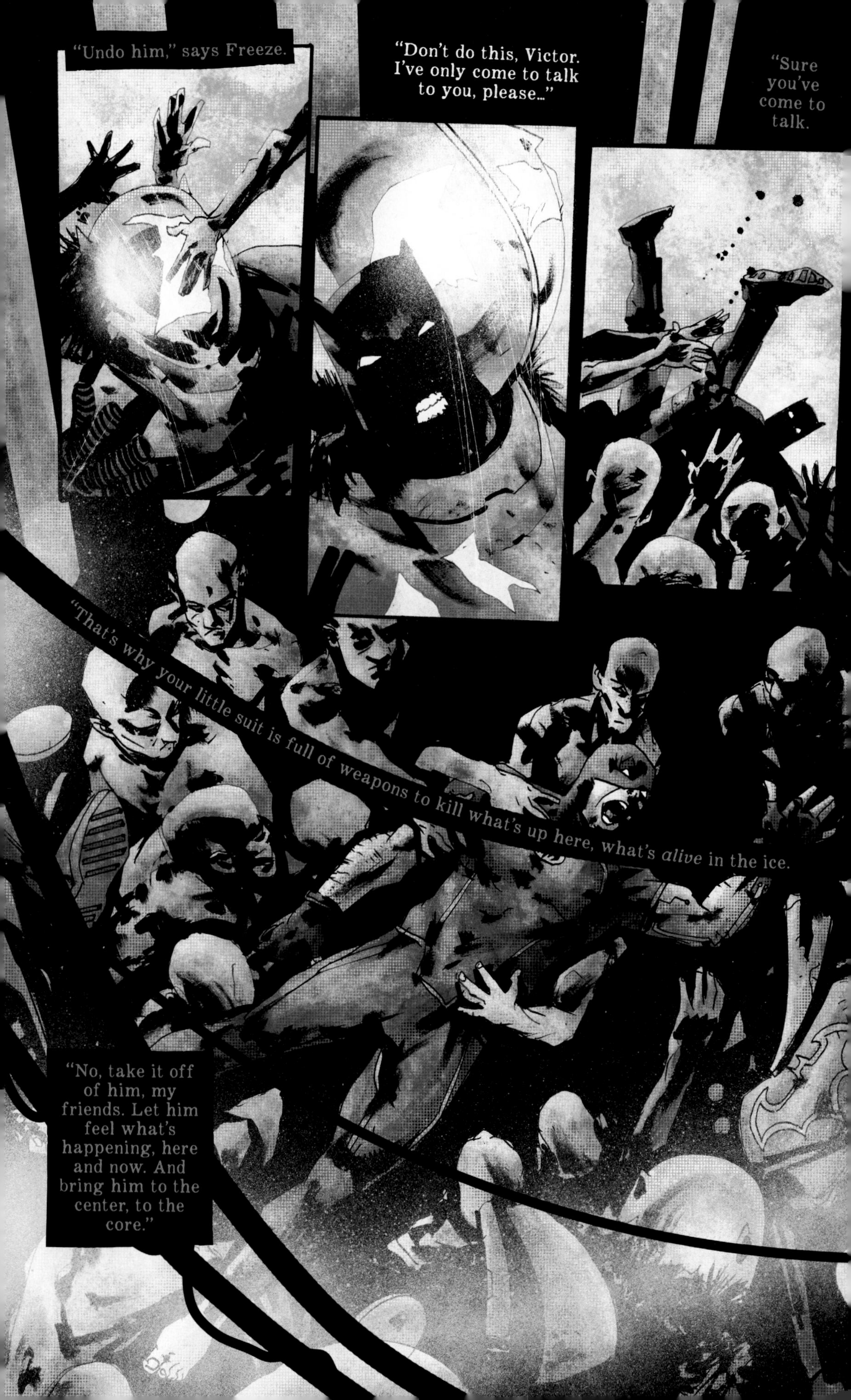
"Undo him," says Freeze.
"Don't do this, Victor. I've only come to talk to you, please..."
"Sure you've come to talk.
That's why your little suit is full of weapons to kill what's up here, what's *alive* in the ice.
"No, take it off of him, my friends. Let him feel what's happening, here and now. And bring him to the center, to the core."

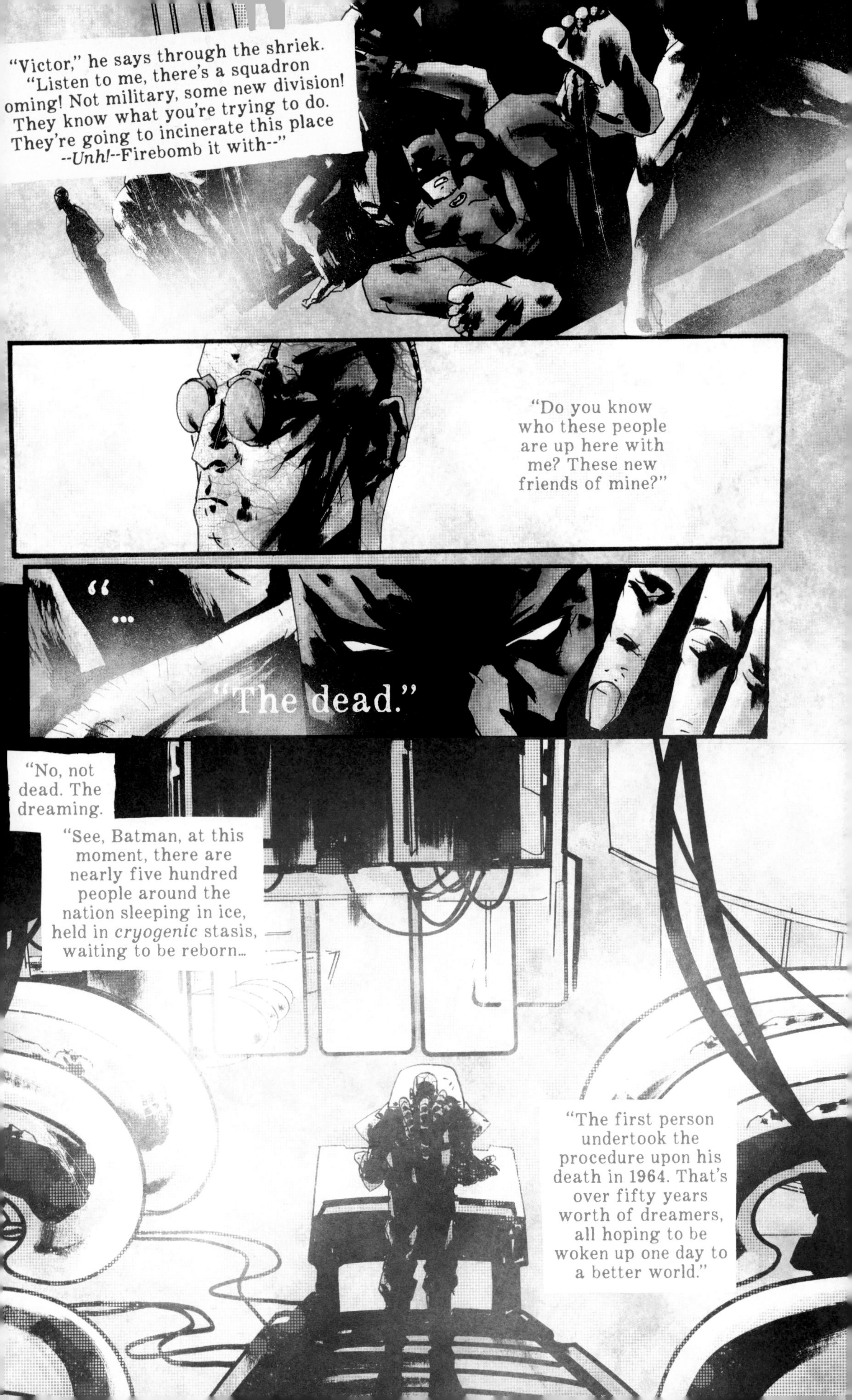

"Victor," he says through the shriek. "Listen to me, there's a squadron oming! Not military, some new division! They know what you're trying to do. They're going to incinerate this place --*Unh!*--Firebomb it with--"
"Do you know who these people are up here with me? These new friends of mine?"
"...
"The dead."
"No, not dead. The dreaming.
"See, Batman, at this moment, there are nearly five hundred people around the nation sleeping in ice, held in *cryogenic* stasis, waiting to be reborn...
"The first person undertook the procedure upon his death in 1964. That's over fifty years worth of dreamers, all hoping to be woken up one day to a better world."

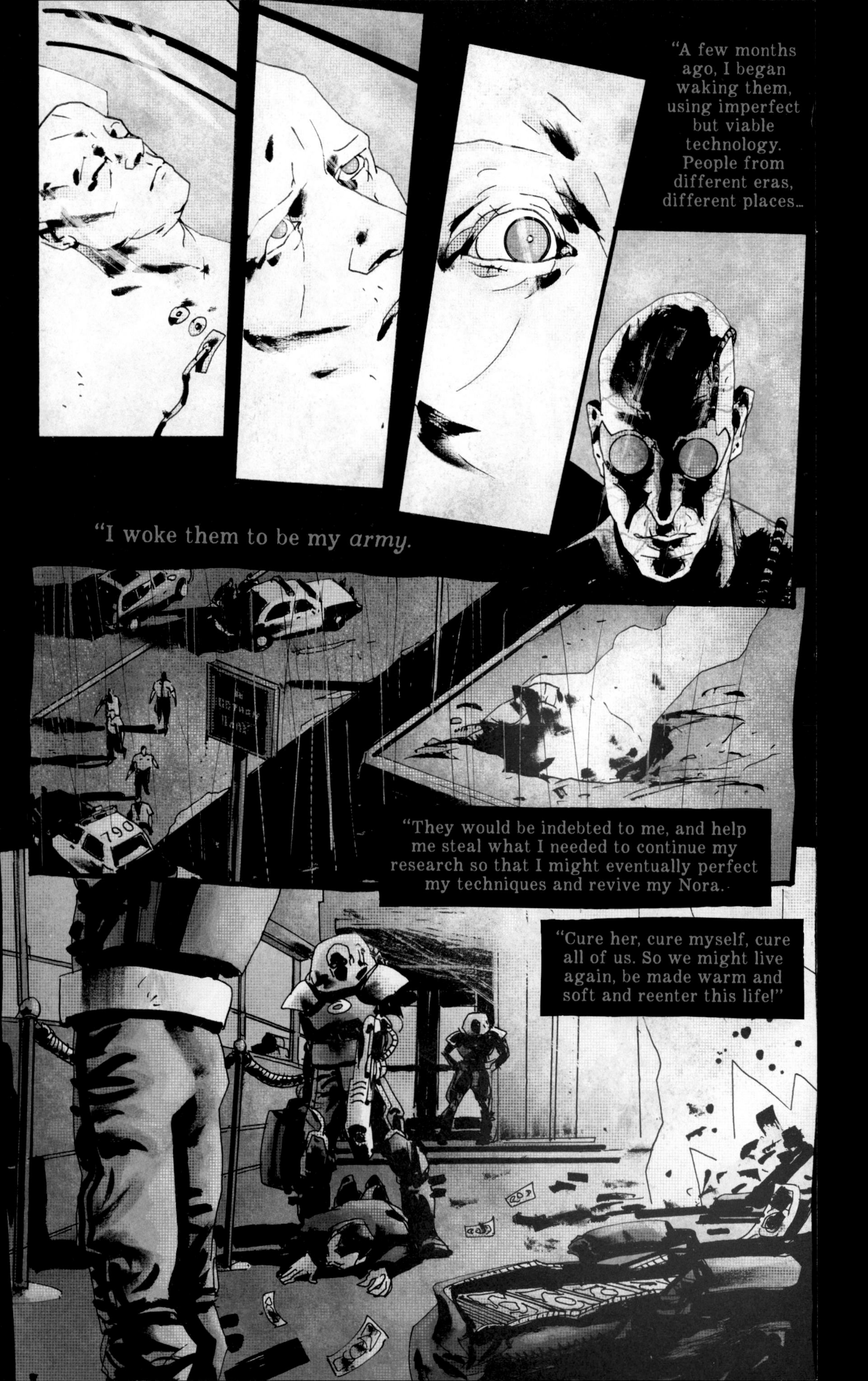
"A few months ago, I began waking them, using imperfect but viable technology. People from different eras, different places...
"I woke them to be my *army.*
"They would be indebted to me, and help me steal what I needed to continue my research so that I might eventually perfect my techniques and revive my Nora.
"Cure her, cure myself, cure all of us. So we might live again, be made warm and soft and reenter this life!"
790

"But look at them, Batman.

"Or rather…*listen* to them.

EEEEEEEEEEEE

"That moan. That sound. A sadness like the creak of grinding teeth.

"I saw then that they were not happy, and I realized, this was because they had put their faith in the cradling ice. They had gone to sleep, to be released by the ice when the world was better. But I had woken them too early.

"That's when I understood, Batman. Understood that this moment, this world, it's overrun with human life; it's dying. Everyone knows this, too. They feel it in the air.

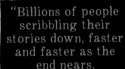

"Billions of people scribbling their stories down, faster and faster as the end nears.

"To wake to this? To wake *her* to this?

"No, I saw that I had been thinking too small. That I had been…myopic."

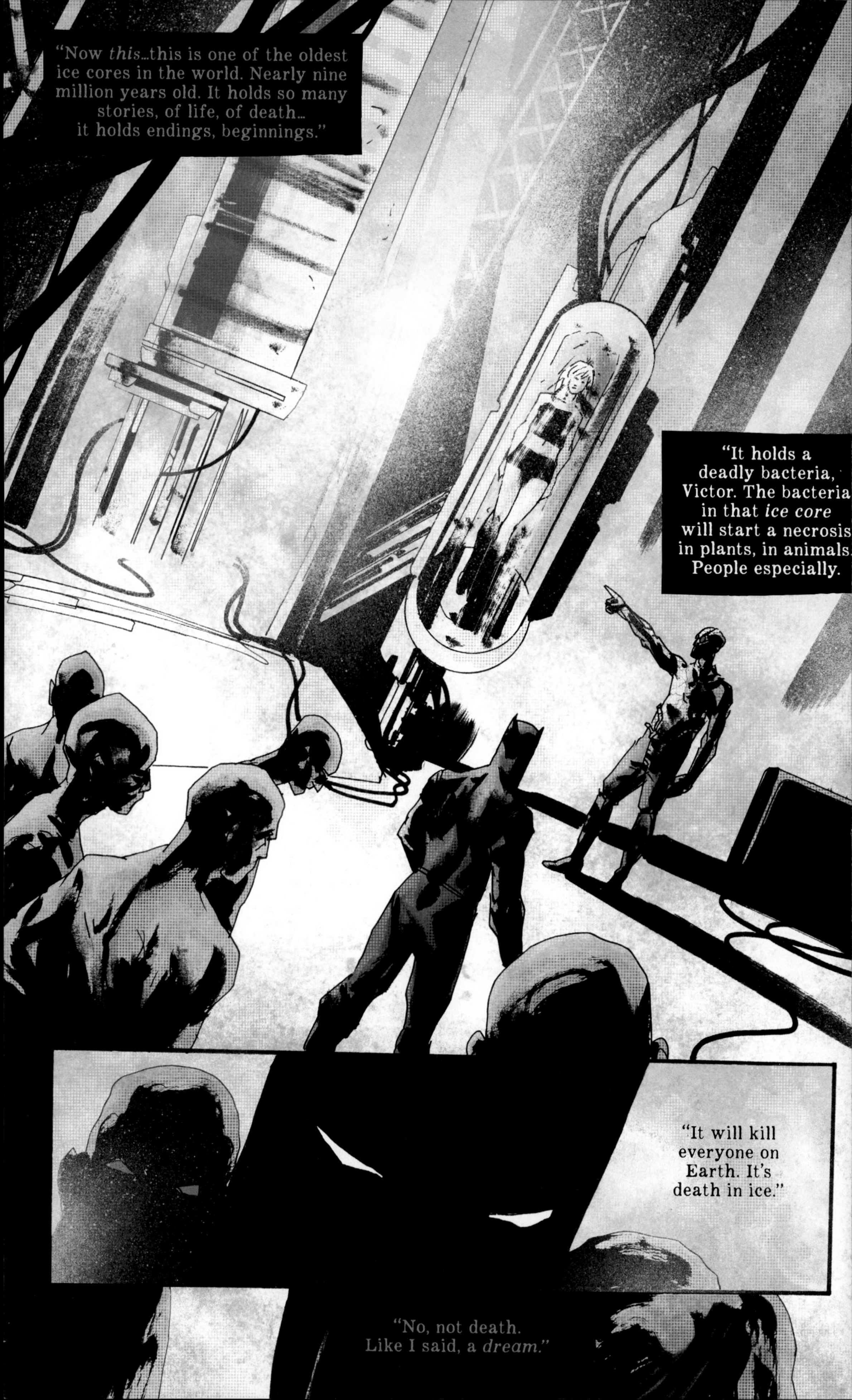
"Now *this*...this is one of the oldest ice cores in the world. Nearly nine million years old. It holds so many stories, of life, of death... it holds endings, beginnings."
"It holds a deadly bacteria, Victor. The bacteria in that *ice core* will start a necrosis in plants, in animals. People especially.
"It will kill everyone on Earth. It's death in ice."
"No, not death. Like I said, a *dream*."

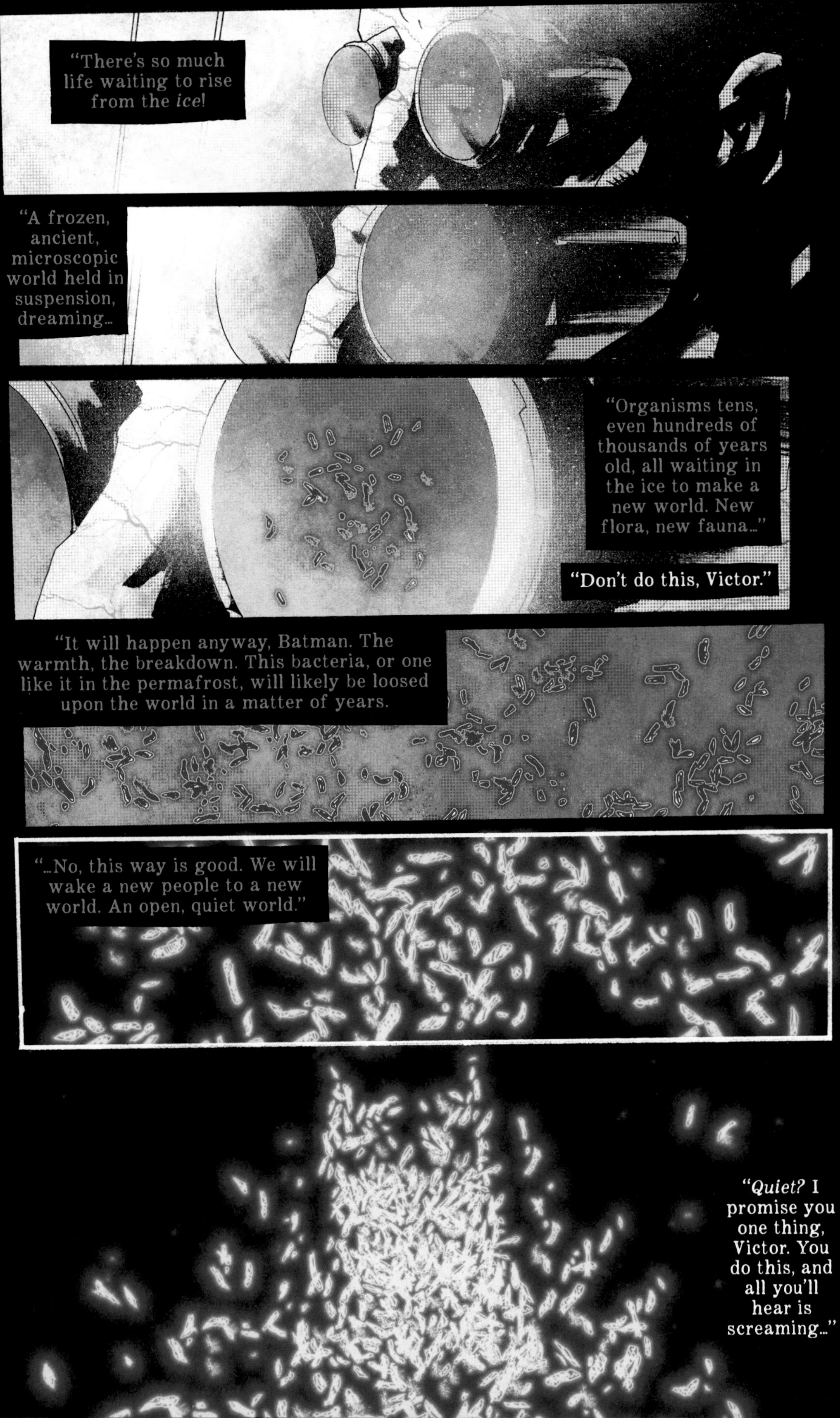
"There's so much life waiting to rise from the *ice*!
"A frozen, ancient, microscopic world held in suspension, dreaming...
"Organisms tens, even hundreds of thousands of years old, all waiting in the ice to make a new world. New flora, new fauna..."
"Don't do this, Victor."
"It will happen anyway, Batman. The warmth, the breakdown. This bacteria, or one like it in the permafrost, will likely be loosed upon the world in a matter of years.
"...No, this way is good. We will wake a new people to a new world. An open, quiet world."
"*Quiet?* I promise you one thing, Victor. You do this, and all you'll hear is screaming..."

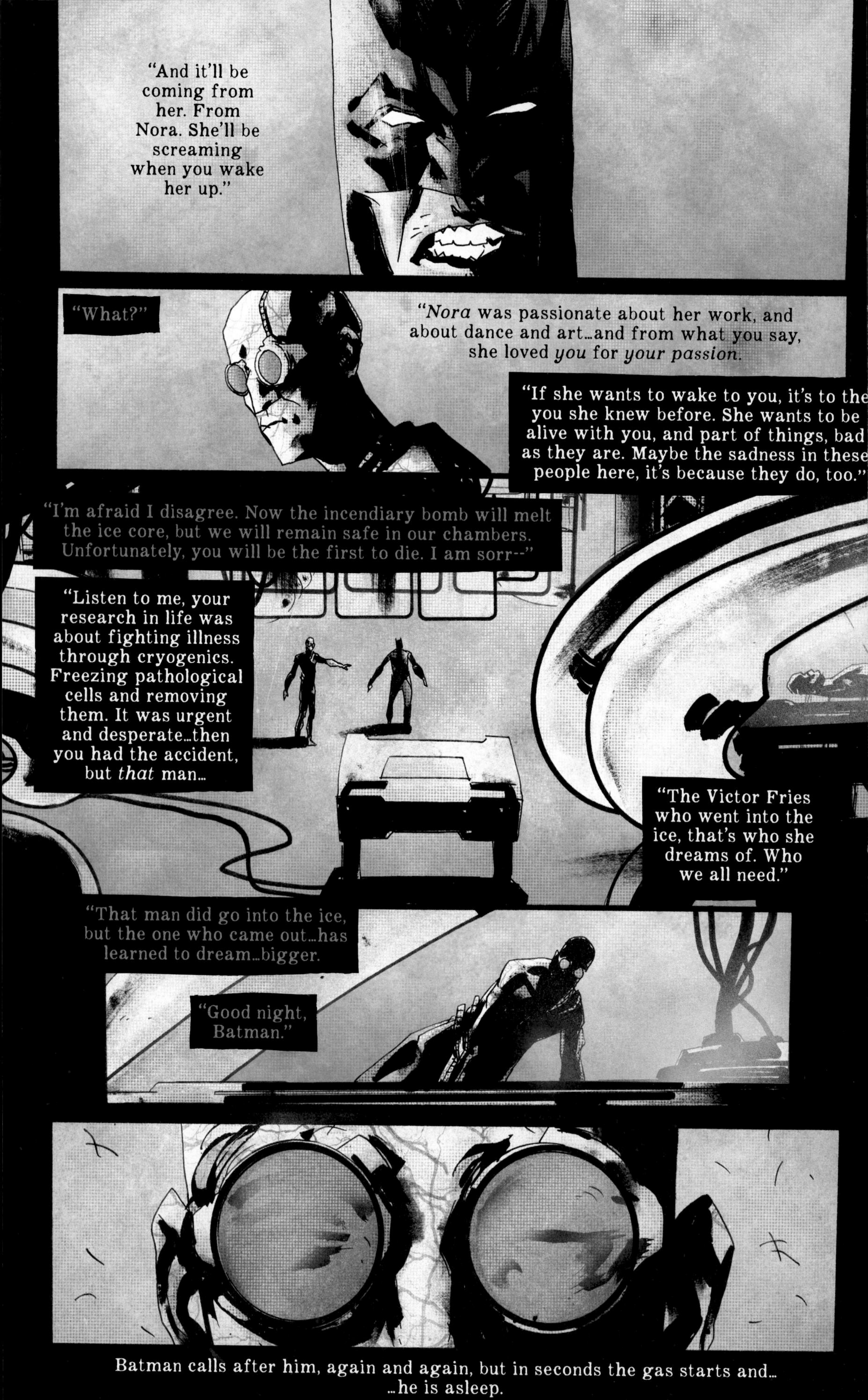
"And it'll be coming from her. From Nora. She'll be screaming when you wake her up."
"What?"
"*Nora* was passionate about her work, and about dance and art...and from what you say, she loved *you* for *your passion*.
"If she wants to wake to you, it's to the you she knew before. She wants to be alive with you, and part of things, bad as they are. Maybe the sadness in these people here, it's because they do, too."
"I'm afraid I disagree. Now the incendiary bomb will melt the ice core, but we will remain safe in our chambers. Unfortunately, you will be the first to die. I am sorr--"
"Listen to me, your research in life was about fighting illness through cryogenics. Freezing pathological cells and removing them. It was urgent and desperate...then you had the accident, but *that* man...
"The Victor Fries who went into the ice, that's who she dreams of. Who we all need."
"That man did go into the ice, but the one who came out...has learned to dream...bigger.
"Good night, Batman."
Batman calls after him, again and again, but in seconds the gas starts and...
...he is asleep.

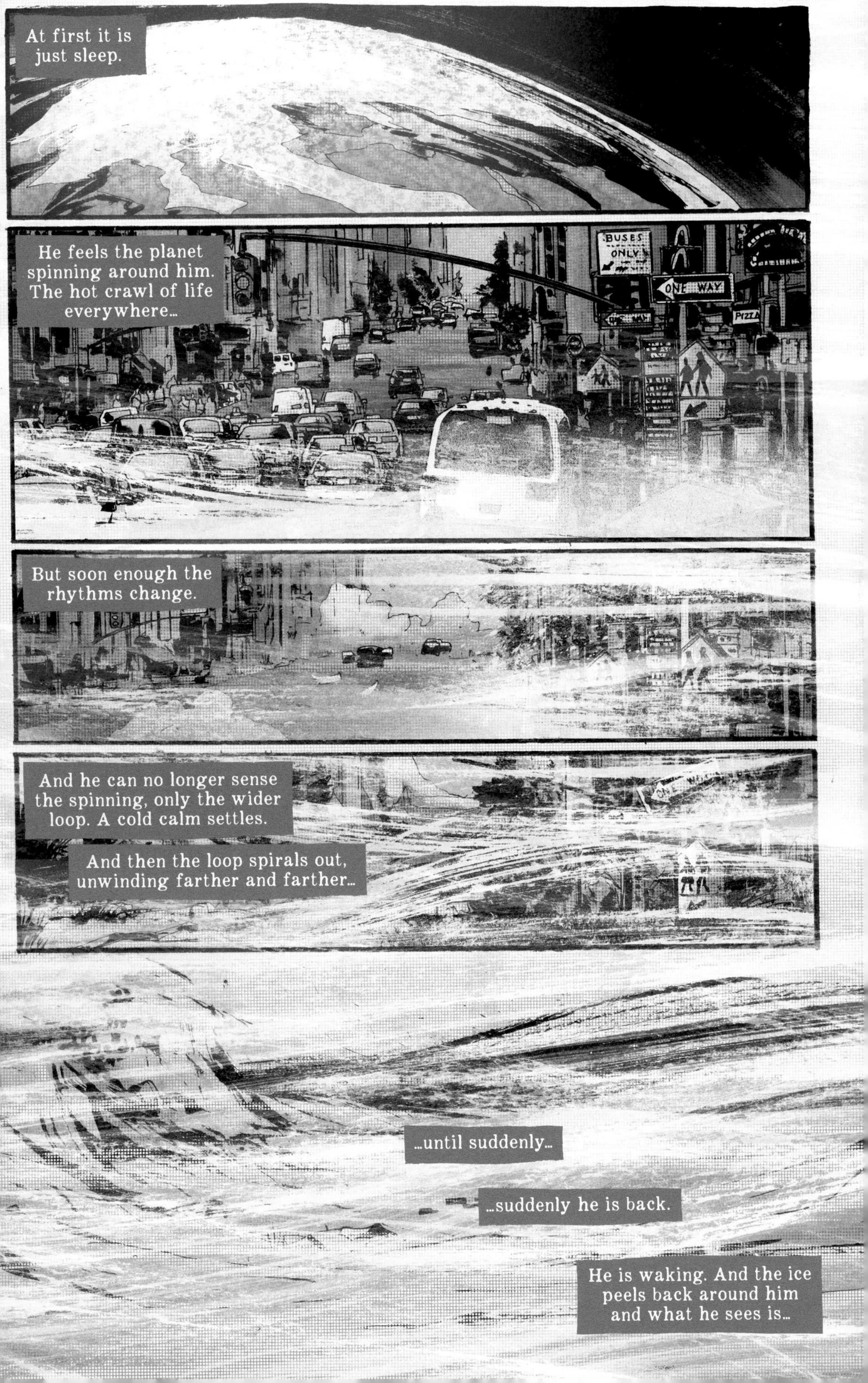
At first it is just sleep.
He feels the planet spinning around him. The hot crawl of life everywhere...
BUSES ONLY
ONE WAY
PIZZA
But soon enough the rhythms change.
And he can no longer sense the spinning, only the wider loop. A cold calm settles.
And then the loop spirals out, unwinding farther and farther...
...until suddenly...
...suddenly he is back.
He is waking. And the ice peels back around him and what he sees is...

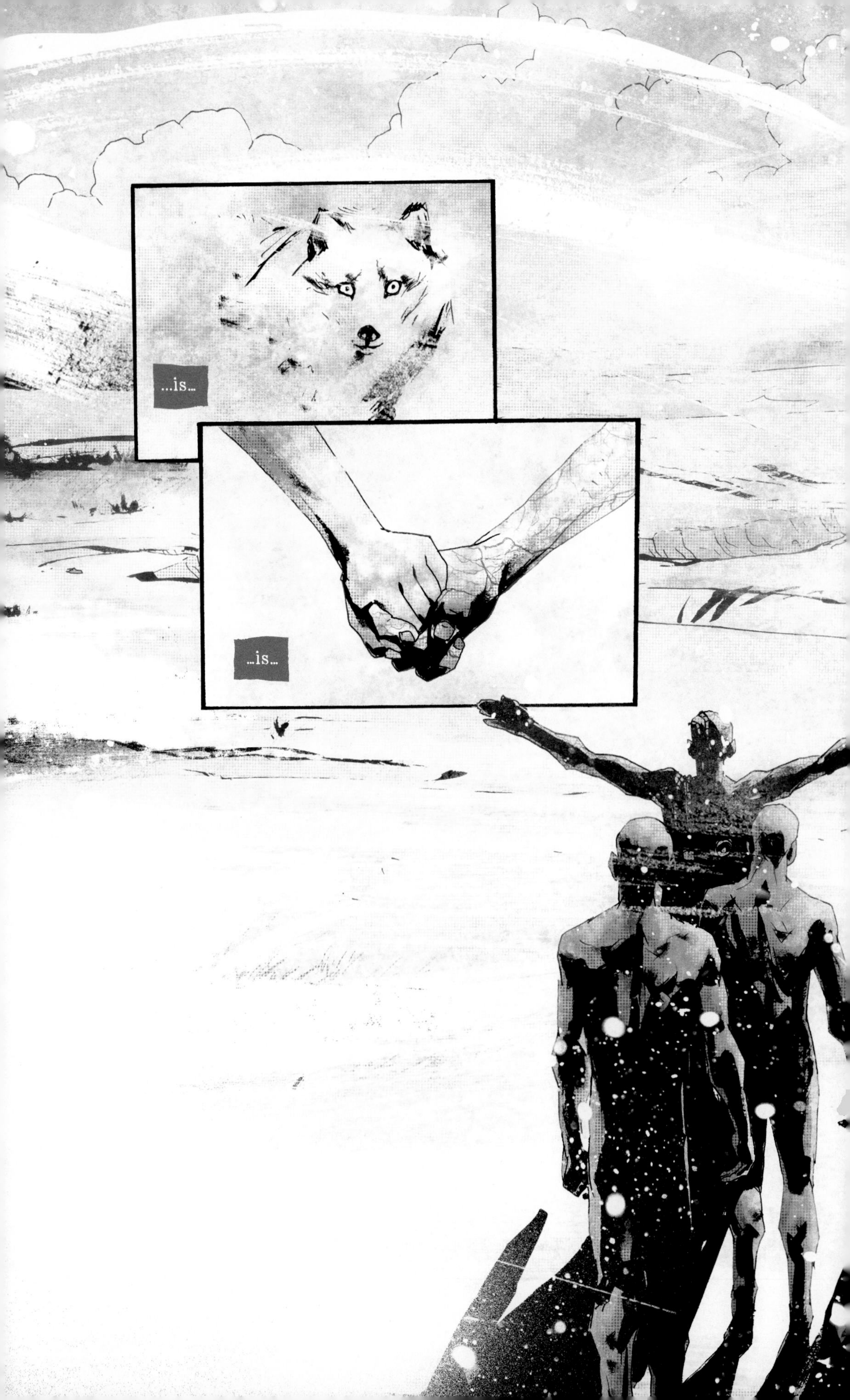
...is...
...is...

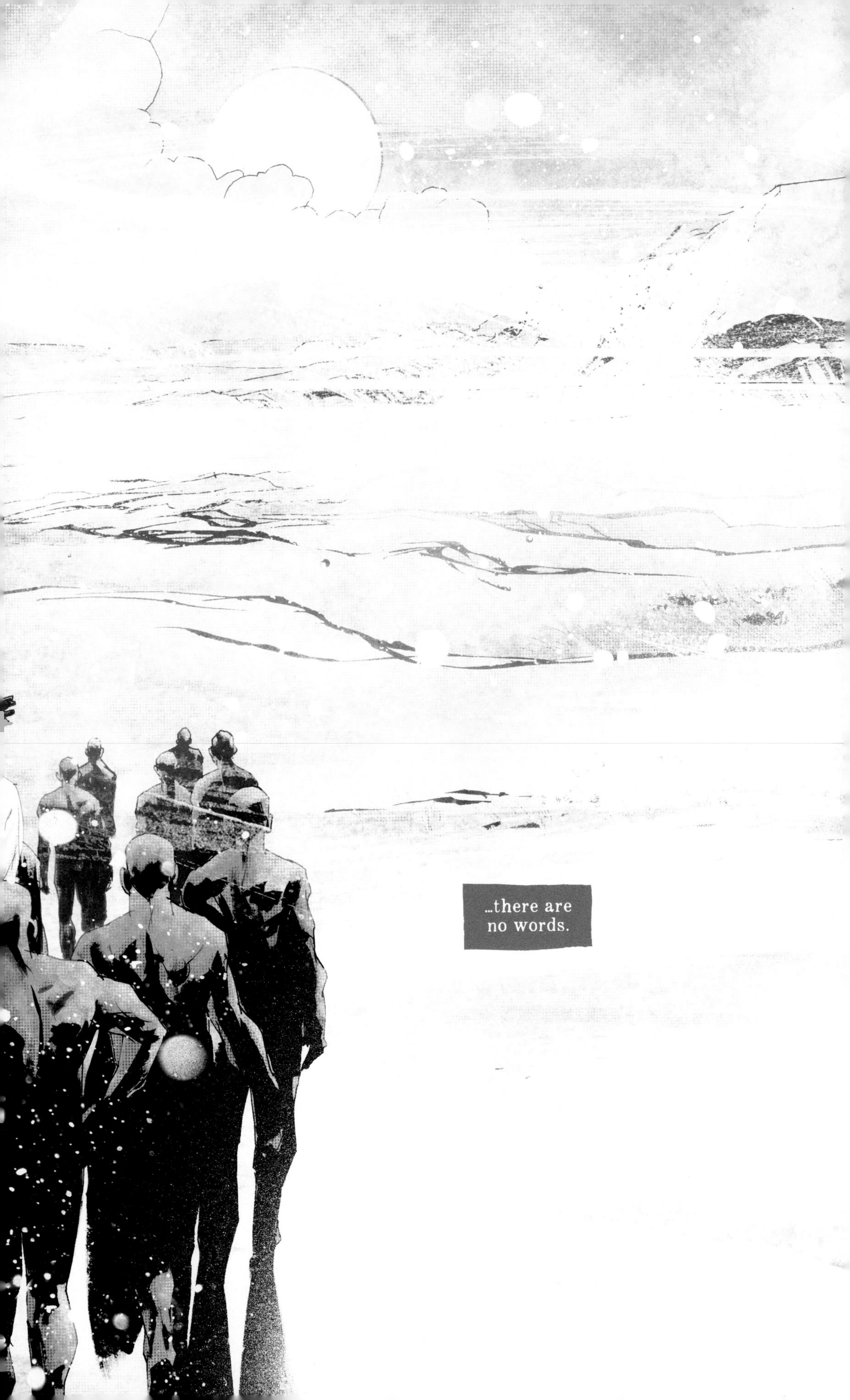
...there are no words.

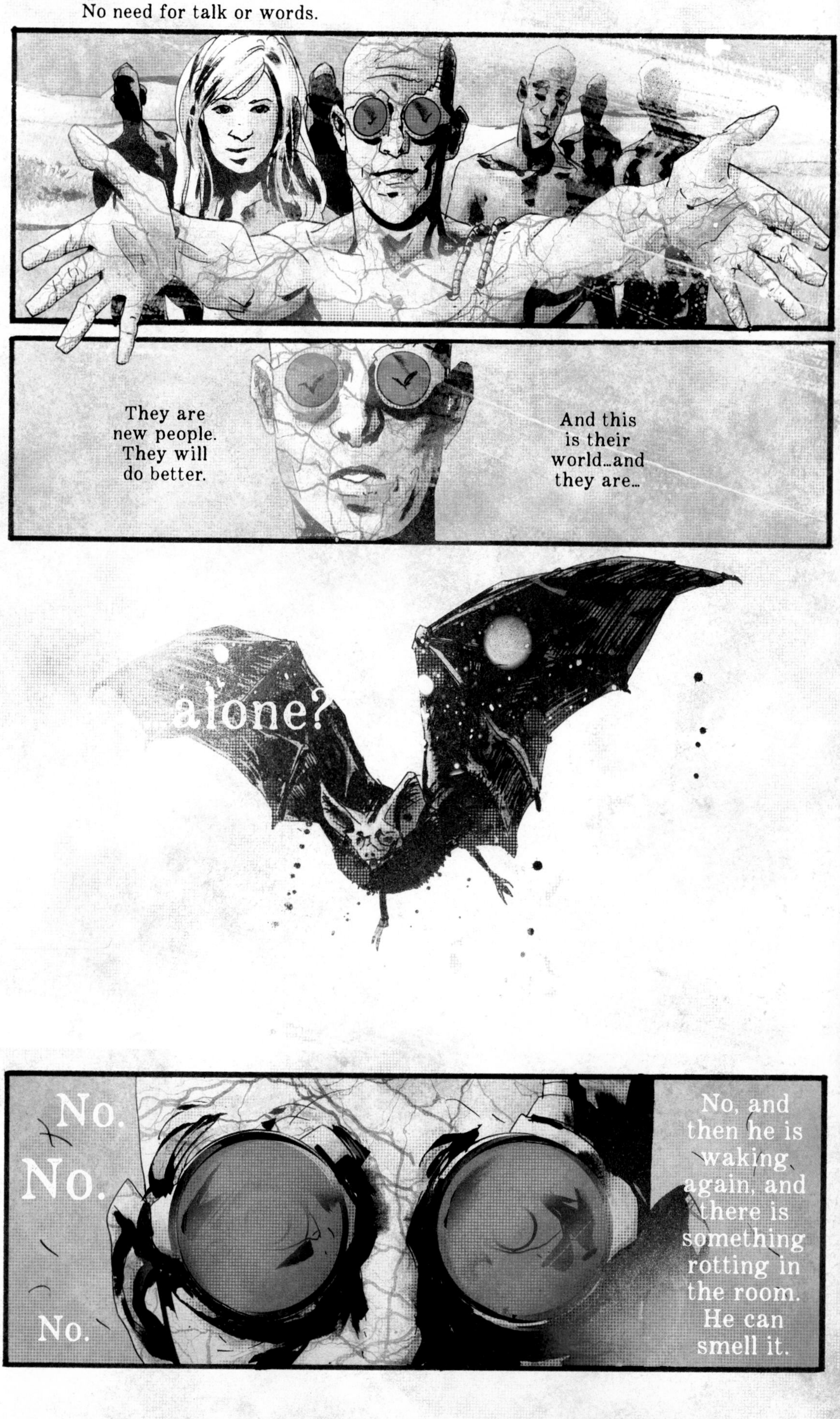
No need for talk or words.
They are new people. They will do better.
And this is their world...and they are...
alone?
No.
No.
No.
No, and then he is waking again, and there is something rotting in the room. He can smell it.

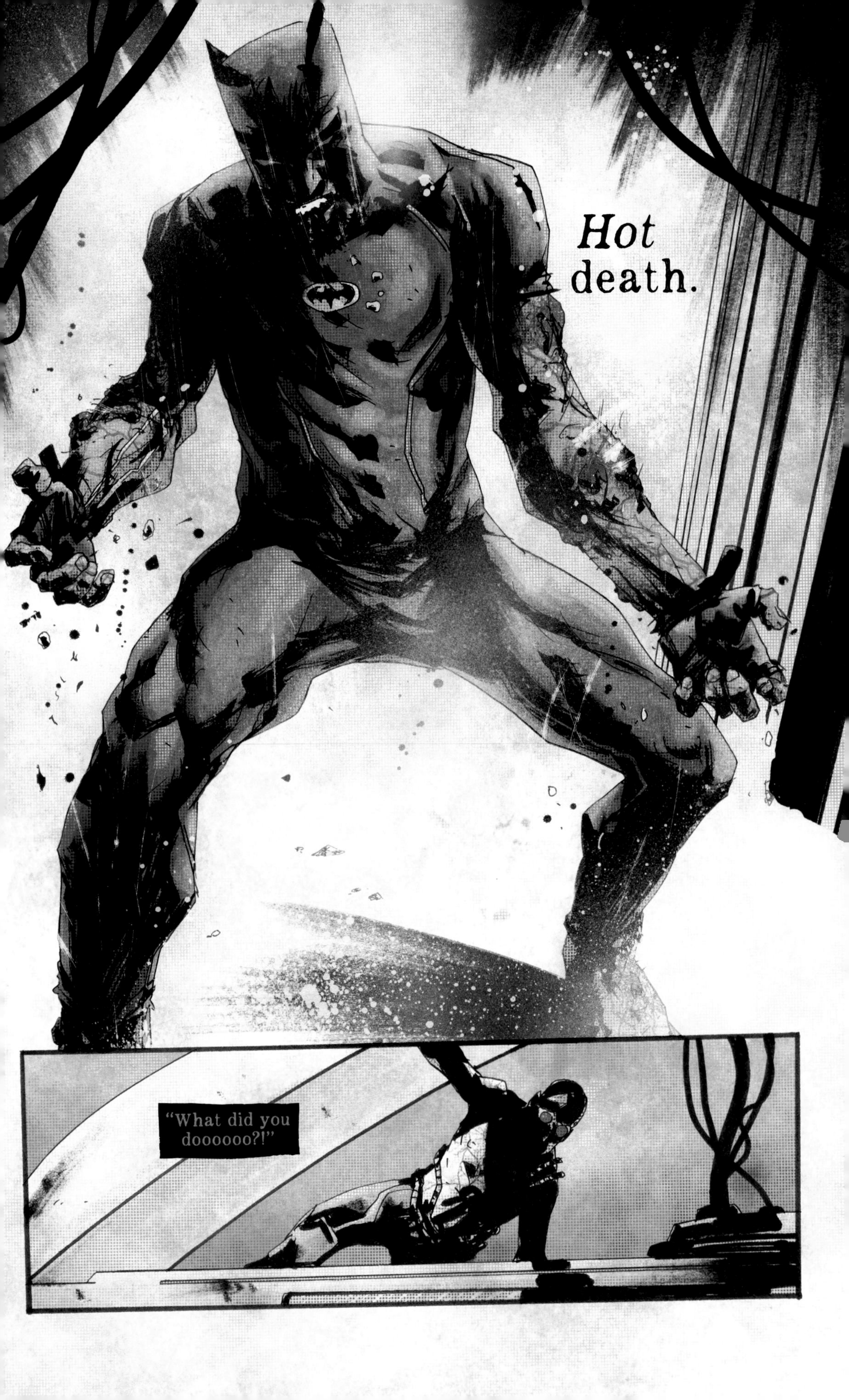
Hot death.
"What did you dooooooo?!"

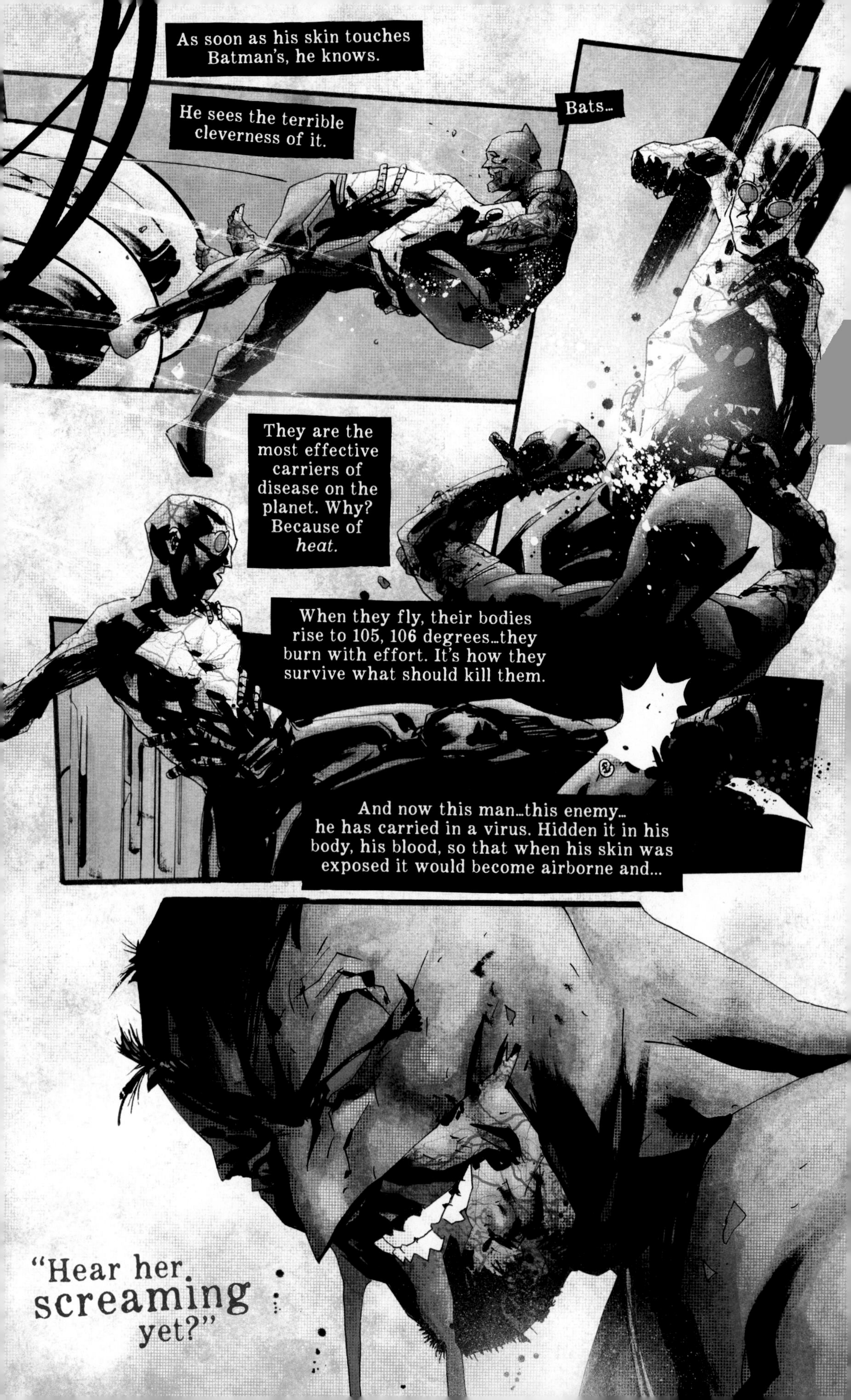

As soon as his skin touches Batman's, he knows.
He sees the terrible cleverness of it.
Bats...
They are the most effective carriers of disease on the planet. Why? Because of *heat.*
When they fly, their bodies rise to 105, 106 degrees...they burn with effort. It's how they survive what should kill them.
And now this man...this enemy... he has carried in a virus. Hidden it in his body, his blood, so that when his skin was exposed it would become airborne and...
"Hear her. screaming yet?"

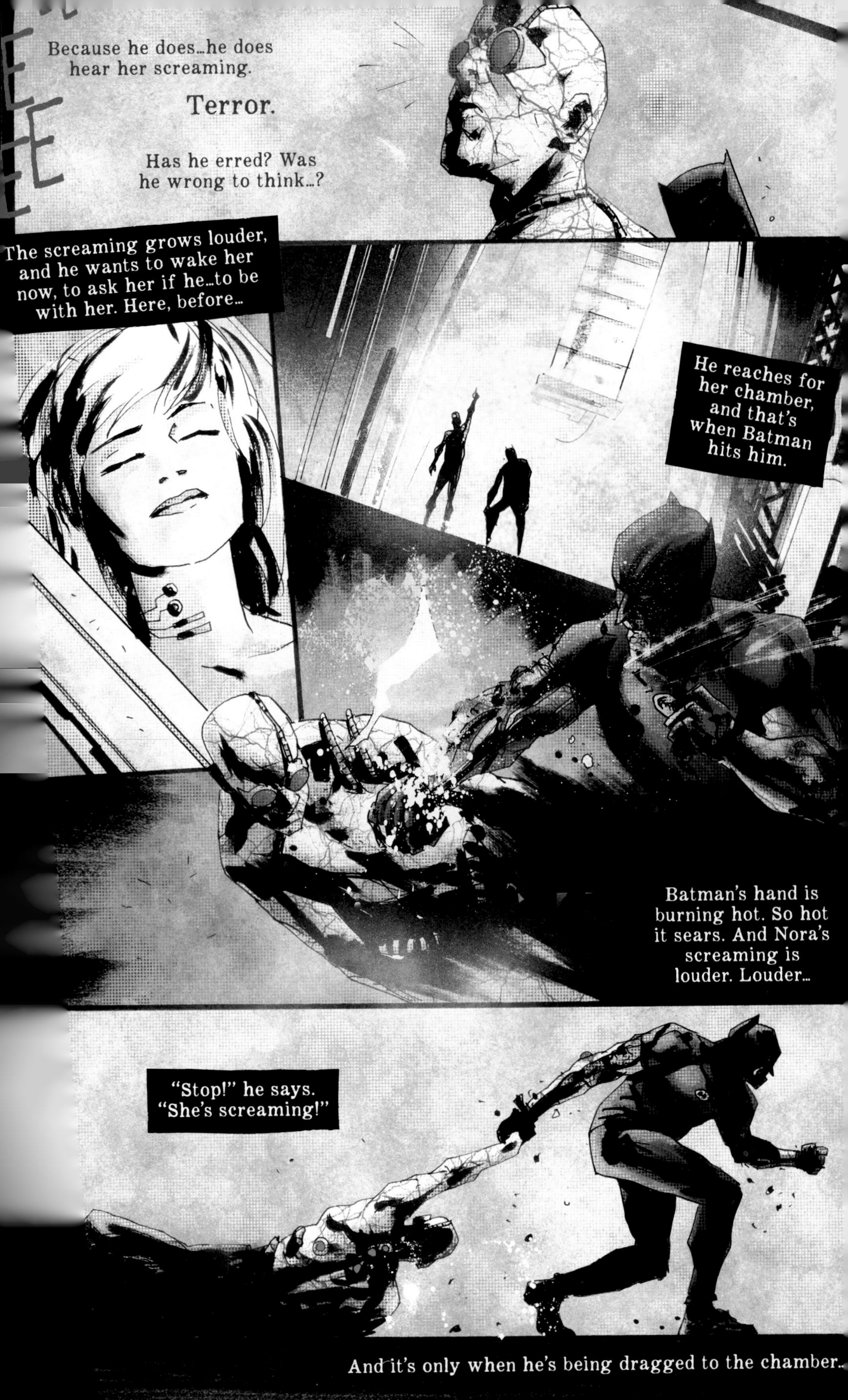

Because he does...he does hear her screaming.
Terror.
Has he erred? Was he wrong to think...?
The screaming grows louder, and he wants to wake her now, to ask her if he...to be with her. Here, before...
He reaches for her chamber, and that's when Batman hits him.
Batman's hand is burning hot. So hot it sears. And Nora's screaming is louder. Louder...
"Stop!" he says. "She's screaming!"
And it's only when he's being dragged to the chamber...

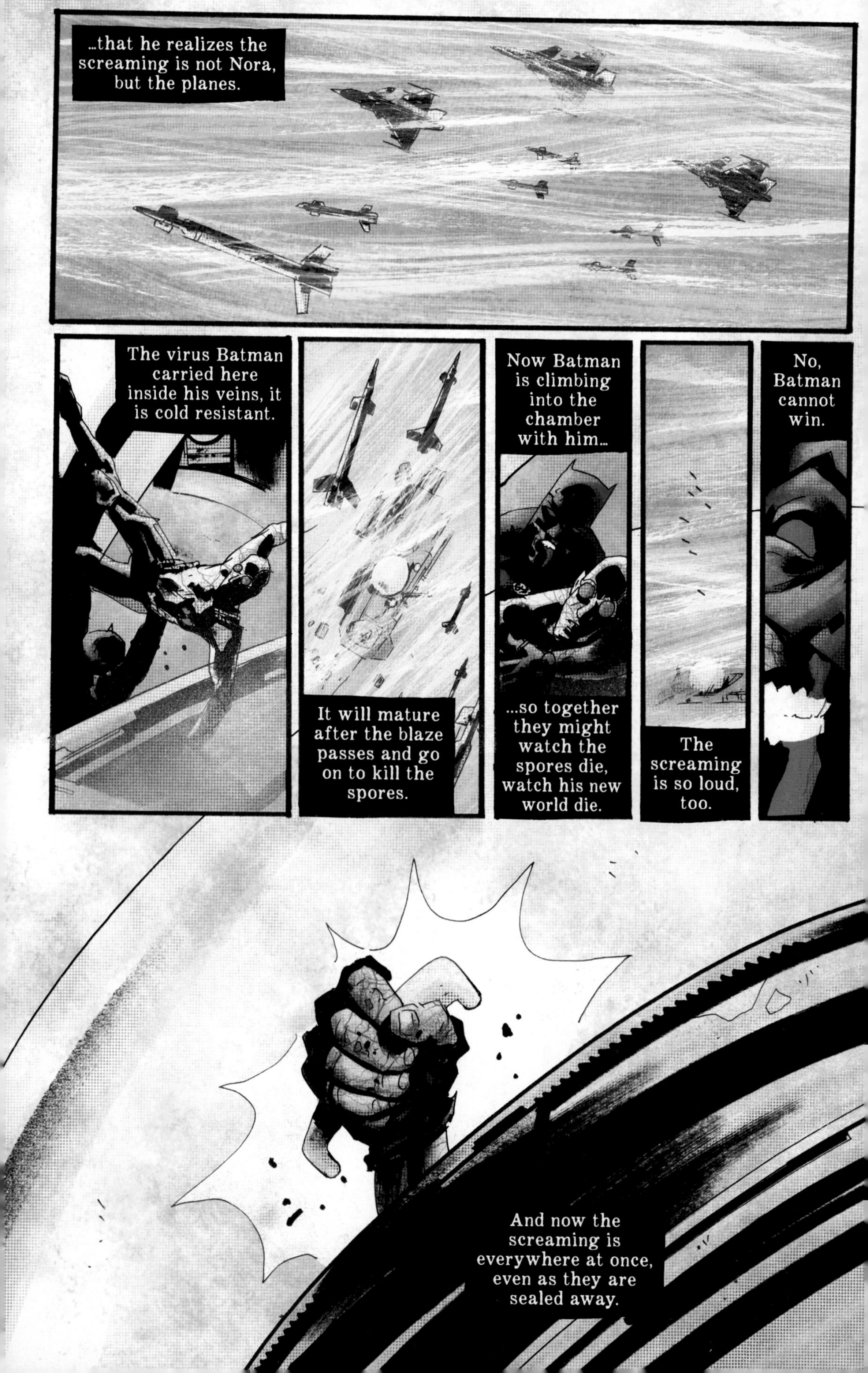
...that he realizes the screaming is not Nora, but the planes.
The virus Batman carried here inside his veins, it is cold resistant.
It will mature after the blaze passes and go on to kill the spores.
Now Batman is climbing into the chamber with him...
...so together they might watch the spores die, watch his new world die.
The screaming is so loud, too.
No, Batman cannot win.
And now the screaming is everywhere at once, even as they are sealed away.

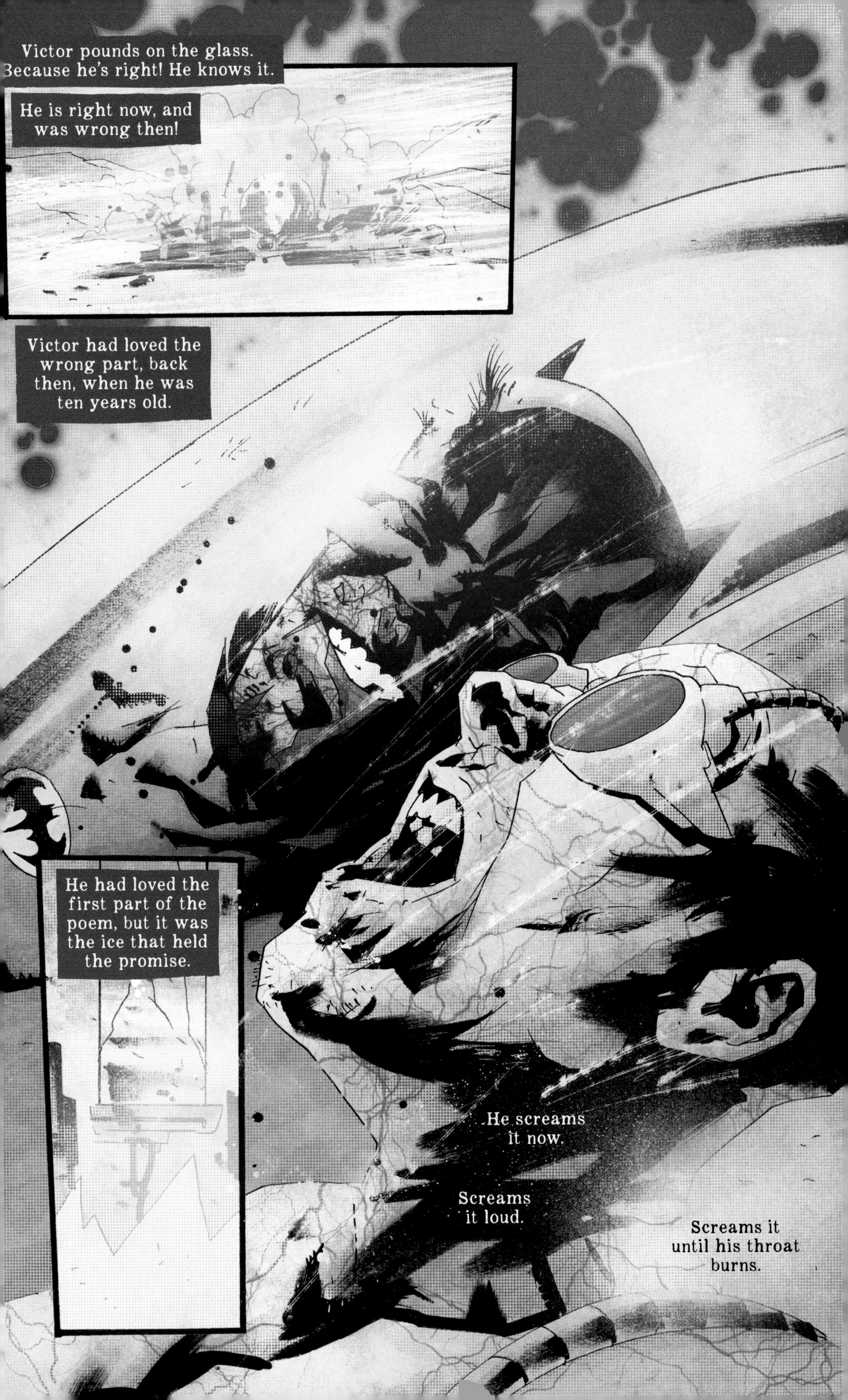
Victor pounds on the glass. Because he's right! He knows it.
He is right now, and was wrong then!
Victor had loved the wrong part, back then, when he was ten years old.
He had loved the first part of the poem, but it was the ice that held the promise.
He screams it now.
Screams it loud.
Screams it until his throat burns.

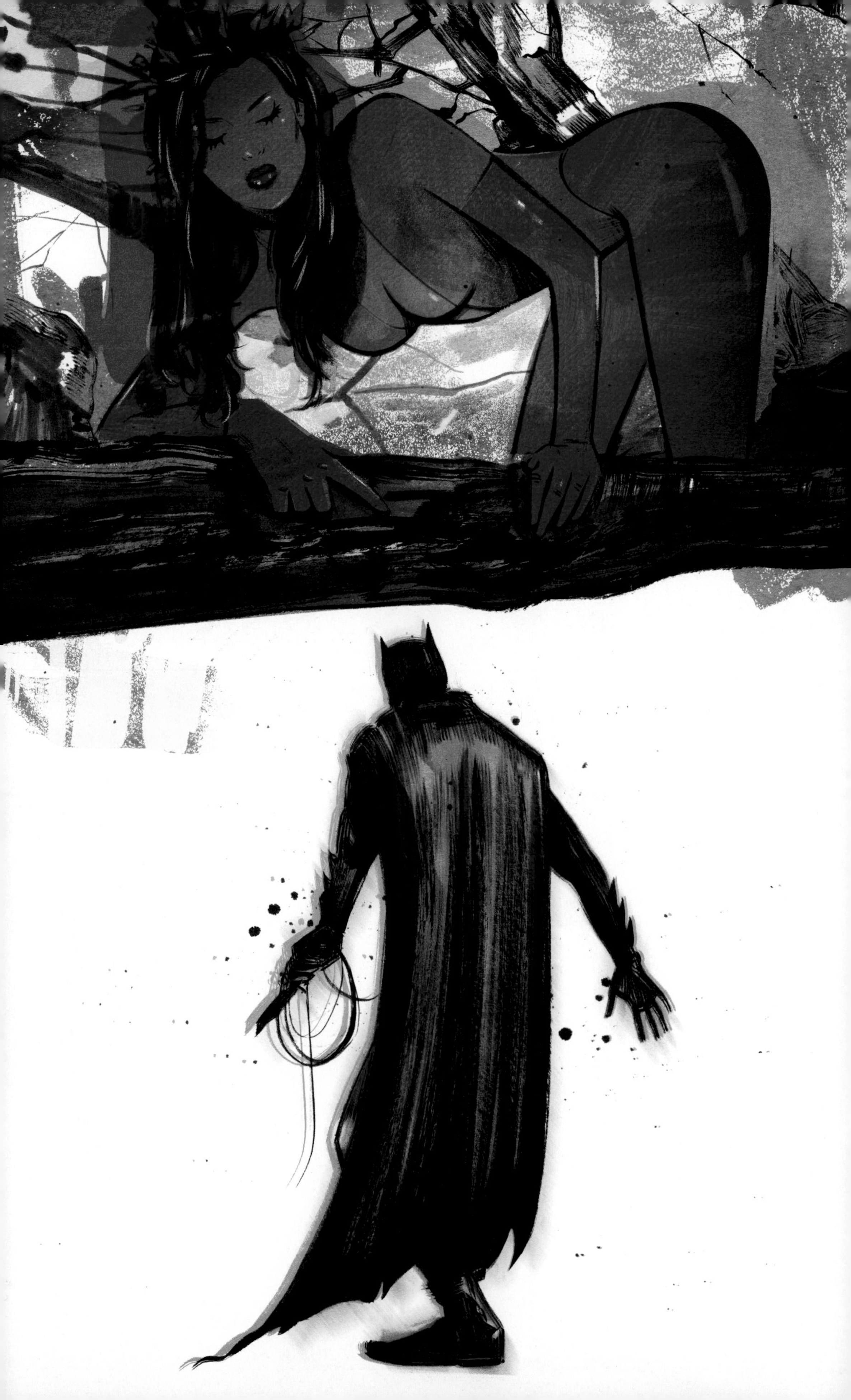

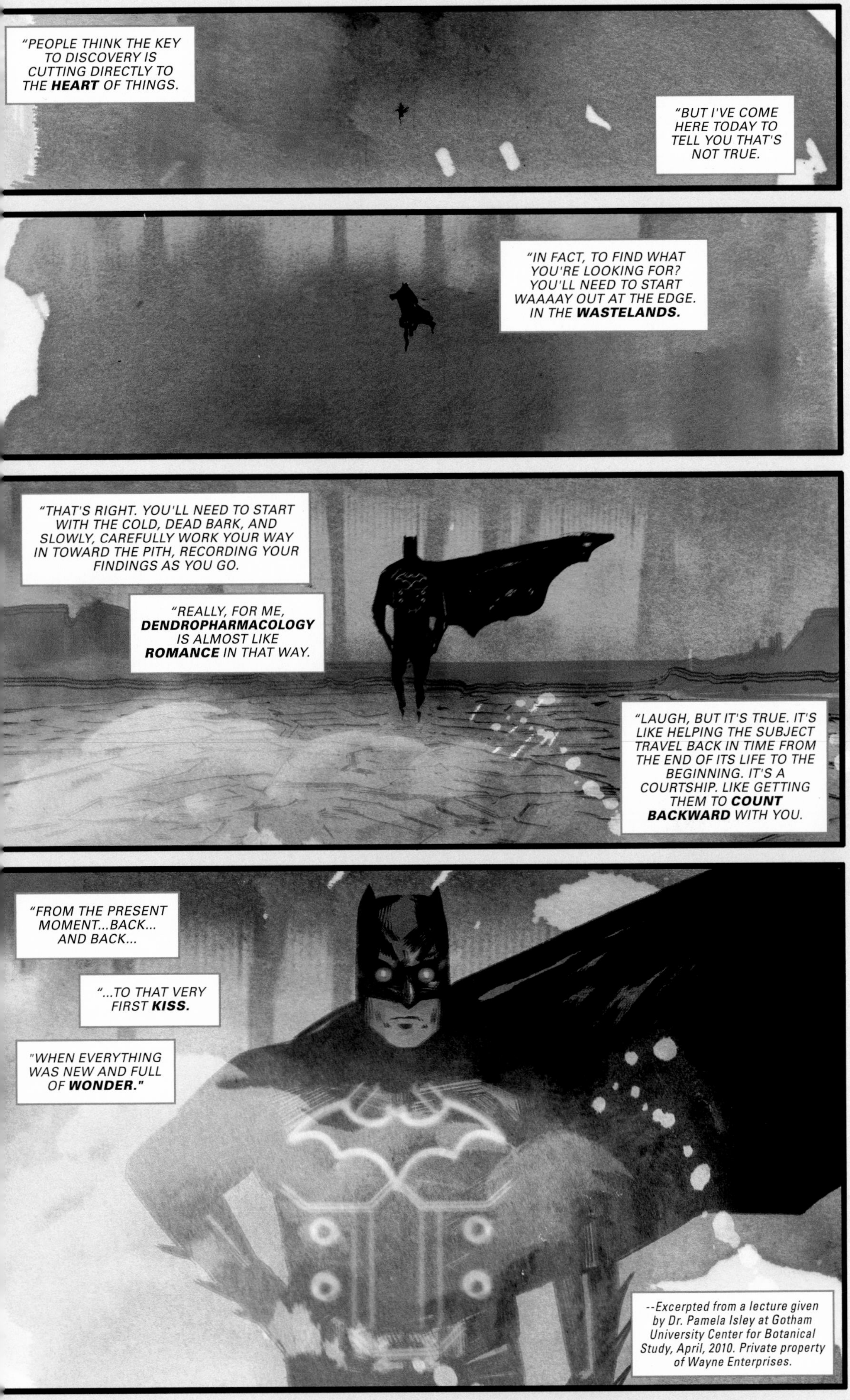
"PEOPLE THINK THE KEY TO DISCOVERY IS CUTTING DIRECTLY TO THE **HEART** OF THINGS.
"BUT I'VE COME HERE TODAY TO TELL YOU THAT'S NOT TRUE.
"IN FACT, TO FIND WHAT YOU'RE LOOKING FOR? YOU'LL NEED TO START WAAAAY OUT AT THE EDGE. IN THE **WASTELANDS.**
"THAT'S RIGHT. YOU'LL NEED TO START WITH THE COLD, DEAD BARK, AND SLOWLY, CAREFULLY WORK YOUR WAY IN TOWARD THE PITH, RECORDING YOUR FINDINGS AS YOU GO.
"REALLY, FOR ME, **DENDROPHARMACOLOGY** IS ALMOST LIKE **ROMANCE** IN THAT WAY.
"LAUGH, BUT IT'S TRUE. IT'S LIKE HELPING THE SUBJECT TRAVEL BACK IN TIME FROM THE END OF ITS LIFE TO THE BEGINNING. IT'S A COURTSHIP. LIKE GETTING THEM TO **COUNT BACKWARD** WITH YOU.
"FROM THE PRESENT MOMENT...BACK... AND BACK...
"...TO THAT VERY FIRST **KISS.**
"WHEN EVERYTHING WAS NEW AND FULL OF **WONDER."**
--Excerpted from a lecture given by Dr. Pamela Isley at Gotham University Center for Botanical Study, April, 2010. Private property of Wayne Enterprises.

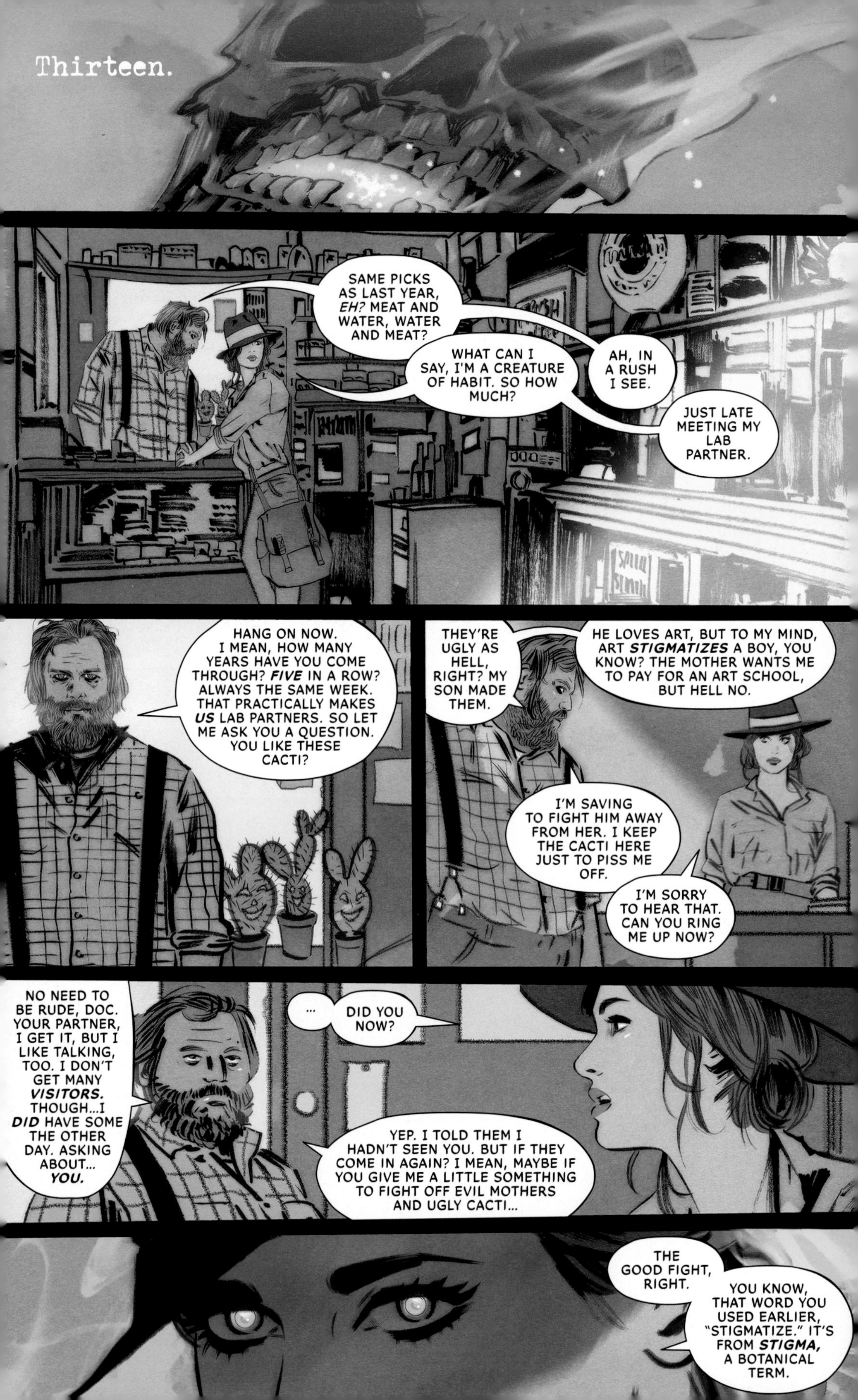
Thirteen.
SAME PICKS AS LAST YEAR, EH? MEAT AND WATER, WATER AND MEAT?
WHAT CAN I SAY, I'M A CREATURE OF HABIT. SO HOW MUCH?
AH, IN A RUSH I SEE.
JUST LATE MEETING MY LAB PARTNER.
HANG ON NOW. I MEAN, HOW MANY YEARS HAVE YOU COME THROUGH? FIVE IN A ROW? ALWAYS THE SAME WEEK. THAT PRACTICALLY MAKES US LAB PARTNERS. SO LET ME ASK YOU A QUESTION. YOU LIKE THESE CACTI?
THEY'RE UGLY AS HELL, RIGHT? MY SON MADE THEM.
HE LOVES ART, BUT TO MY MIND, ART STIGMATIZES A BOY, YOU KNOW? THE MOTHER WANTS ME TO PAY FOR AN ART SCHOOL, BUT HELL NO.
I'M SAVING TO FIGHT HIM AWAY FROM HER. I KEEP THE CACTI HERE JUST TO PISS ME OFF.
I'M SORRY TO HEAR THAT. CAN YOU RING ME UP NOW?
NO NEED TO BE RUDE, DOC. YOUR PARTNER, I GET IT, BUT I LIKE TALKING, TOO. I DON'T GET MANY VISITORS. THOUGH...I DID HAVE SOME THE OTHER DAY. ASKING ABOUT... YOU.
...
DID YOU NOW?
YEP. I TOLD THEM I HADN'T SEEN YOU. BUT IF THEY COME IN AGAIN? I MEAN, MAYBE IF YOU GIVE ME A LITTLE SOMETHING TO FIGHT OFF EVIL MOTHERS AND UGLY CACTI...
THE GOOD FIGHT, RIGHT.
YOU KNOW, THAT WORD YOU USED EARLIER, "STIGMATIZE." IT'S FROM STIGMA, A BOTANICAL TERM.

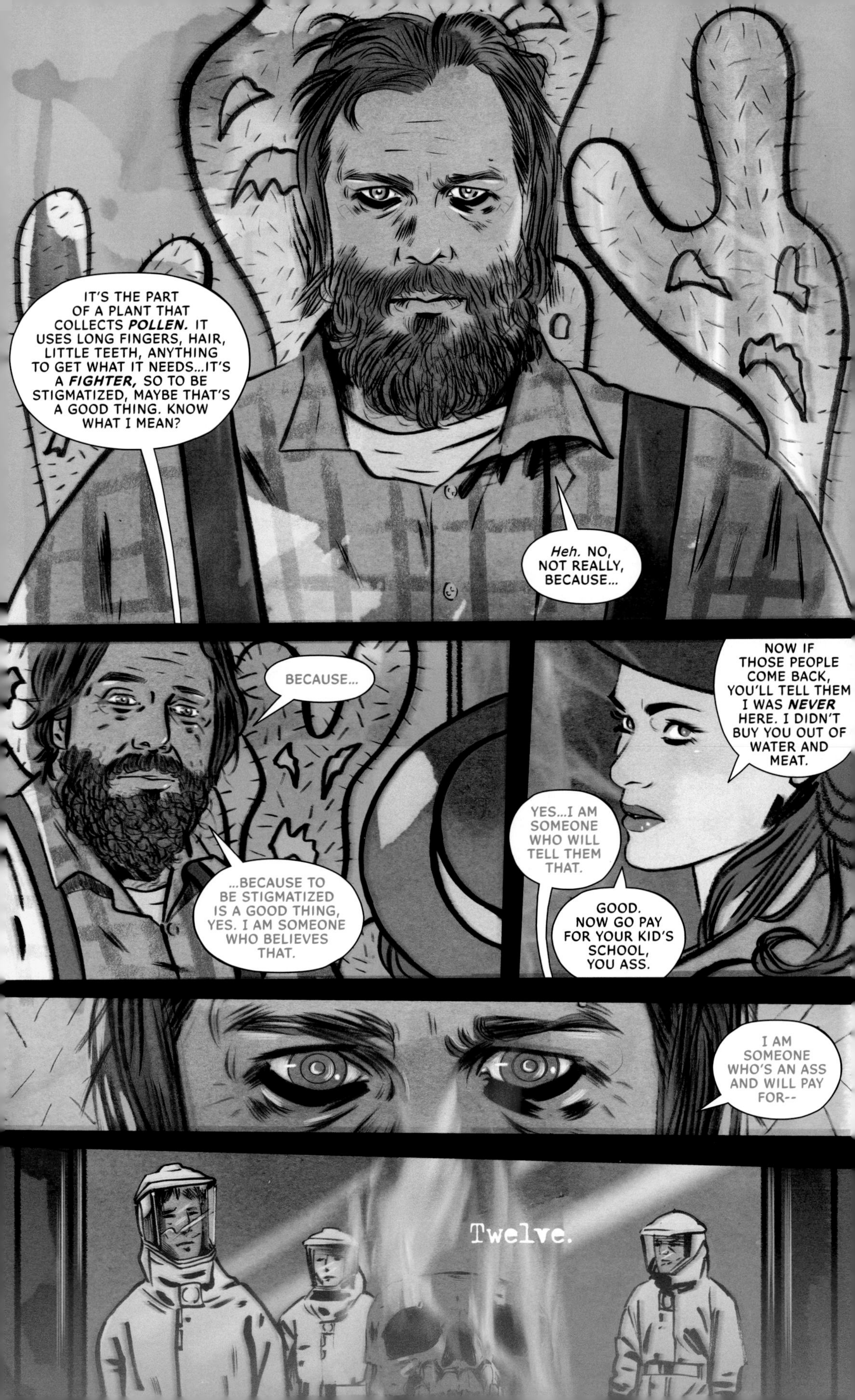
IT'S THE PART OF A PLANT THAT COLLECTS *POLLEN.* IT USES LONG FINGERS, HAIR, LITTLE TEETH, ANYTHING TO GET WHAT IT NEEDS...IT'S A *FIGHTER,* SO TO BE STIGMATIZED, MAYBE THAT'S A GOOD THING. KNOW WHAT I MEAN?
*Heh.* NO, NOT REALLY, BECAUSE...
BECAUSE...
...BECAUSE TO BE STIGMATIZED IS A GOOD THING, YES. I AM SOMEONE WHO BELIEVES THAT.
NOW IF THOSE PEOPLE COME BACK, YOU'LL TELL THEM I WAS *NEVER* HERE. I DIDN'T BUY YOU OUT OF WATER AND MEAT.
YES...I AM SOMEONE WHO WILL TELL THEM THAT.
GOOD. NOW GO PAY FOR YOUR KID'S SCHOOL, YOU ASS.
I AM SOMEONE WHO'S AN ASS AND WILL PAY FOR--
Twelve.

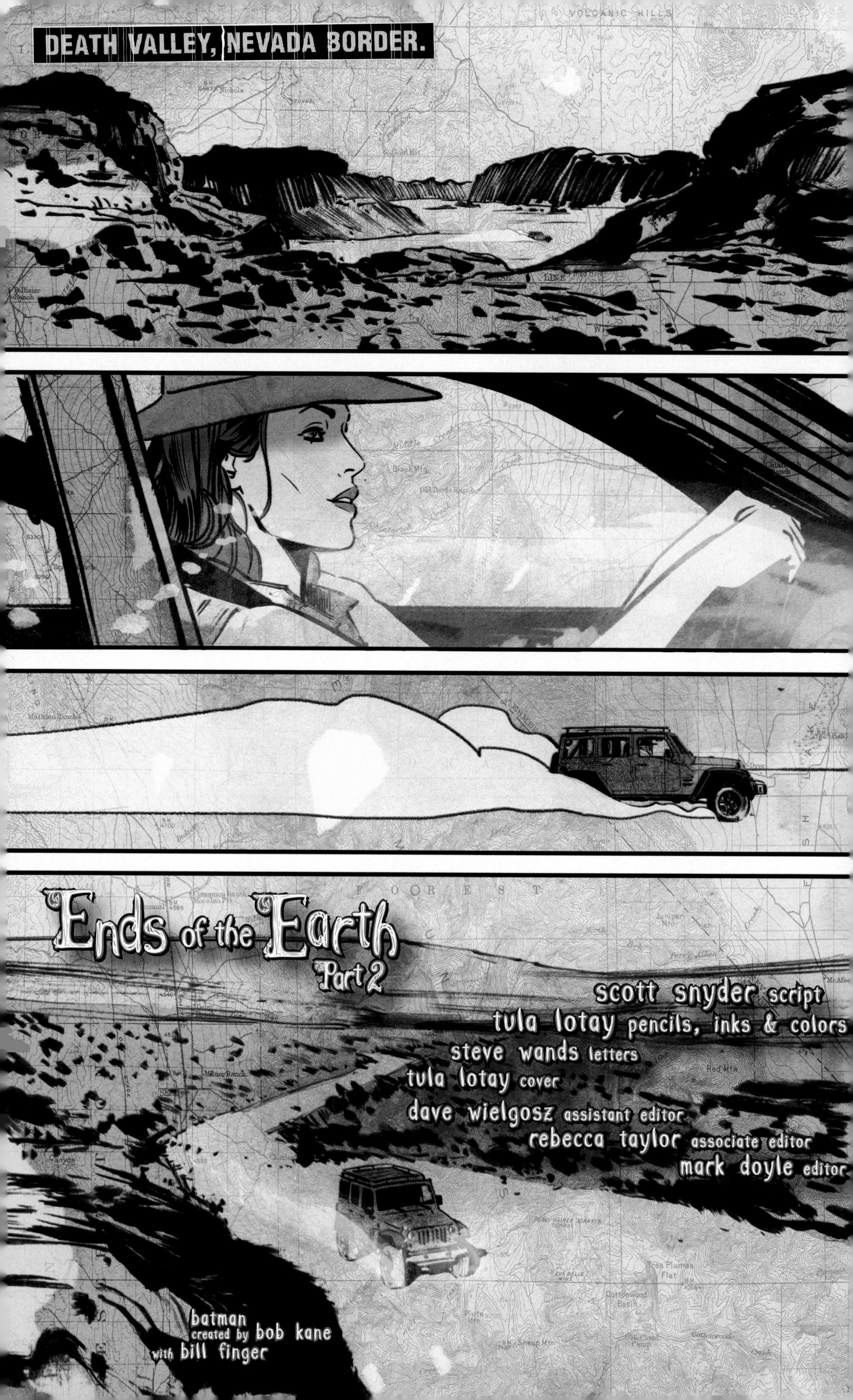

DEATH VALLEY, NEVADA BORDER.
Ends of the Earth
Part 2
scott snyder script
tula lotay pencils, inks & colors
steve wands letters
tula lotay cover
dave wielgosz assistant editor
rebecca taylor associate editor
mark doyle editor
batman
created by bob kane
with bill finger

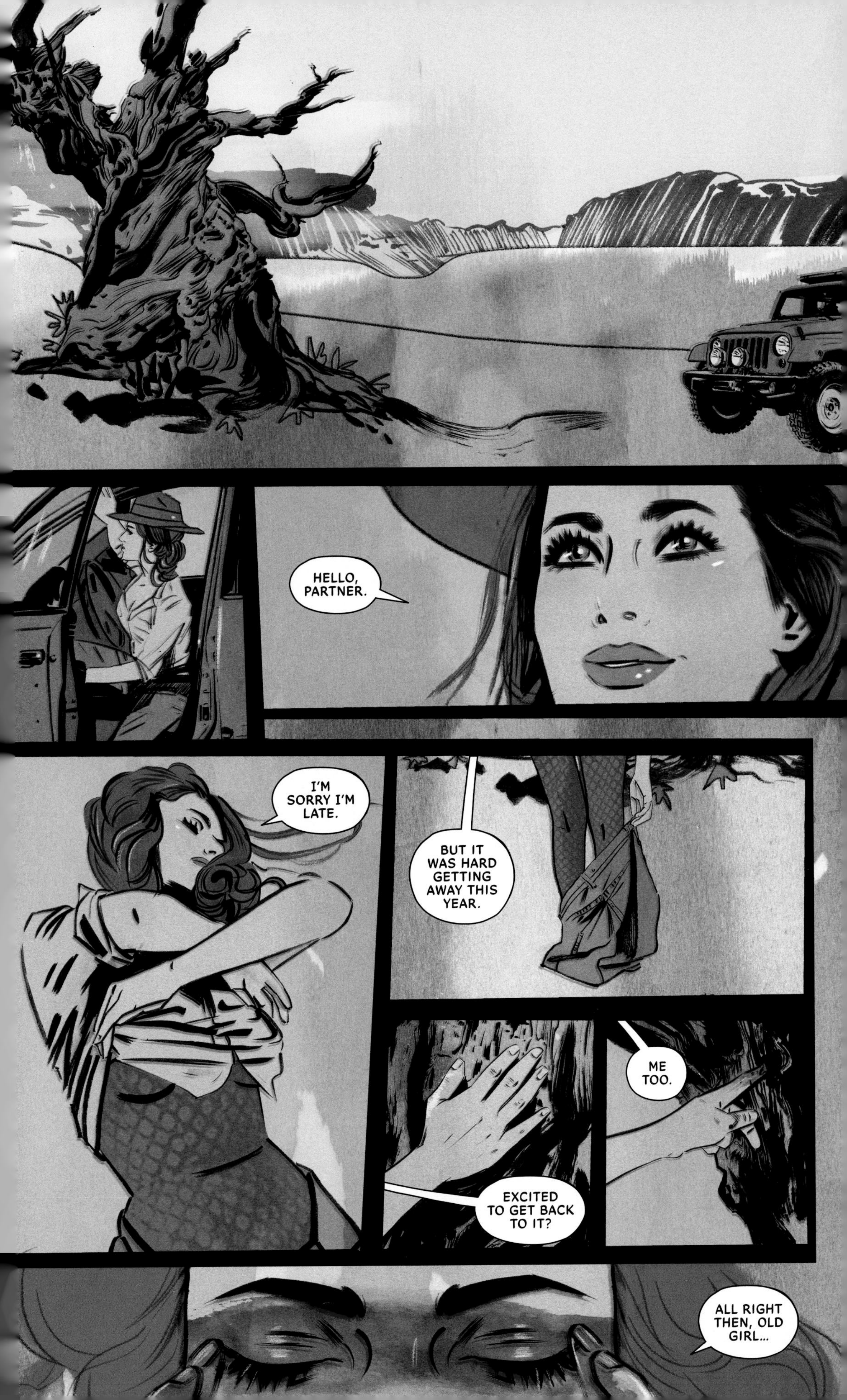
HELLO, PARTNER.
I'M SORRY I'M LATE.
BUT IT WAS HARD GETTING AWAY THIS YEAR.
EXCITED TO GET BACK TO IT?
ME TOO.
ALL RIGHT THEN, OLD GIRL...

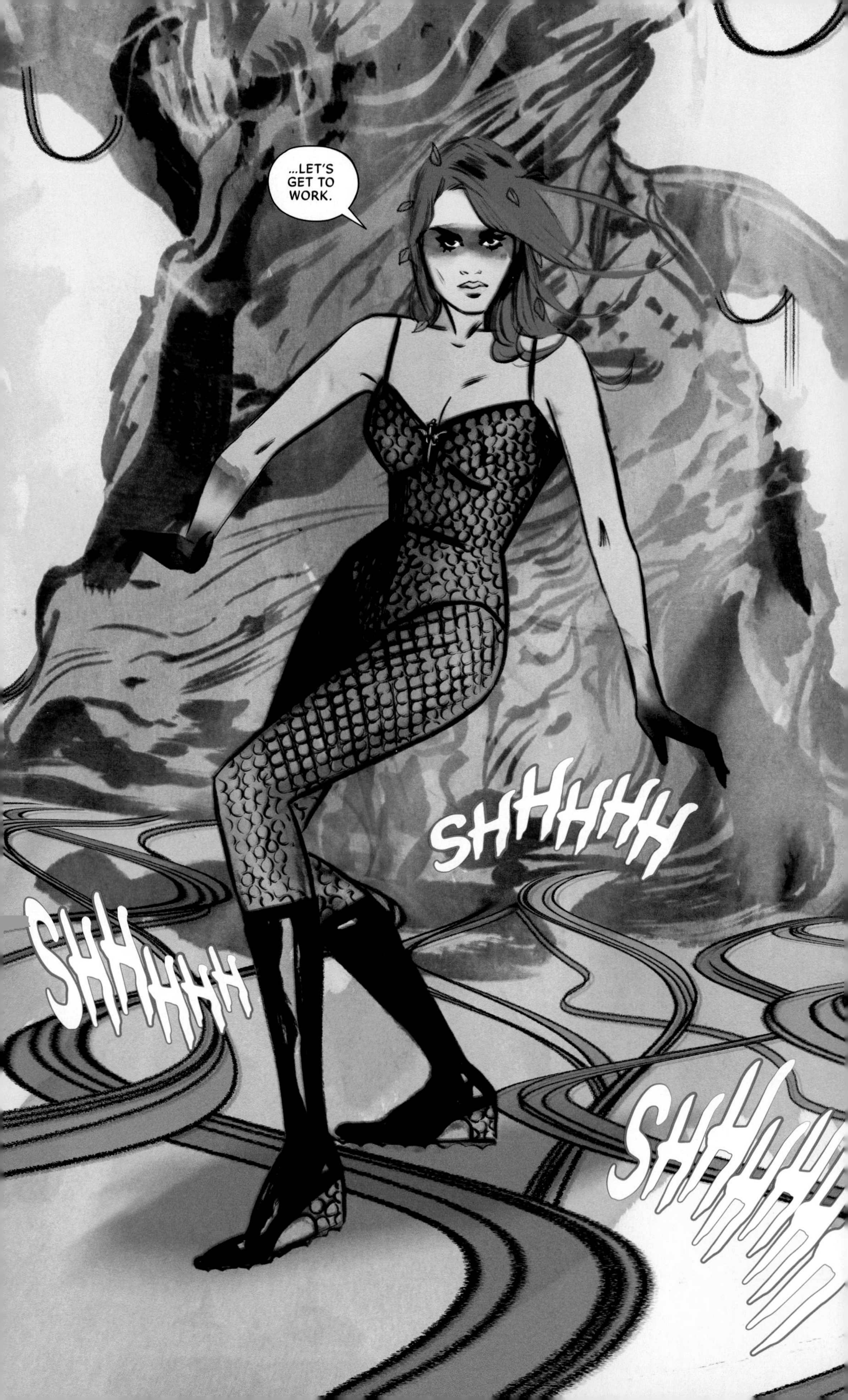
...LET'S GET TO WORK.
SHHHHH
SHHHHH
SHHHHH

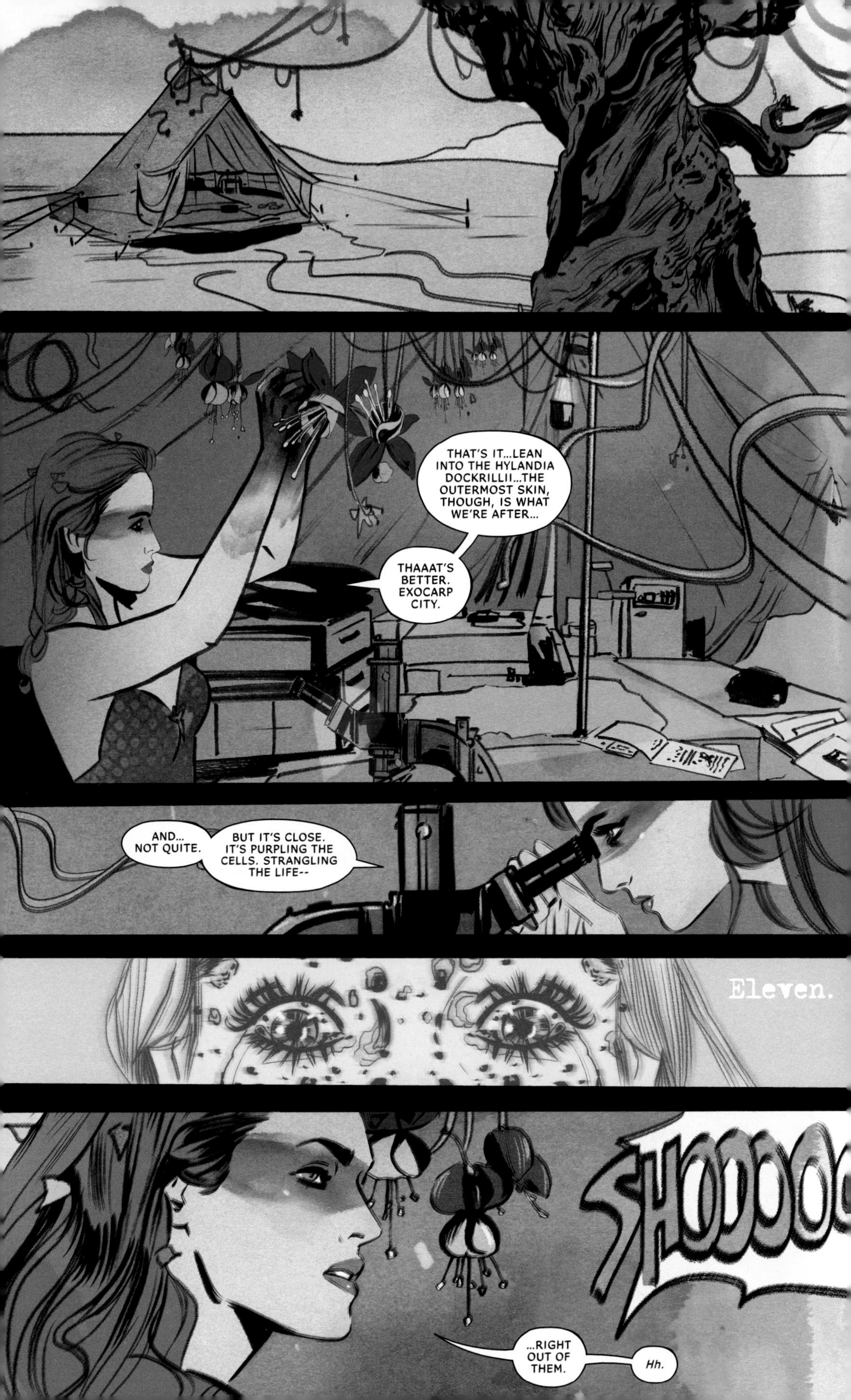
THAT'S IT...LEAN INTO THE HYLANDIA DOCKRILLII...THE OUTERMOST SKIN, THOUGH, IS WHAT WE'RE AFTER...
THAAAT'S BETTER. EXOCARP CITY.
AND... NOT QUITE.
BUT IT'S CLOSE. IT'S PURPLING THE CELLS. STRANGLING THE LIFE--
Eleven.
SHOOOOO
...RIGHT OUT OF THEM.
Hh.

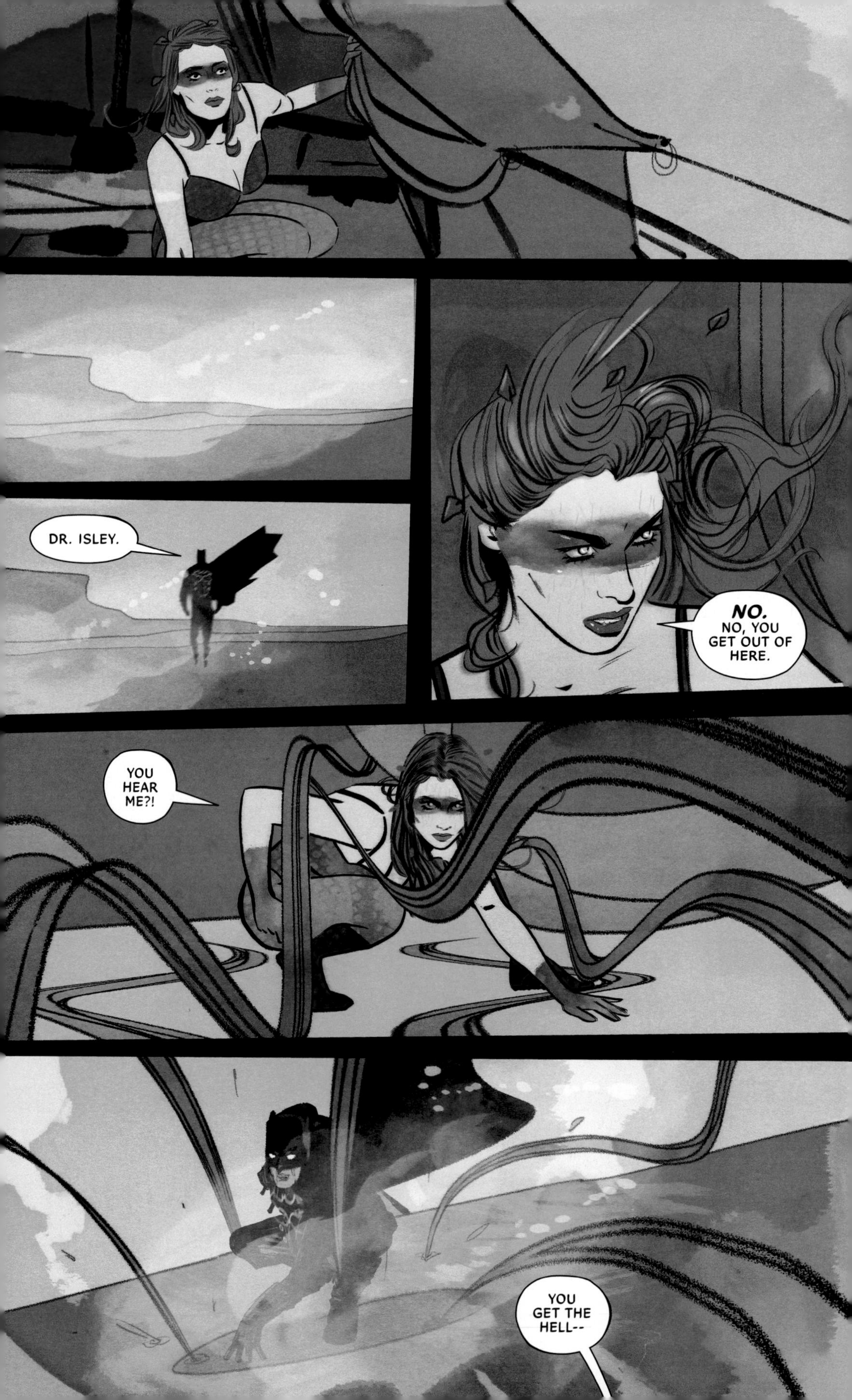
DR. ISLEY.
NO. NO, YOU GET OUT OF HERE.
YOU HEAR ME?!
YOU GET THE HELL--

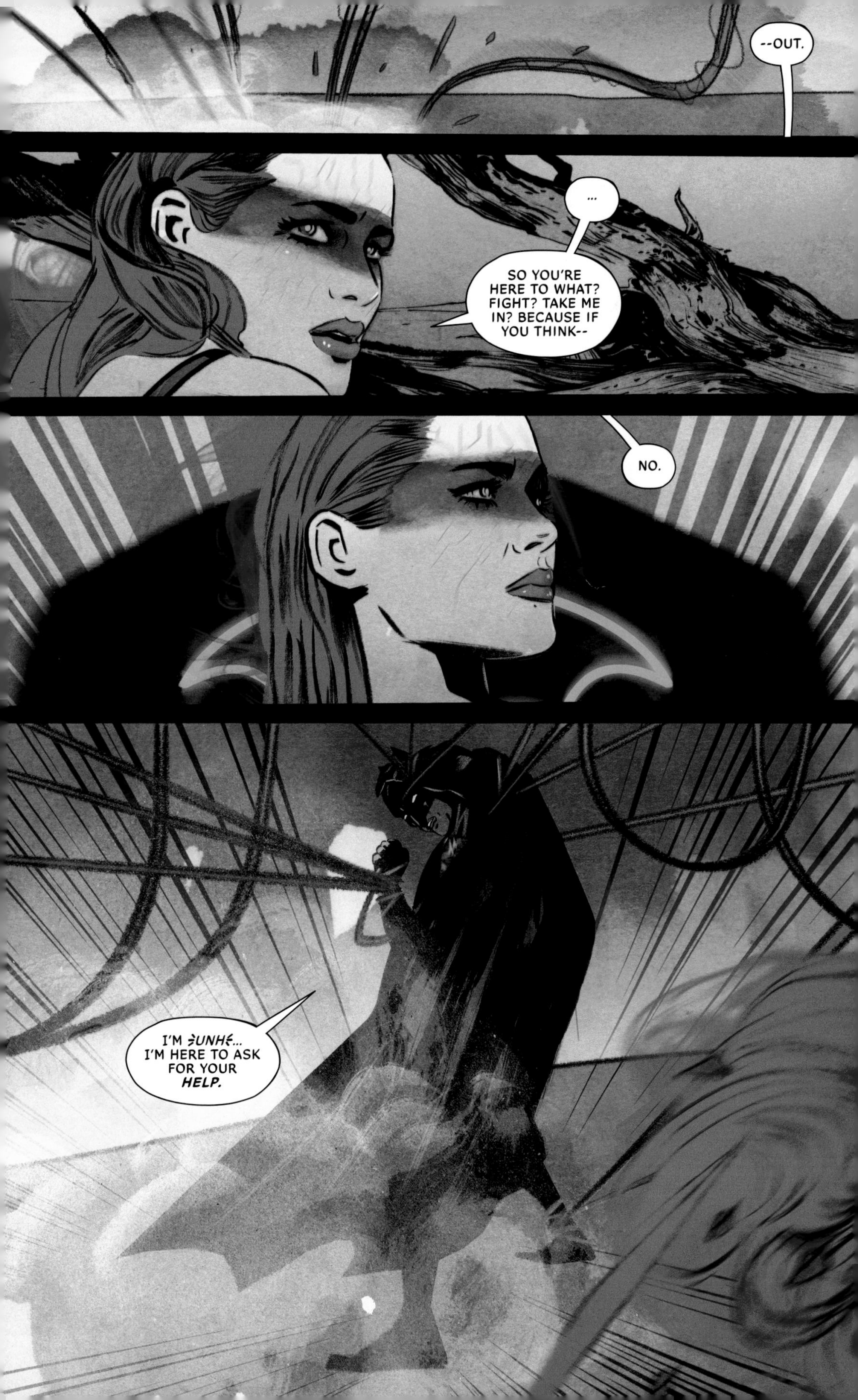
--OUT.
...
SO YOU'RE HERE TO WHAT? FIGHT? TAKE ME IN? BECAUSE IF YOU THINK--
NO.
I'M *UNH*... I'M HERE TO ASK FOR YOUR ***HELP.***

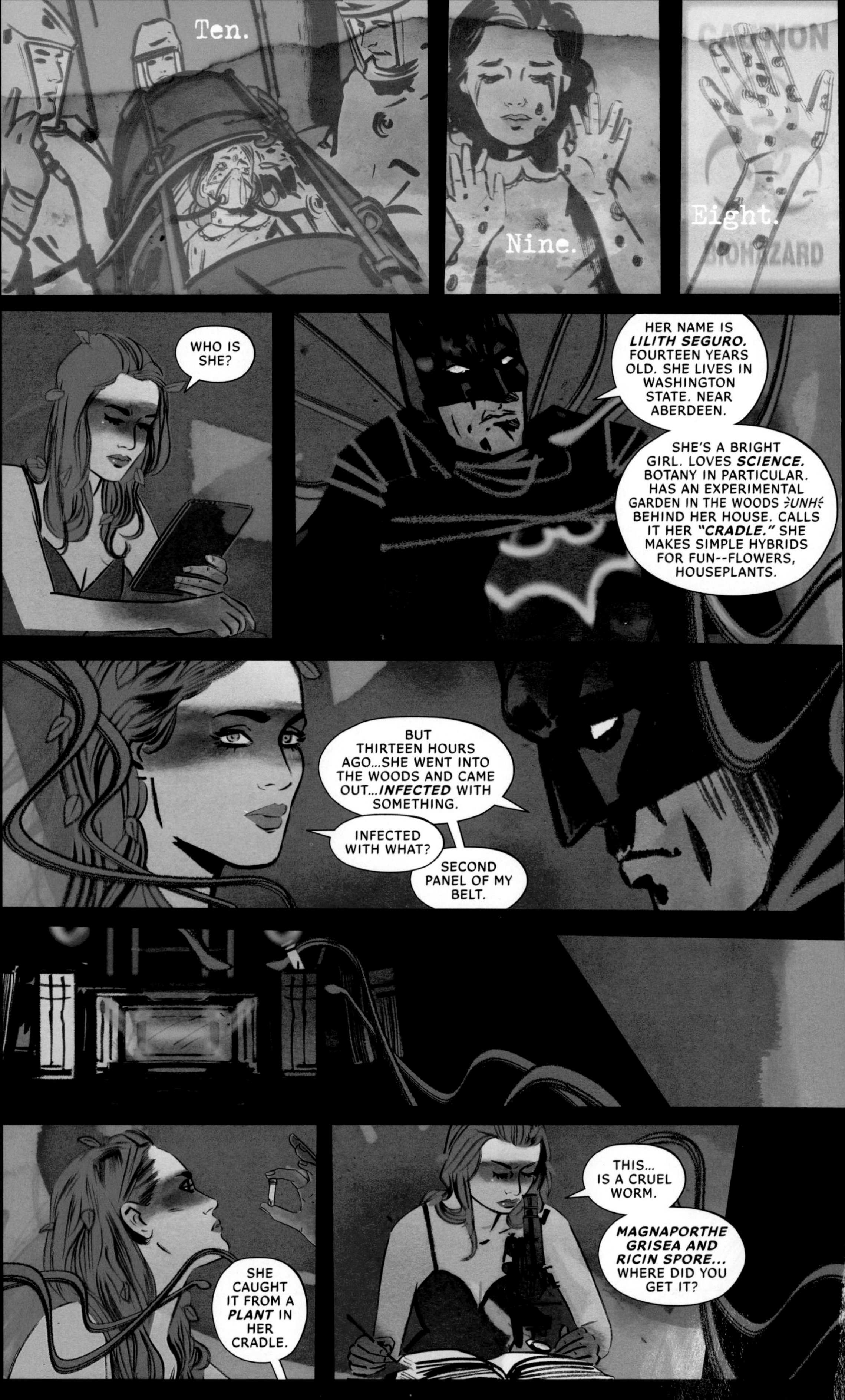
Ten.
Nine.
CAUTION
Eight.
BIOHAZARD
WHO IS SHE?
HER NAME IS LILITH SEGURO. FOURTEEN YEARS OLD. SHE LIVES IN WASHINGTON STATE. NEAR ABERDEEN.
SHE'S A BRIGHT GIRL. LOVES SCIENCE. BOTANY IN PARTICULAR. HAS AN EXPERIMENTAL GARDEN IN THE WOODS ⋟UNH⋞ BEHIND HER HOUSE. CALLS IT HER "CRADLE." SHE MAKES SIMPLE HYBRIDS FOR FUN--FLOWERS, HOUSEPLANTS.
BUT THIRTEEN HOURS AGO...SHE WENT INTO THE WOODS AND CAME OUT...INFECTED WITH SOMETHING.
INFECTED WITH WHAT?
SECOND PANEL OF MY BELT.
SHE CAUGHT IT FROM A PLANT IN HER CRADLE.
THIS... IS A CRUEL WORM.
MAGNAPORTHE GRISEA AND RICIN SPORE... WHERE DID YOU GET IT?

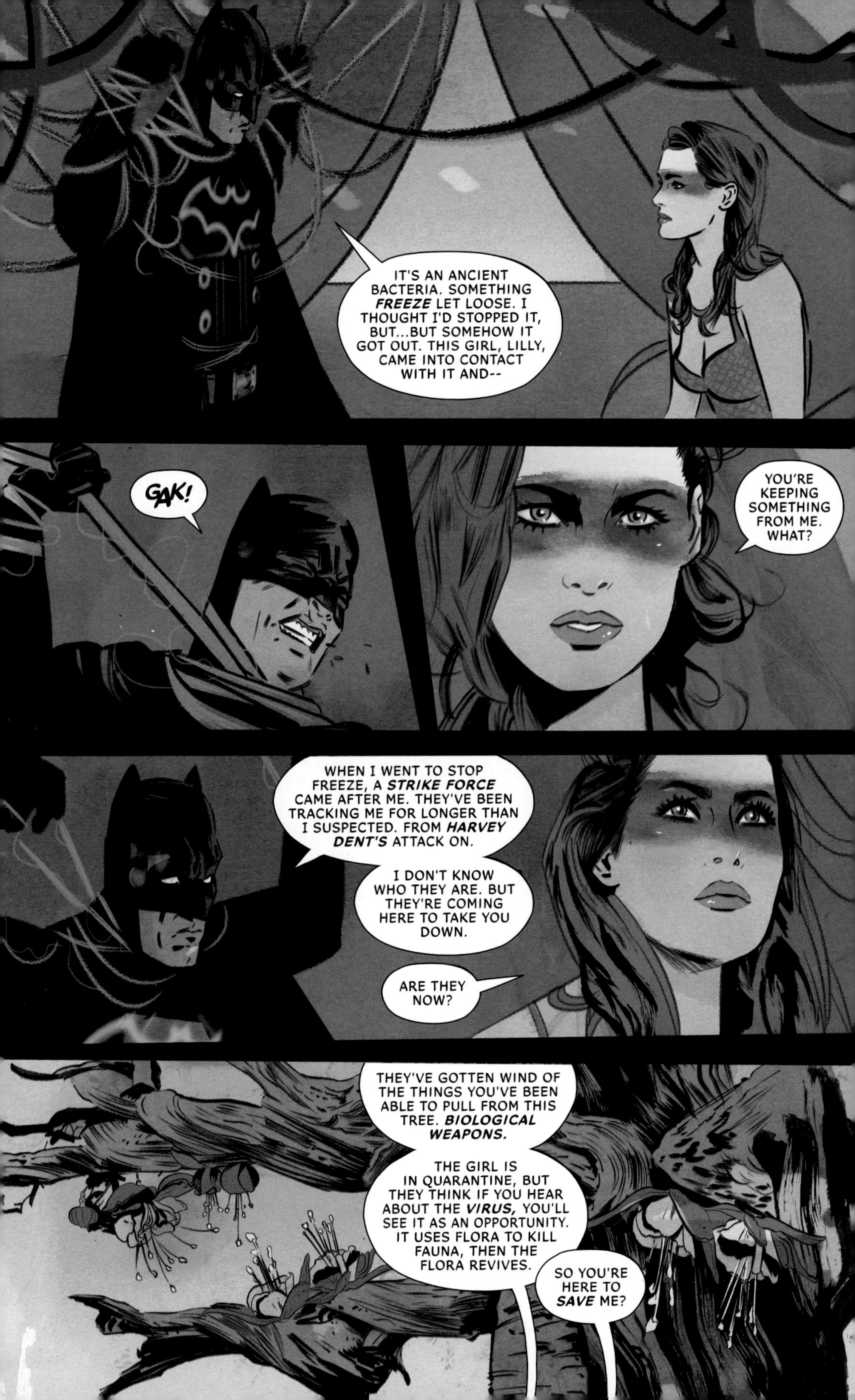
IT'S AN ANCIENT BACTERIA. SOMETHING FREEZE LET LOOSE. I THOUGHT I'D STOPPED IT, BUT...BUT SOMEHOW IT GOT OUT. THIS GIRL, LILLY, CAME INTO CONTACT WITH IT AND--
GAK!
YOU'RE KEEPING SOMETHING FROM ME. WHAT?
WHEN I WENT TO STOP FREEZE, A STRIKE FORCE CAME AFTER ME. THEY'VE BEEN TRACKING ME FOR LONGER THAN I SUSPECTED. FROM HARVEY DENT'S ATTACK ON.
I DON'T KNOW WHO THEY ARE. BUT THEY'RE COMING HERE TO TAKE YOU DOWN.
ARE THEY NOW?
THEY'VE GOTTEN WIND OF THE THINGS YOU'VE BEEN ABLE TO PULL FROM THIS TREE. BIOLOGICAL WEAPONS.
THE GIRL IS IN QUARANTINE, BUT THEY THINK IF YOU HEAR ABOUT THE VIRUS, YOU'LL SEE IT AS AN OPPORTUNITY. IT USES FLORA TO KILL FAUNA, THEN THE FLORA REVIVES.
SO YOU'RE HERE TO SAVE ME?

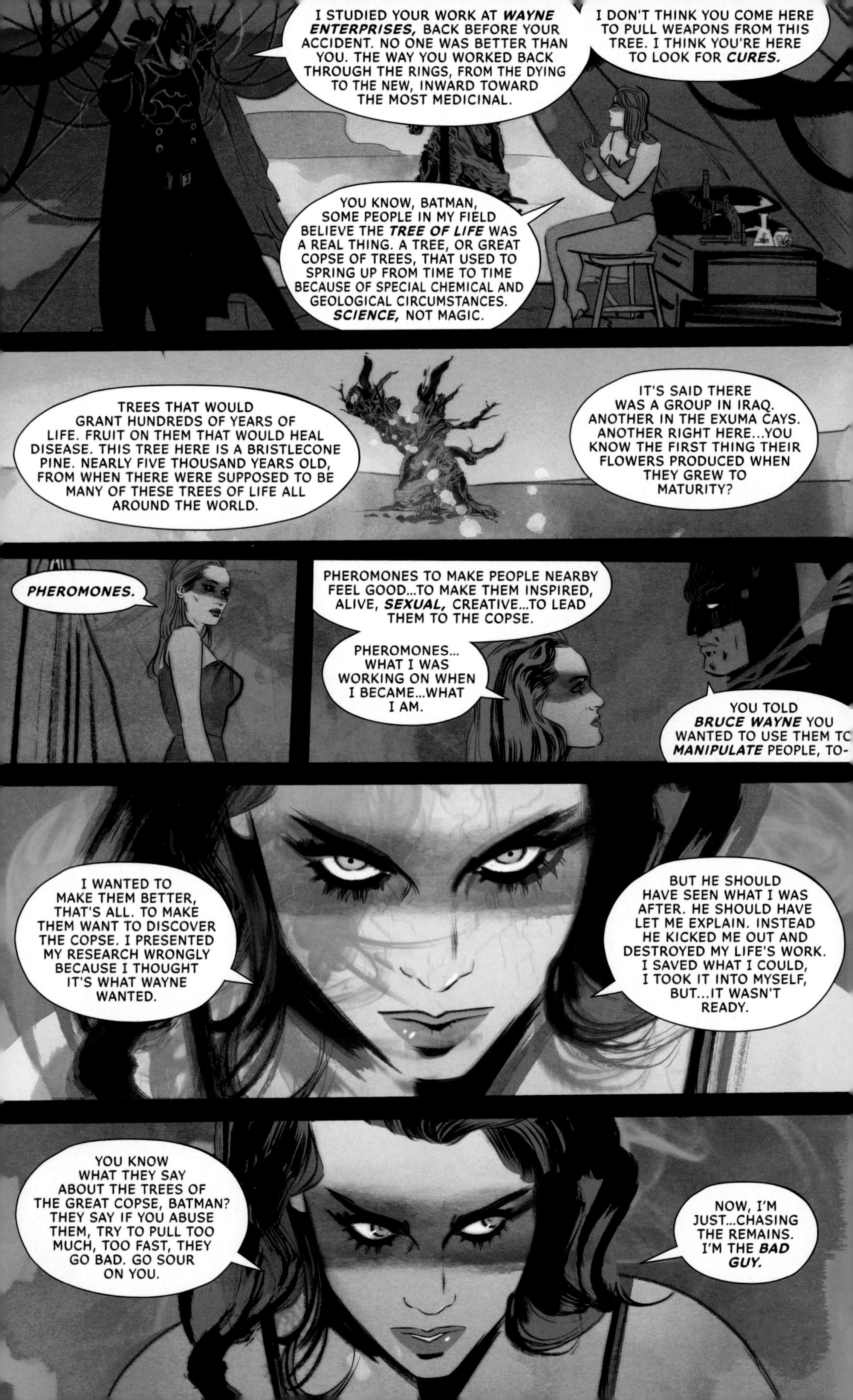
I STUDIED YOUR WORK AT WAYNE ENTERPRISES, BACK BEFORE YOUR ACCIDENT. NO ONE WAS BETTER THAN YOU. THE WAY YOU WORKED BACK THROUGH THE RINGS, FROM THE DYING TO THE NEW, INWARD TOWARD THE MOST MEDICINAL.
I DON'T THINK YOU COME HERE TO PULL WEAPONS FROM THIS TREE. I THINK YOU'RE HERE TO LOOK FOR CURES.
YOU KNOW, BATMAN, SOME PEOPLE IN MY FIELD BELIEVE THE TREE OF LIFE WAS A REAL THING. A TREE, OR GREAT COPSE OF TREES, THAT USED TO SPRING UP FROM TIME TO TIME BECAUSE OF SPECIAL CHEMICAL AND GEOLOGICAL CIRCUMSTANCES. SCIENCE, NOT MAGIC.
TREES THAT WOULD GRANT HUNDREDS OF YEARS OF LIFE. FRUIT ON THEM THAT WOULD HEAL DISEASE. THIS TREE HERE IS A BRISTLECONE PINE. NEARLY FIVE THOUSAND YEARS OLD, FROM WHEN THERE WERE SUPPOSED TO BE MANY OF THESE TREES OF LIFE ALL AROUND THE WORLD.
IT'S SAID THERE WAS A GROUP IN IRAQ. ANOTHER IN THE EXUMA CAYS. ANOTHER RIGHT HERE...YOU KNOW THE FIRST THING THEIR FLOWERS PRODUCED WHEN THEY GREW TO MATURITY?
PHEROMONES.
PHEROMONES TO MAKE PEOPLE NEARBY FEEL GOOD...TO MAKE THEM INSPIRED, ALIVE, SEXUAL, CREATIVE...TO LEAD THEM TO THE COPSE.
PHEROMONES... WHAT I WAS WORKING ON WHEN I BECAME...WHAT I AM.
YOU TOLD BRUCE WAYNE YOU WANTED TO USE THEM TO MANIPULATE PEOPLE, TO-
I WANTED TO MAKE THEM BETTER, THAT'S ALL. TO MAKE THEM WANT TO DISCOVER THE COPSE. I PRESENTED MY RESEARCH WRONGLY BECAUSE I THOUGHT IT'S WHAT WAYNE WANTED.
BUT HE SHOULD HAVE SEEN WHAT I WAS AFTER. HE SHOULD HAVE LET ME EXPLAIN. INSTEAD HE KICKED ME OUT AND DESTROYED MY LIFE'S WORK. I SAVED WHAT I COULD, I TOOK IT INTO MYSELF, BUT...IT WASN'T READY.
YOU KNOW WHAT THEY SAY ABOUT THE TREES OF THE GREAT COPSE, BATMAN? THEY SAY IF YOU ABUSE THEM, TRY TO PULL TOO MUCH, TOO FAST, THEY GO BAD. GO SOUR ON YOU.
NOW, I'M JUST...CHASING THE REMAINS. I'M THE BAD GUY.

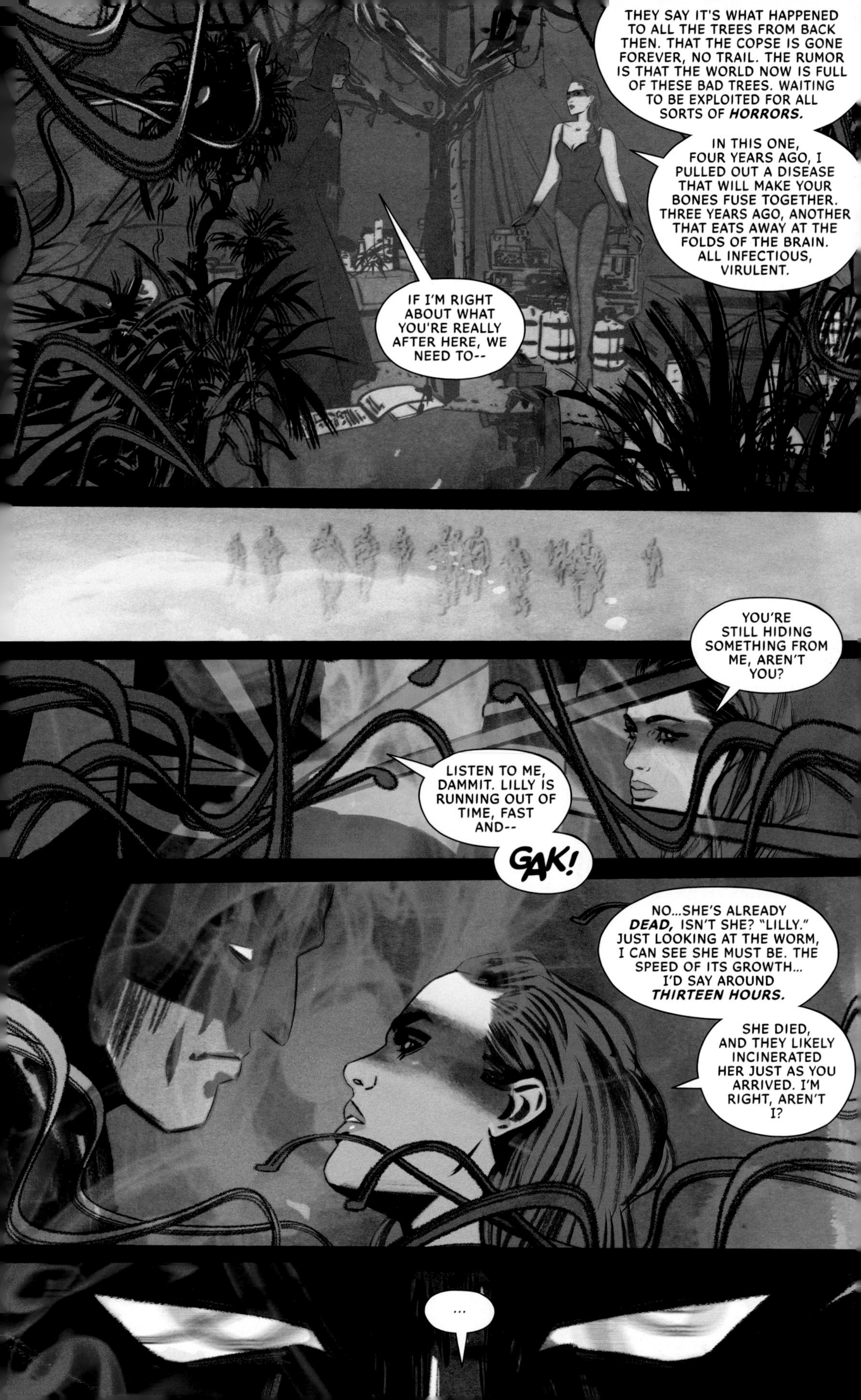
THEY SAY IT'S WHAT HAPPENED TO ALL THE TREES FROM BACK THEN. THAT THE COPSE IS GONE FOREVER, NO TRAIL. THE RUMOR IS THAT THE WORLD NOW IS FULL OF THESE BAD TREES. WAITING TO BE EXPLOITED FOR ALL SORTS OF *HORRORS.*
IN THIS ONE, FOUR YEARS AGO, I PULLED OUT A DISEASE THAT WILL MAKE YOUR BONES FUSE TOGETHER. THREE YEARS AGO, ANOTHER THAT EATS AWAY AT THE FOLDS OF THE BRAIN. ALL INFECTIOUS, VIRULENT.
IF I'M RIGHT ABOUT WHAT YOU'RE REALLY AFTER HERE, WE NEED TO--
YOU'RE STILL HIDING SOMETHING FROM ME, AREN'T YOU?
LISTEN TO ME, DAMMIT. LILLY IS RUNNING OUT OF TIME, FAST AND--
GAK!
NO...SHE'S ALREADY *DEAD,* ISN'T SHE? "LILLY." JUST LOOKING AT THE WORM, I CAN SEE SHE MUST BE. THE SPEED OF ITS GROWTH... I'D SAY AROUND *THIRTEEN HOURS.*
SHE DIED, AND THEY LIKELY INCINERATED HER JUST AS YOU ARRIVED. I'M RIGHT, AREN'T I?
...

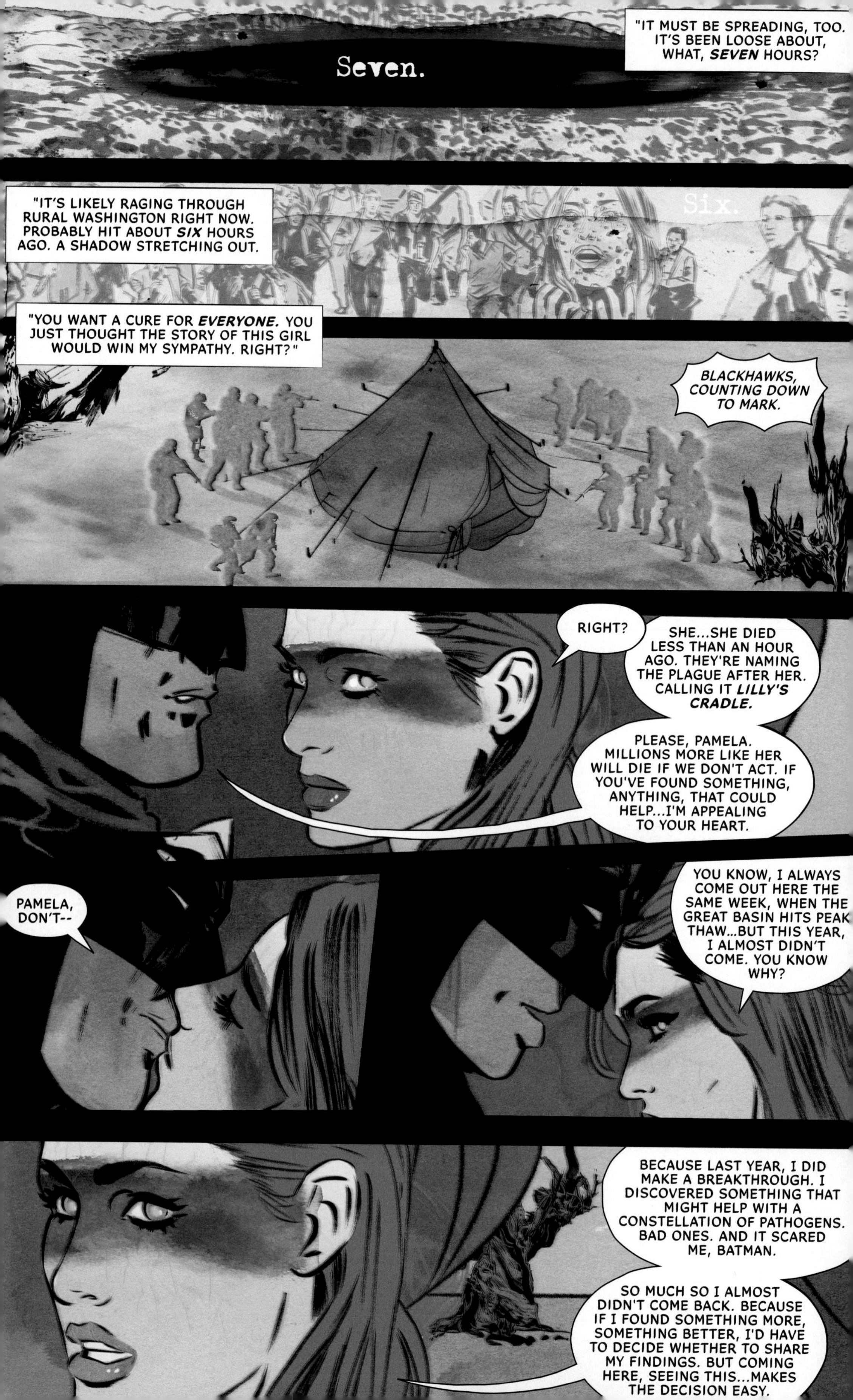
Seven.
"IT MUST BE SPREADING, TOO. IT'S BEEN LOOSE ABOUT, WHAT, SEVEN HOURS?
Six.
"IT'S LIKELY RAGING THROUGH RURAL WASHINGTON RIGHT NOW. PROBABLY HIT ABOUT SIX HOURS AGO. A SHADOW STRETCHING OUT.
"YOU WANT A CURE FOR EVERYONE. YOU JUST THOUGHT THE STORY OF THIS GIRL WOULD WIN MY SYMPATHY. RIGHT?"
BLACKHAWKS, COUNTING DOWN TO MARK.
RIGHT?
SHE...SHE DIED LESS THAN AN HOUR AGO. THEY'RE NAMING THE PLAGUE AFTER HER. CALLING IT LILLY'S CRADLE.
PLEASE, PAMELA. MILLIONS MORE LIKE HER WILL DIE IF WE DON'T ACT. IF YOU'VE FOUND SOMETHING, ANYTHING, THAT COULD HELP...I'M APPEALING TO YOUR HEART.
PAMELA, DON'T--
YOU KNOW, I ALWAYS COME OUT HERE THE SAME WEEK, WHEN THE GREAT BASIN HITS PEAK THAW...BUT THIS YEAR, I ALMOST DIDN'T COME. YOU KNOW WHY?
BECAUSE LAST YEAR, I DID MAKE A BREAKTHROUGH. I DISCOVERED SOMETHING THAT MIGHT HELP WITH A CONSTELLATION OF PATHOGENS. BAD ONES. AND IT SCARED ME, BATMAN.
SO MUCH SO I ALMOST DIDN'T COME BACK. BECAUSE IF I FOUND SOMETHING MORE, SOMETHING BETTER, I'D HAVE TO DECIDE WHETHER TO SHARE MY FINDINGS. BUT COMING HERE, SEEING THIS...MAKES THE DECISION EASY.

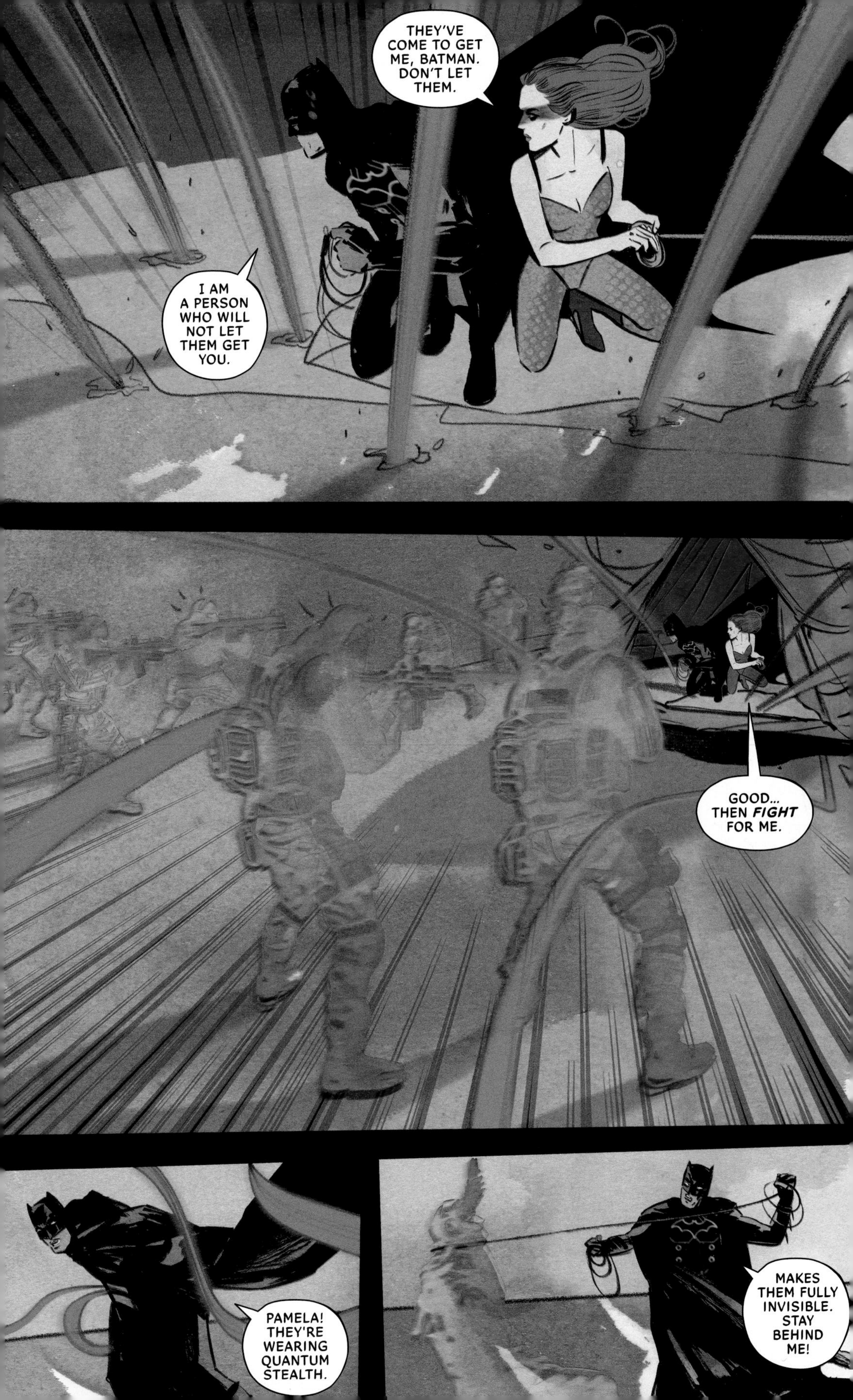
THEY'VE COME TO GET ME, BATMAN. DON'T LET THEM.
I AM A PERSON WHO WILL NOT LET THEM GET YOU.
GOOD... THEN *FIGHT* FOR ME.
PAMELA! THEY'RE WEARING QUANTUM STEALTH.
MAKES THEM FULLY INVISIBLE. STAY BEHIND ME!

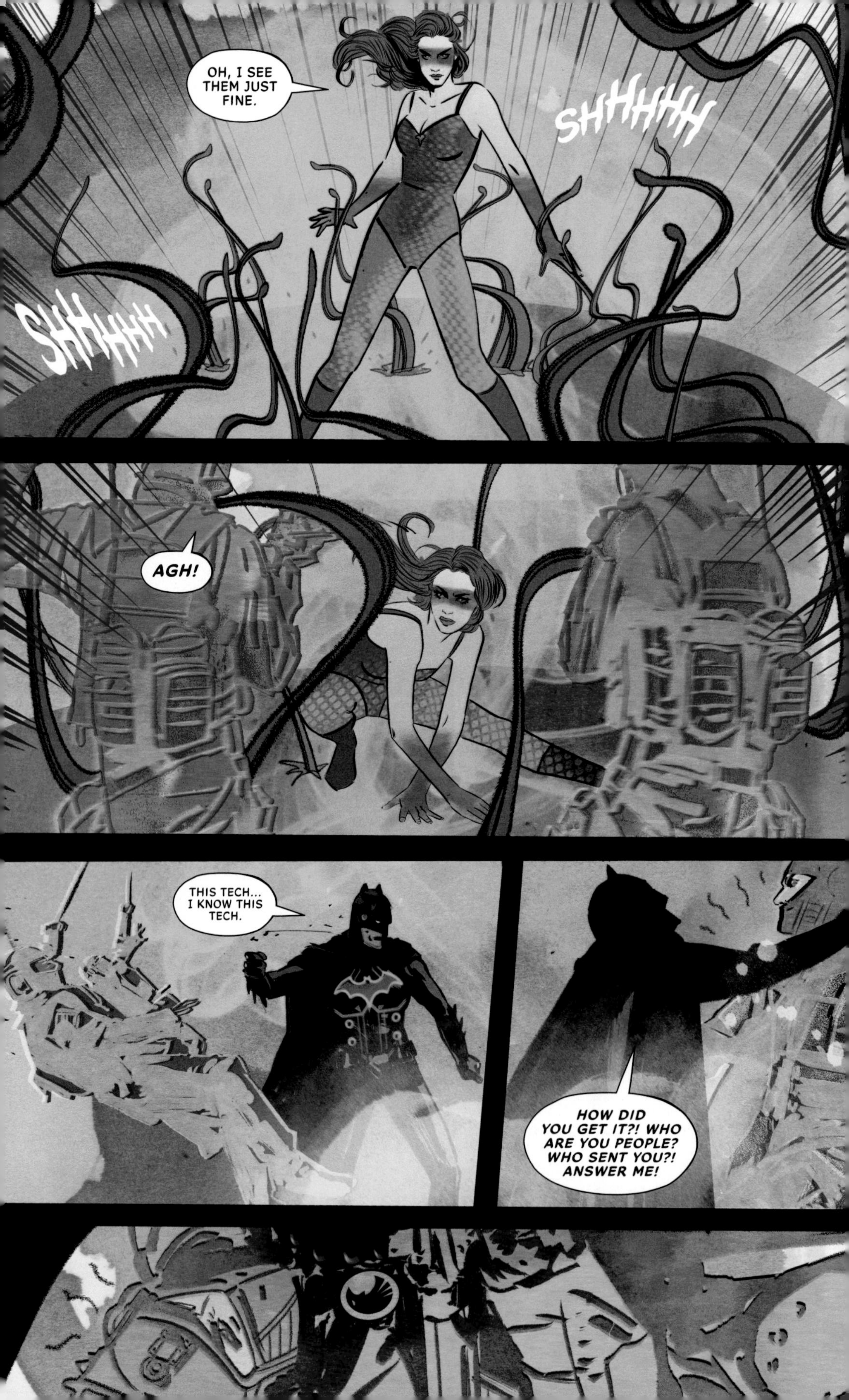
OH, I SEE THEM JUST FINE.
SHHHHHH
SHHHHH
AGH!
THIS TECH... I KNOW THIS TECH.
HOW DID YOU GET IT?! WHO ARE YOU PEOPLE? WHO SENT YOU?! ANSWER ME!

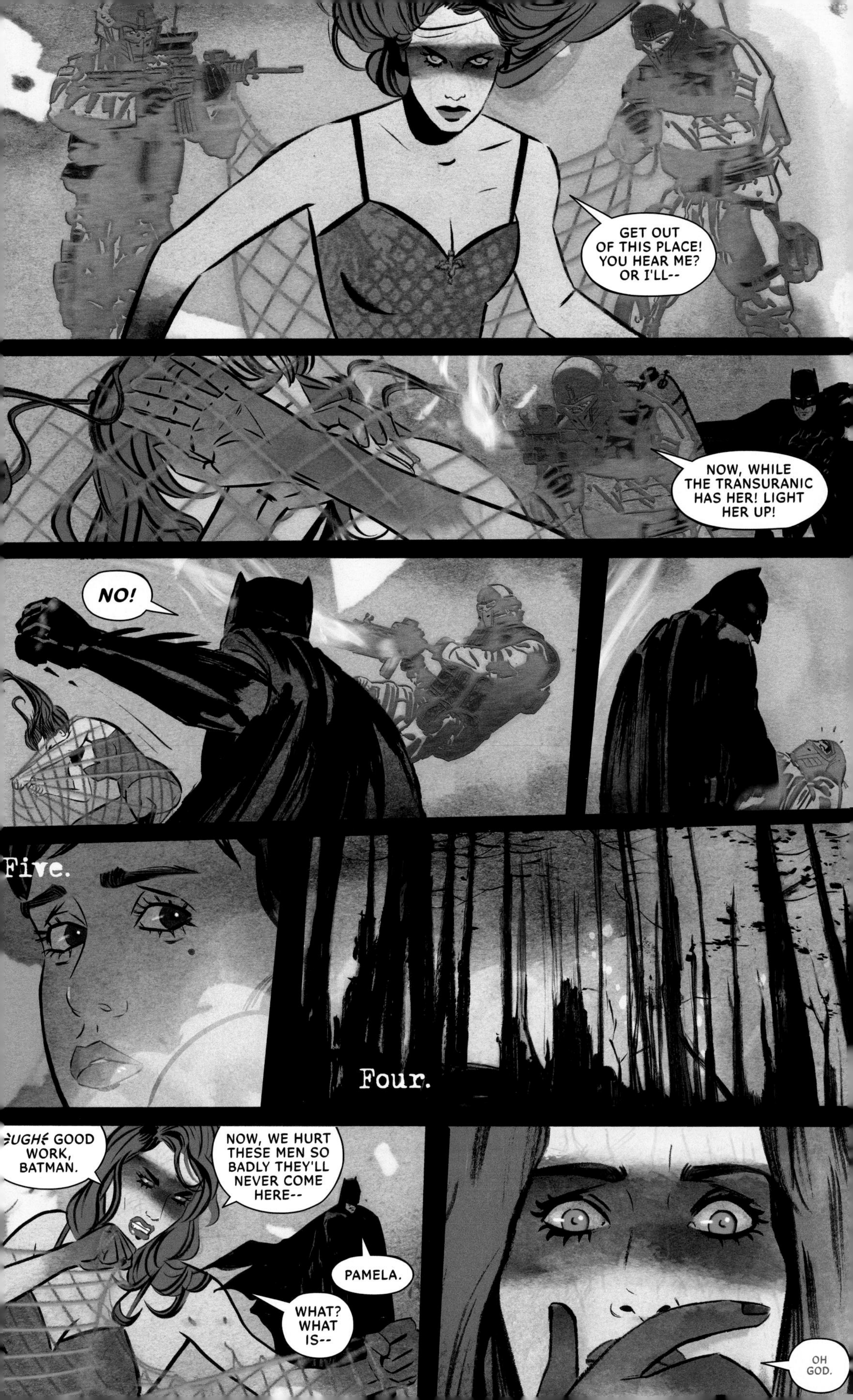
GET OUT OF THIS PLACE! YOU HEAR ME? OR I'LL--
NOW, WHILE THE TRANSURANIC HAS HER! LIGHT HER UP!
NO!
Five.
Four.
UGH GOOD WORK, BATMAN.
NOW, WE HURT THESE MEN SO BADLY THEY'LL NEVER COME HERE--
PAMELA.
WHAT? WHAT IS--
OH GOD.

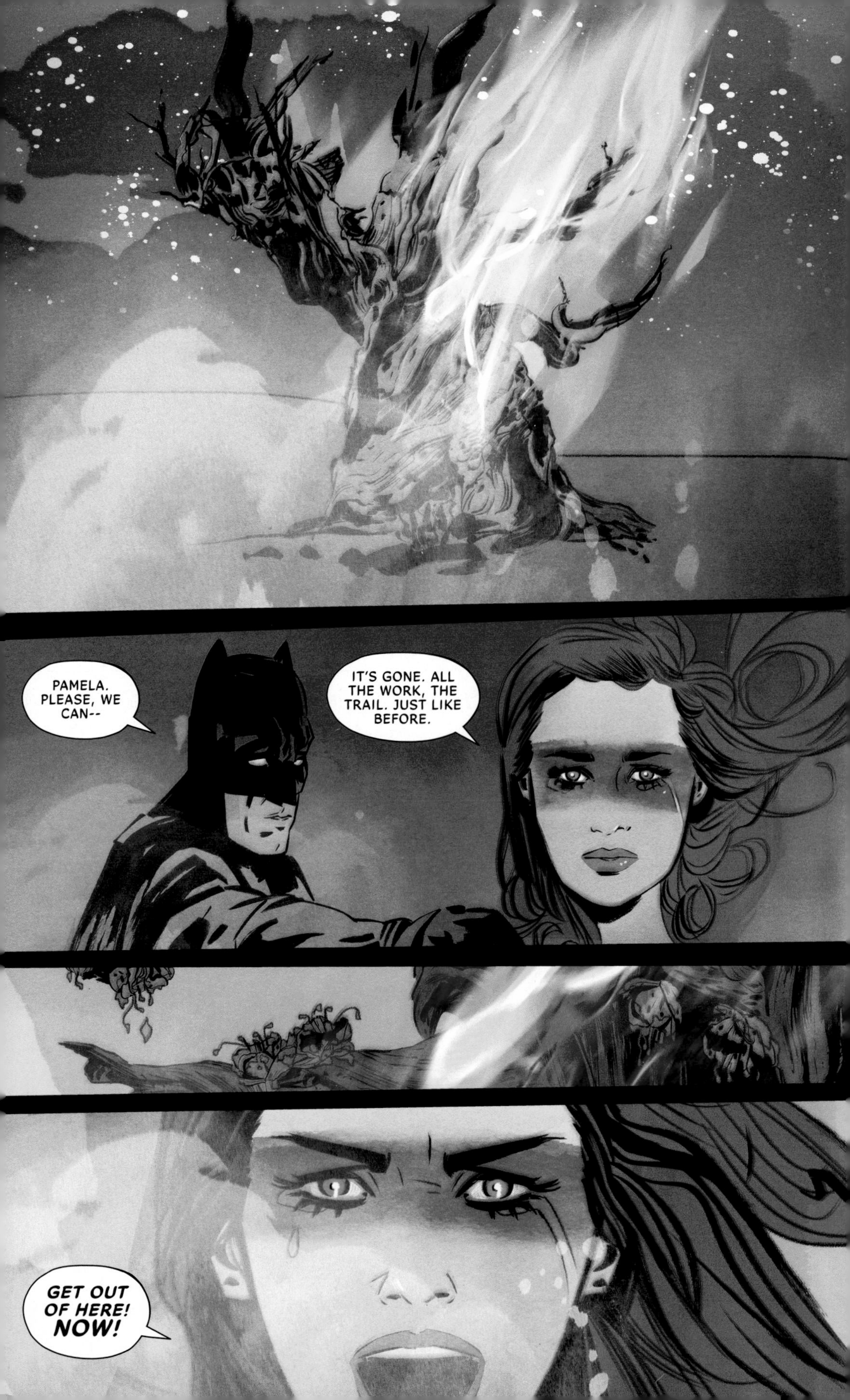
PAMELA. PLEASE, WE CAN--
IT'S GONE. ALL THE WORK, THE TRAIL. JUST LIKE BEFORE.
GET OUT OF HERE! NOW!

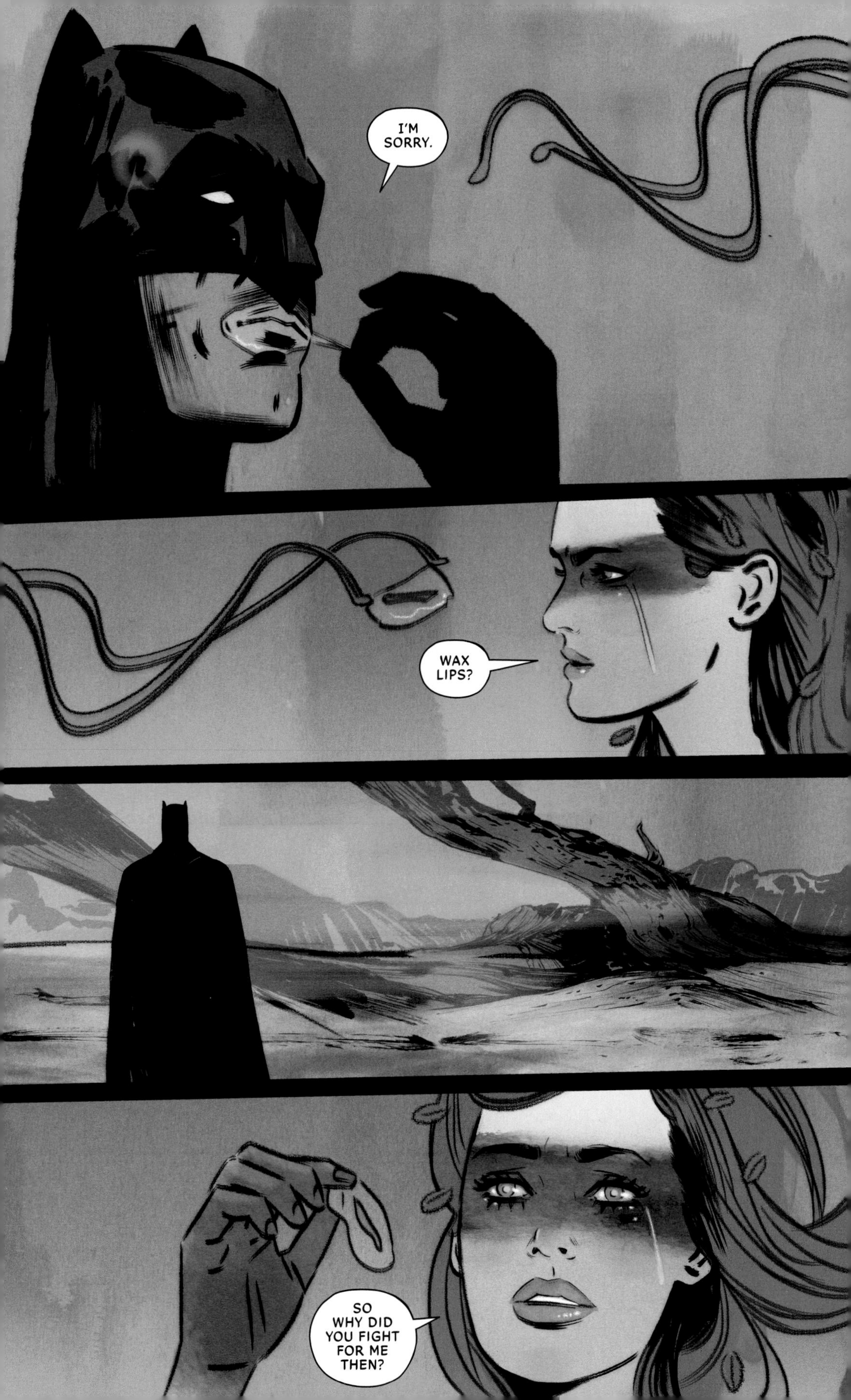
I'M SORRY.
WAX LIPS?
SO WHY DID YOU FIGHT FOR ME THEN?

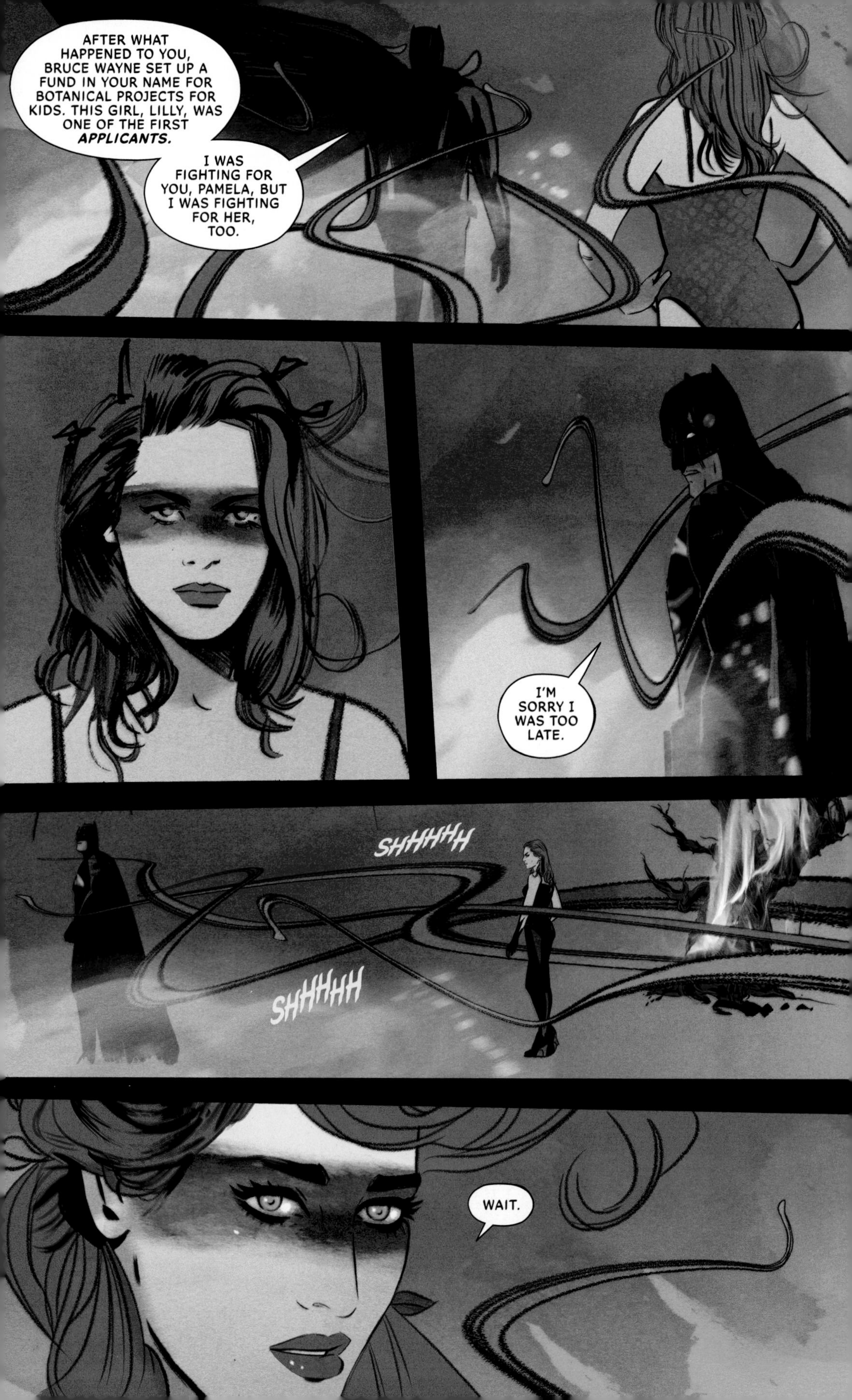
AFTER WHAT HAPPENED TO YOU, BRUCE WAYNE SET UP A FUND IN YOUR NAME FOR BOTANICAL PROJECTS FOR KIDS. THIS GIRL, LILLY, WAS ONE OF THE FIRST *APPLICANTS.*
I WAS FIGHTING FOR YOU, PAMELA, BUT I WAS FIGHTING FOR HER, TOO.
I'M SORRY I WAS TOO LATE.
SHHHHH
SHHHHH
WAIT.

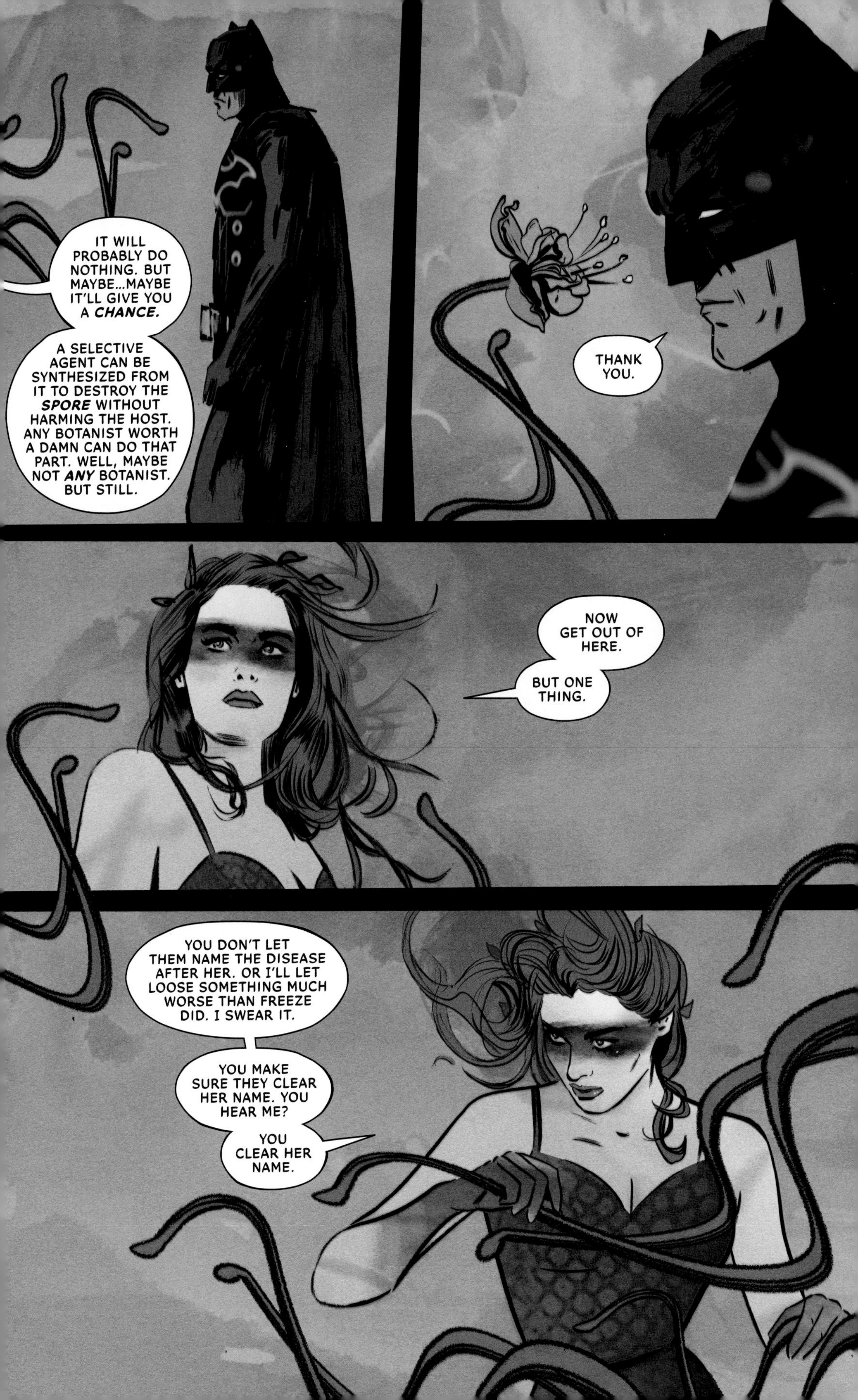
IT WILL PROBABLY DO NOTHING. BUT MAYBE...MAYBE IT'LL GIVE YOU A *CHANCE.*
A SELECTIVE AGENT CAN BE SYNTHESIZED FROM IT TO DESTROY THE *SPORE* WITHOUT HARMING THE HOST. ANY BOTANIST WORTH A DAMN CAN DO THAT PART. WELL, MAYBE NOT *ANY* BOTANIST. BUT STILL.
THANK YOU.
NOW GET OUT OF HERE.
BUT ONE THING.
YOU DON'T LET THEM NAME THE DISEASE AFTER HER. OR I'LL LET LOOSE SOMETHING MUCH WORSE THAN FREEZE DID. I SWEAR IT.
YOU MAKE SURE THEY CLEAR HER NAME. YOU HEAR ME?
YOU CLEAR HER NAME.

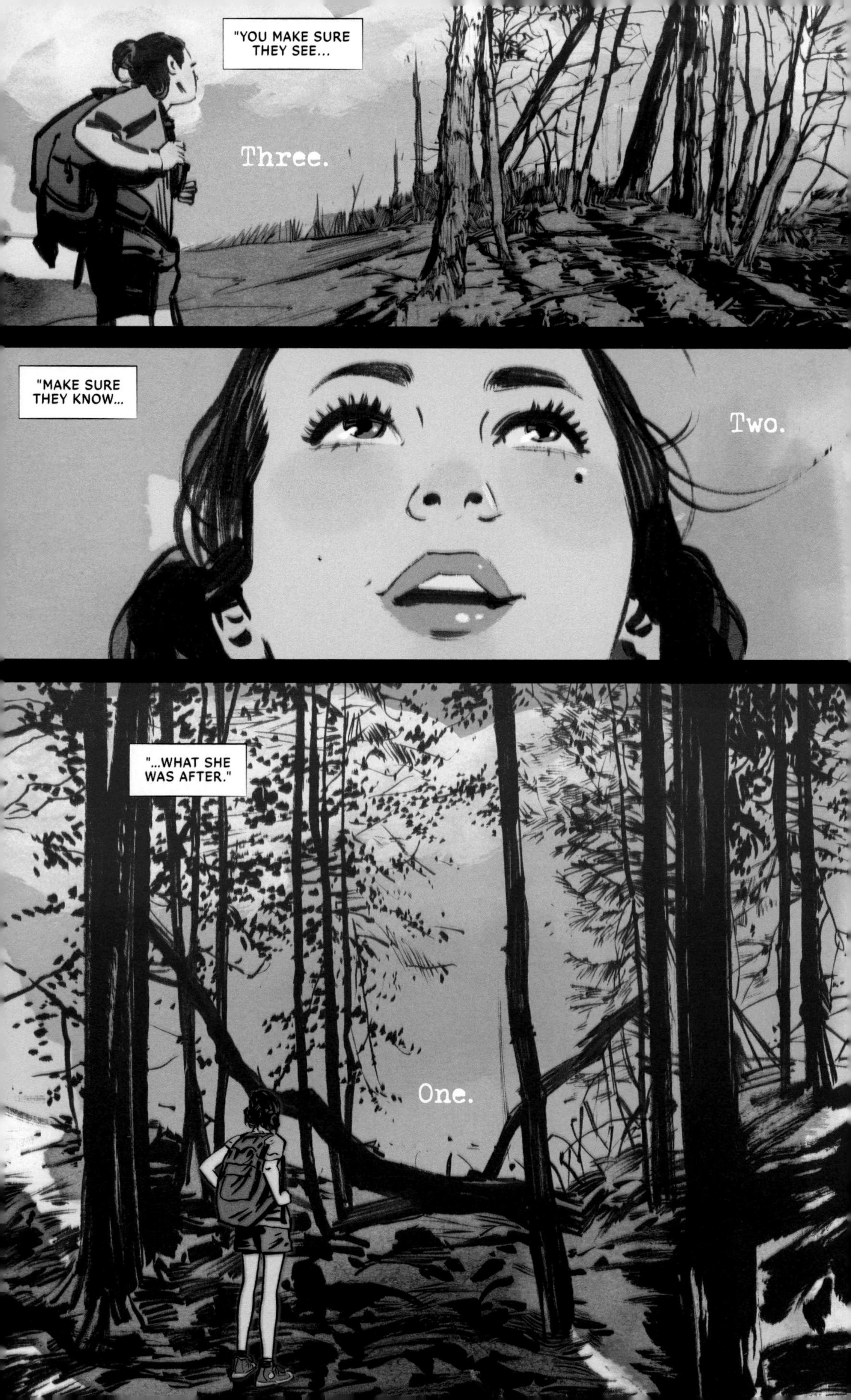
"YOU MAKE SURE THEY SEE...
Three.
"MAKE SURE THEY KNOW...
Two.
"...WHAT SHE WAS AFTER."
One.

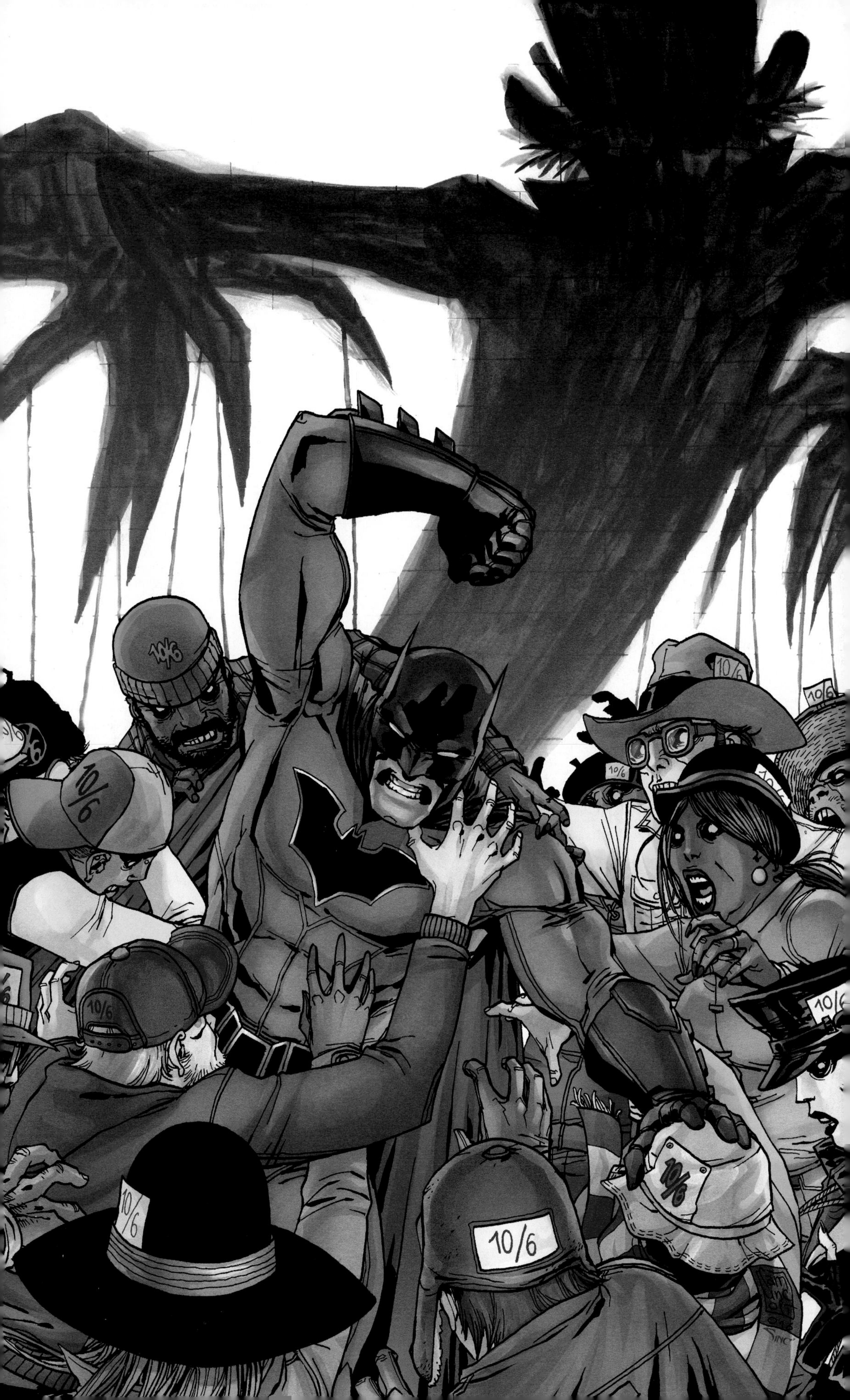
10/6
10/6
10/6
10/6
10/6
10/6
10/6
10/6
10/6
10/6

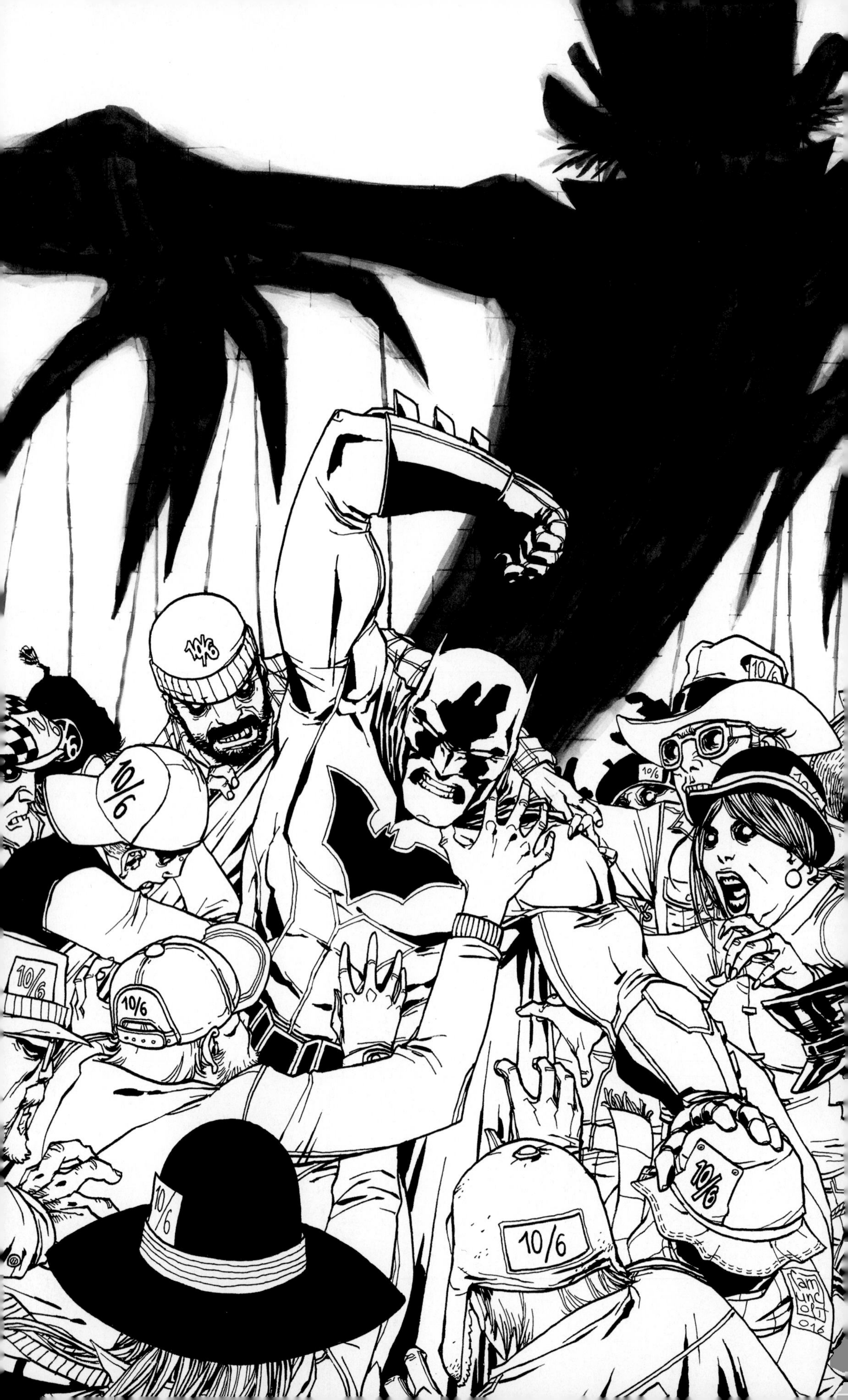
10/6

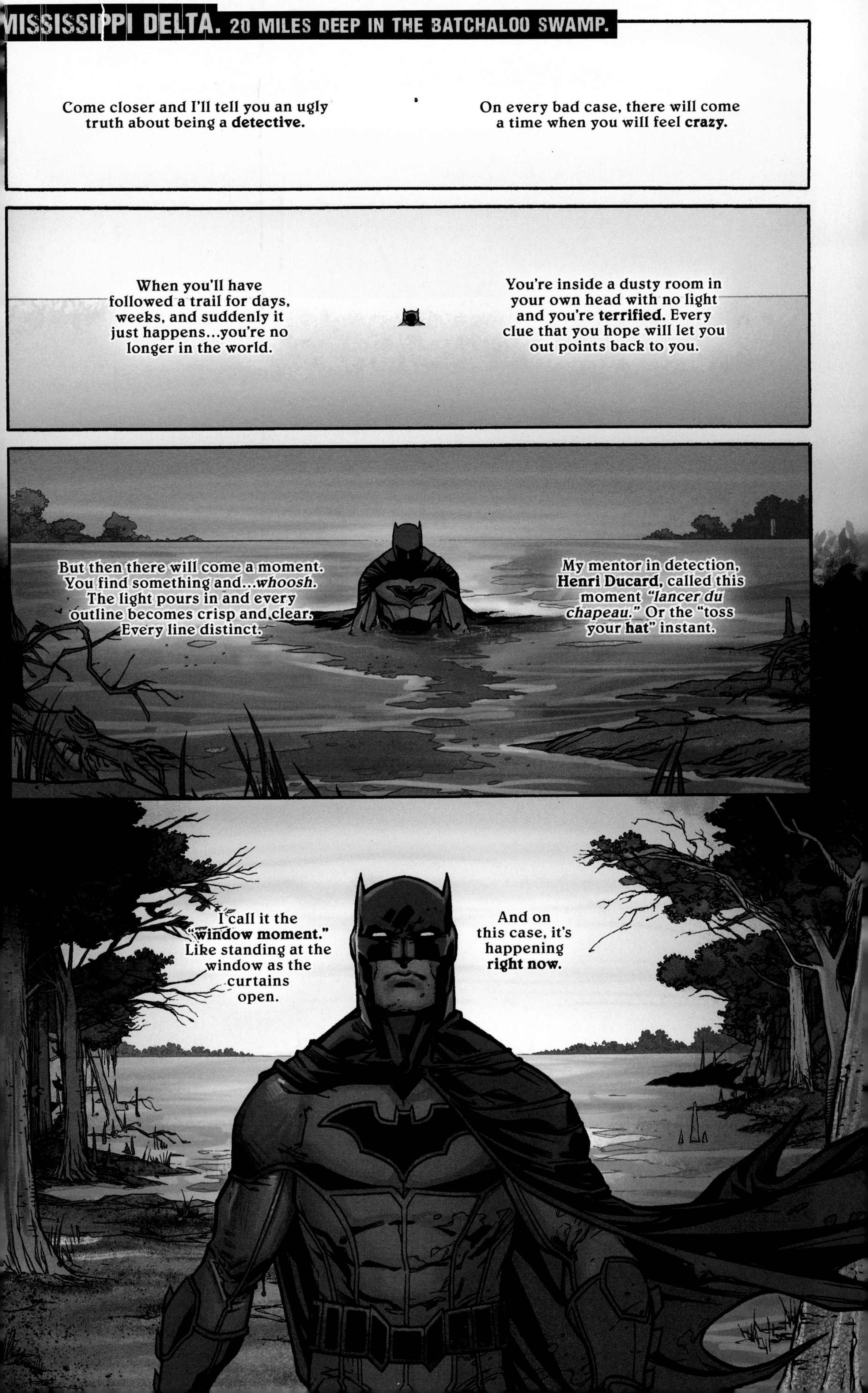
MISSISSIPPI DELTA. 20 MILES DEEP IN THE BATCHALOO SWAMP.
Come closer and I'll tell you an ugly truth about being a **detective.**
On every bad case, there will come a time when you will feel **crazy.**
When you'll have followed a trail for days, weeks, and suddenly it just happens...you're no longer in the world.
You're inside a dusty room in your own head with no light and you're **terrified.** Every clue that you hope will let you out points back to you.
But then there will come a moment. You find something and...*whoosh.* The light pours in and every outline becomes crisp and clear. Every line distinct.
My mentor in detection, **Henri Ducard,** called this moment *"lancer du chapeau."* Or the "toss your **hat**" instant.
I call it the "**window moment.**" Like standing at the window as the curtains open.
And on this case, it's happening **right now.**

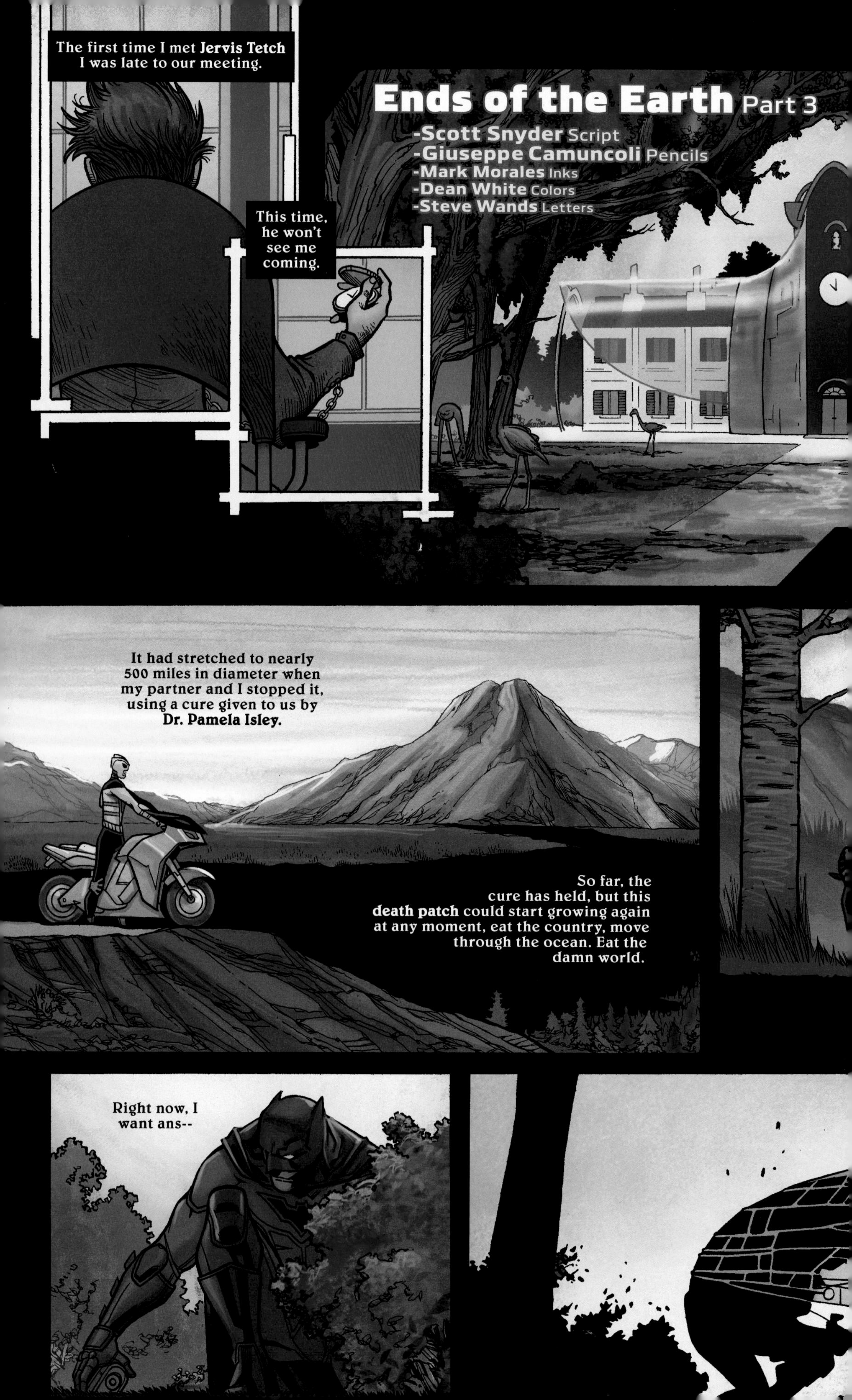

The first time I met Jervis Tetch I was late to our meeting.
Ends of the Earth Part 3
-Scott Snyder Script
-Giuseppe Camuncoli Pencils
-Mark Morales Inks
-Dean White Colors
-Steve Wands Letters
This time, he won't see me coming.
It had stretched to nearly 500 miles in diameter when my partner and I stopped it, using a cure given to us by Dr. Pamela Isley.
So far, the cure has held, but this death patch could start growing again at any moment, eat the country, move through the ocean. Eat the damn world.
Right now, I want ans--

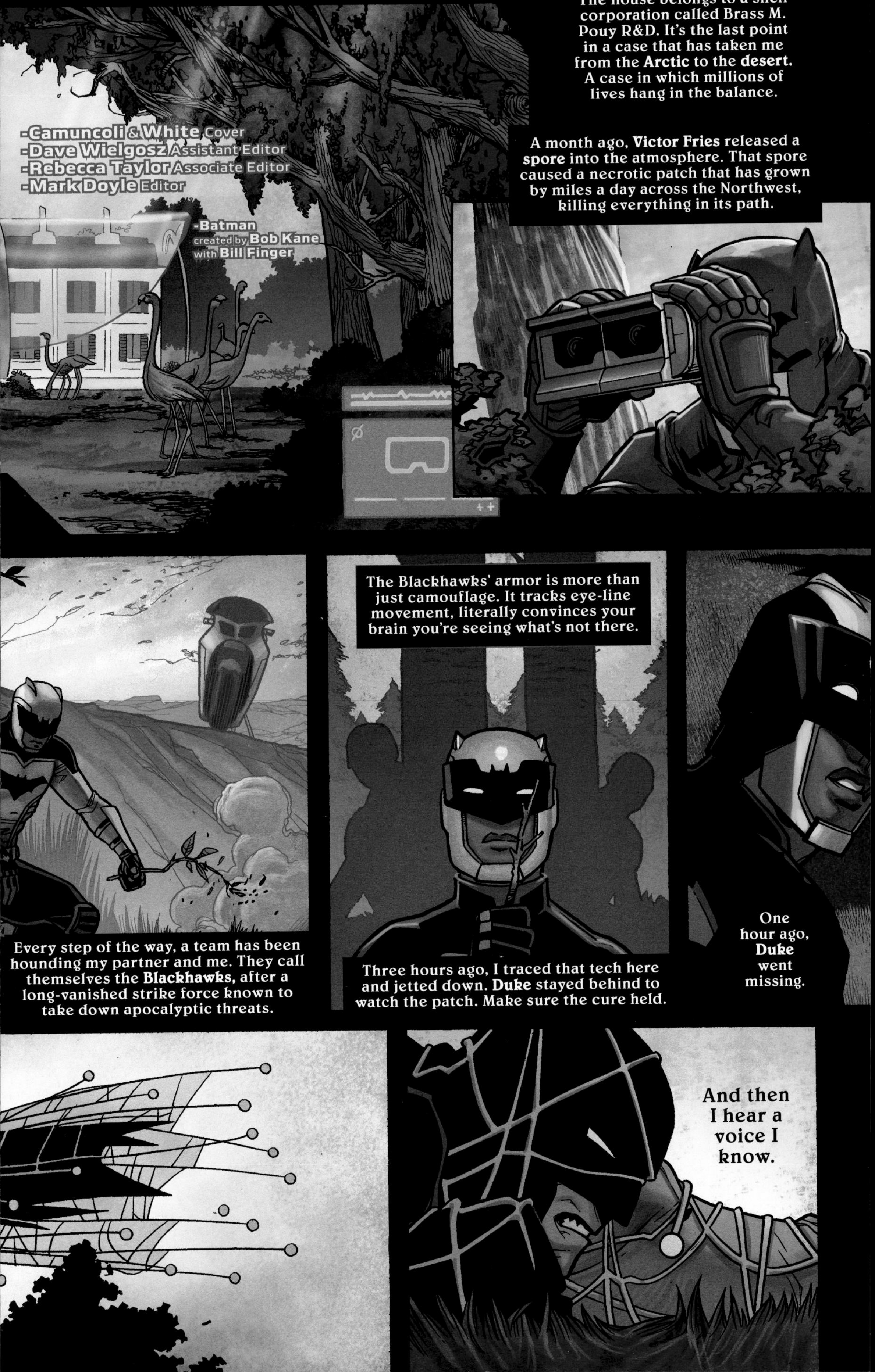
corporation called Brass M. Pouy R&D. It's the last point in a case that has taken me from the Arctic to the desert. A case in which millions of lives hang in the balance.
-Camuncoli & White Cover
-Dave Wielgosz Assistant Editor
-Rebecca Taylor Associate Editor
-Mark Doyle Editor
-Batman created by Bob Kane with Bill Finger
A month ago, Victor Fries released a spore into the atmosphere. That spore caused a necrotic patch that has grown by miles a day across the Northwest, killing everything in its path.
Every step of the way, a team has been hounding my partner and me. They call themselves the Blackhawks, after a long-vanished strike force known to take down apocalyptic threats.
The Blackhawks' armor is more than just camouflage. It tracks eye-line movement, literally convinces your brain you're seeing what's not there.
Three hours ago, I traced that tech here and jetted down. Duke stayed behind to watch the patch. Make sure the cure held.
One hour ago, Duke went missing.
And then I hear a voice I know.

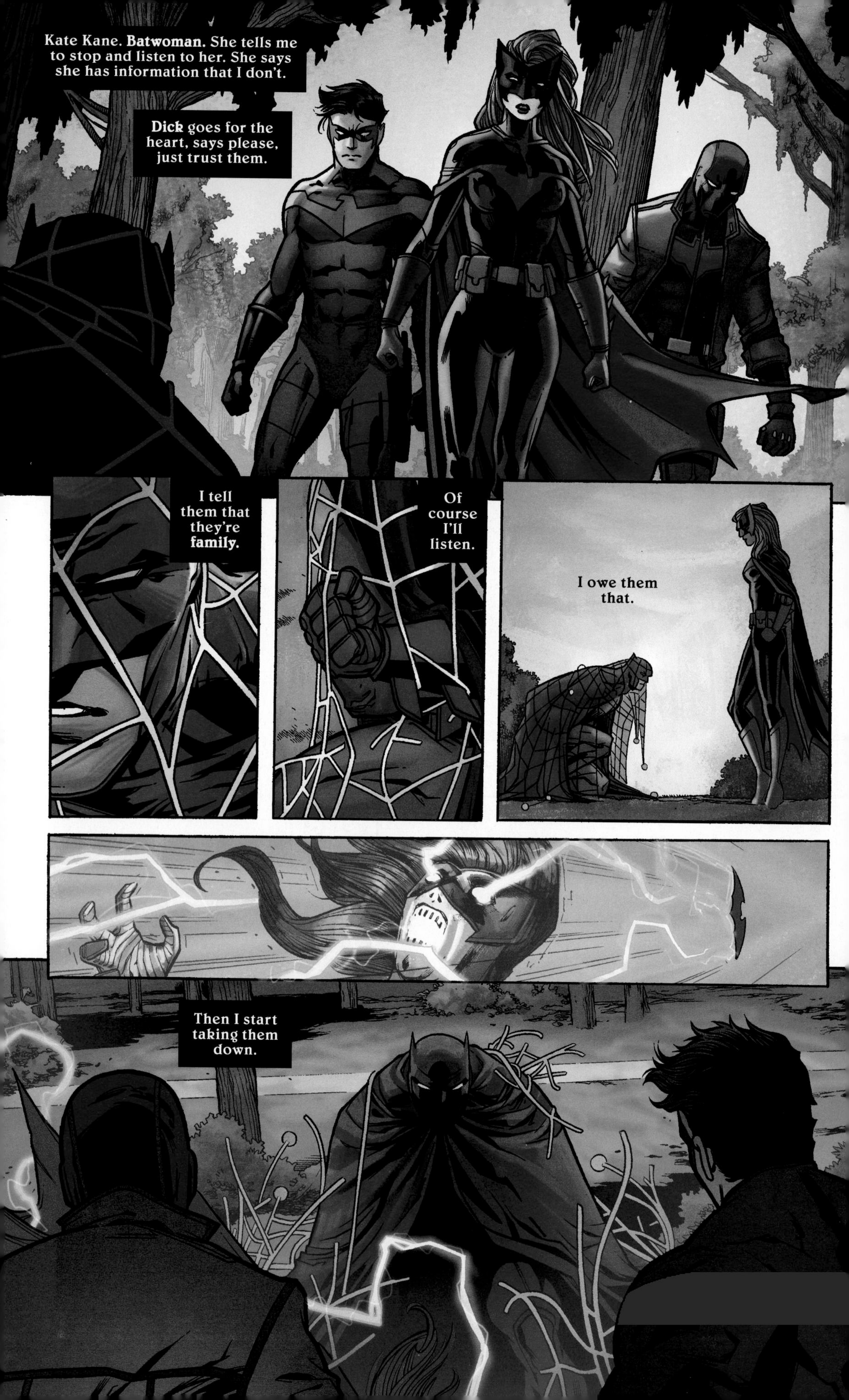

Kate Kane. Batwoman. She tells me to stop and listen to her. She says she has information that I don't.
Dick goes for the heart, says please, just trust them.
I tell them that they're family.
Of course I'll listen.
I owe them that.
Then I start taking them down.

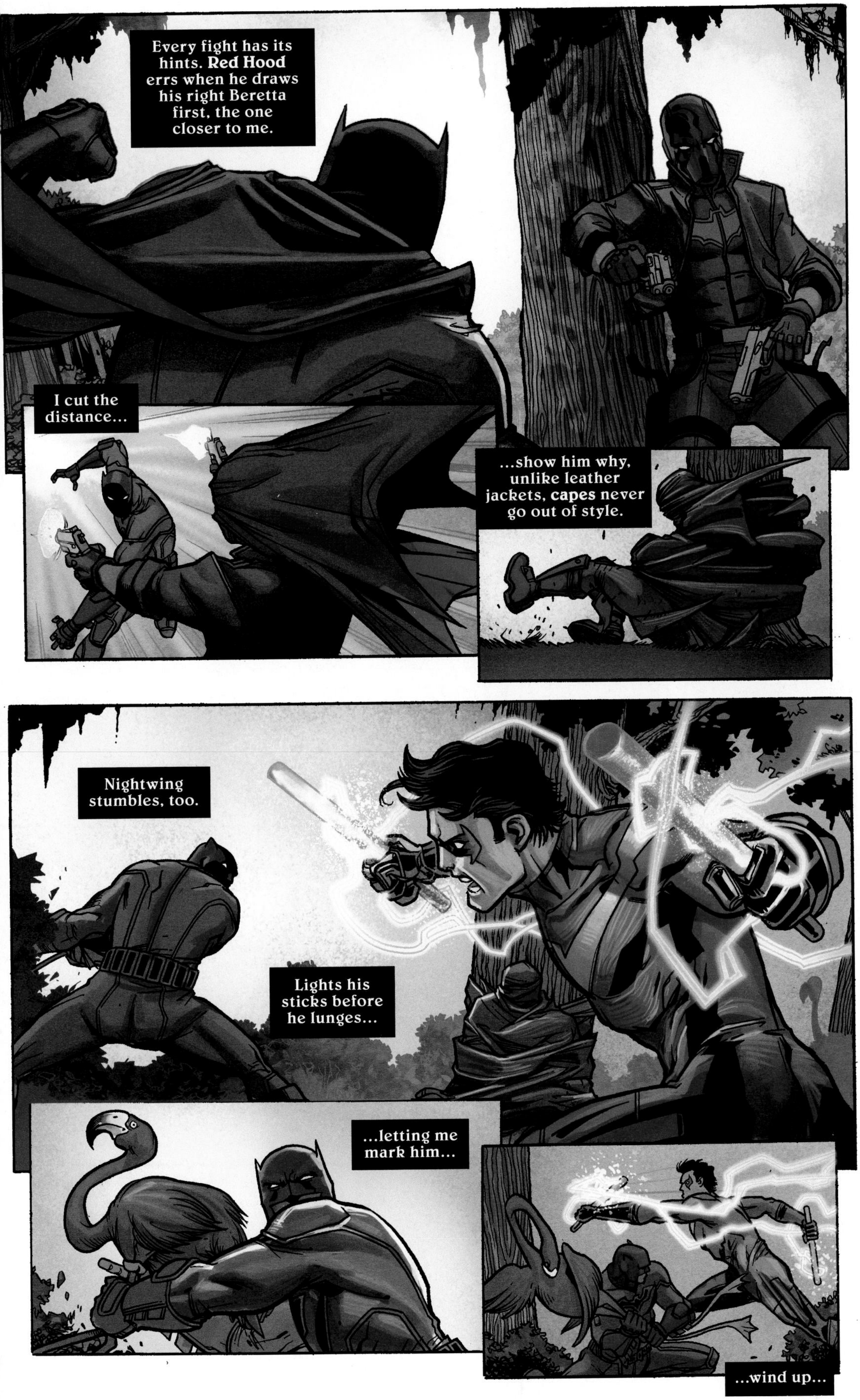
Every fight has its hints. **Red Hood** errs when he draws his right Beretta first, the one closer to me.
I cut the distance...
...show him why, unlike leather jackets, **capes** never go out of style.
Nightwing stumbles, too.
Lights his sticks before he lunges...
...letting me mark him...
...wind up...

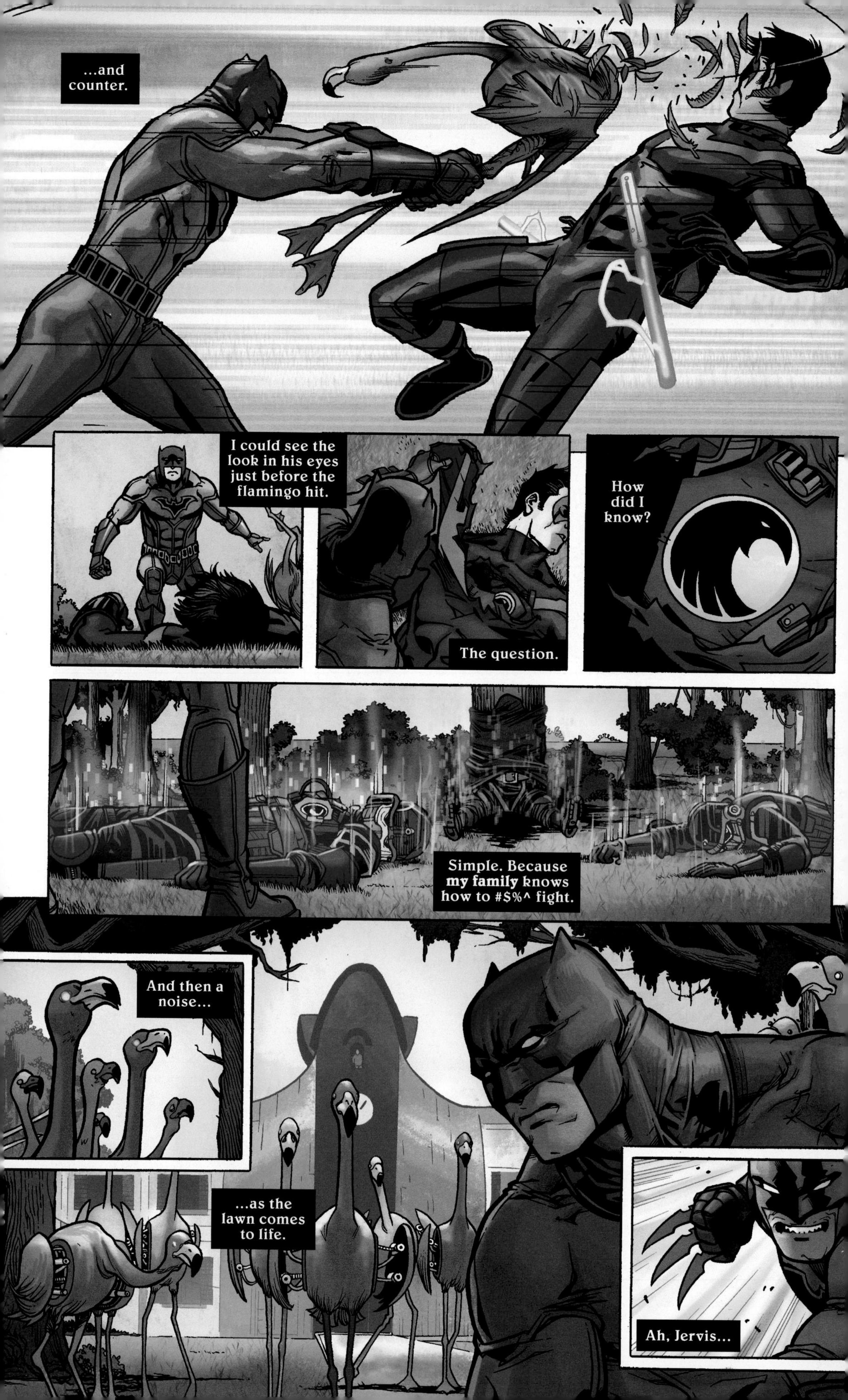
...and counter.
I could see the look in his eyes just before the flamingo hit.
The question.
How did I know?
Simple. Because **my family** knows how to #$%^ fight.
And then a noise...
...as the lawn comes to life.
Ah, Jervis...

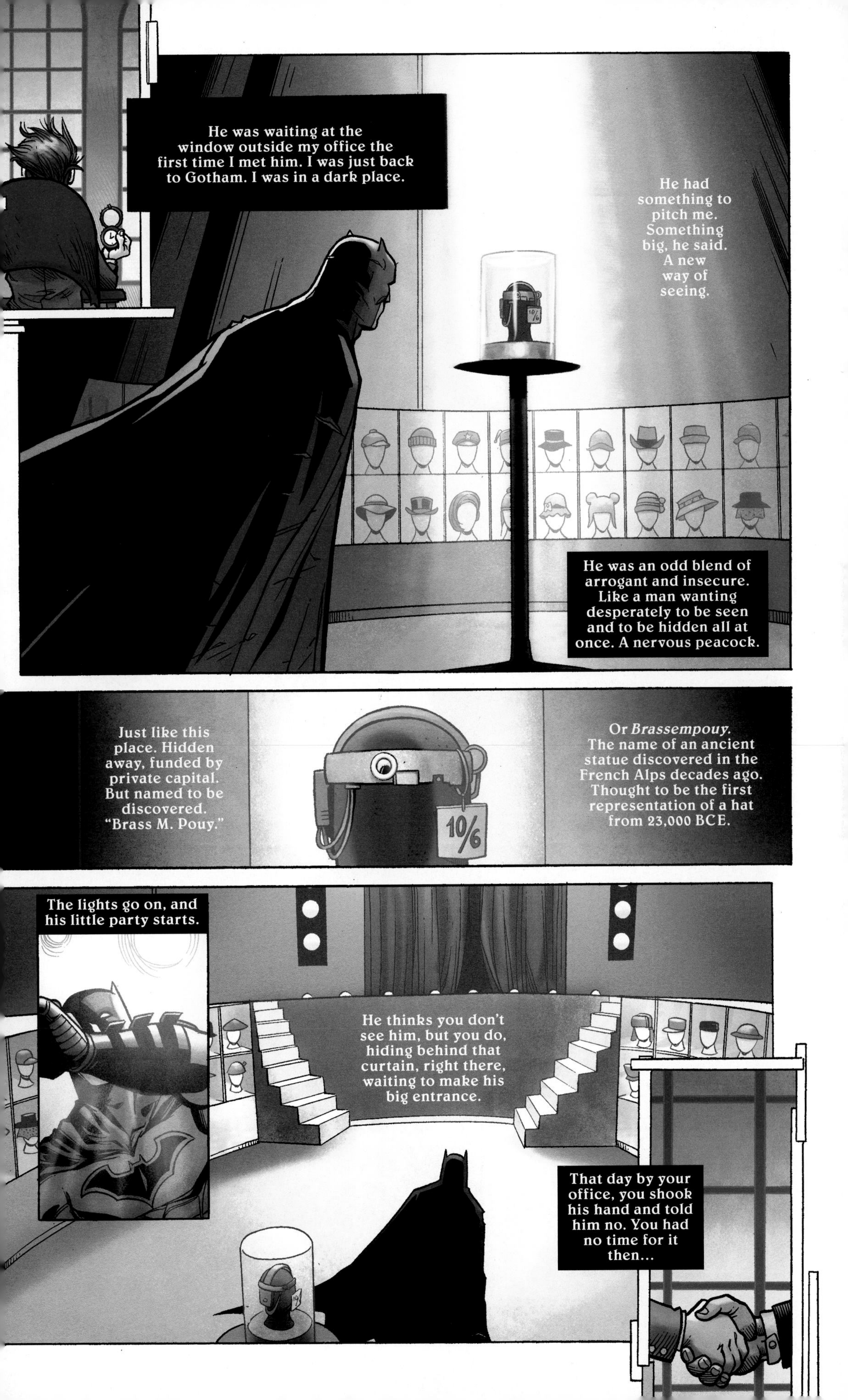
He was waiting at the window outside my office the first time I met him. I was just back to Gotham. I was in a dark place.
He had something to pitch me. Something big, he said. A new way of seeing.
10/6
He was an odd blend of arrogant and insecure. Like a man wanting desperately to be seen and to be hidden all at once. A nervous peacock.
Just like this place. Hidden away, funded by private capital. But named to be discovered. "Brass M. Pouy."
10/6
Or *Brassempouy*. The name of an ancient statue discovered in the French Alps decades ago. Thought to be the first representation of a hat from 23,000 BCE.
The lights go on, and his little party starts.
He thinks you don't see him, but you do, hiding behind that curtain, right there, waiting to make his big entrance.
That day by your office, you shook his hand and told him no. You had no time for it then...

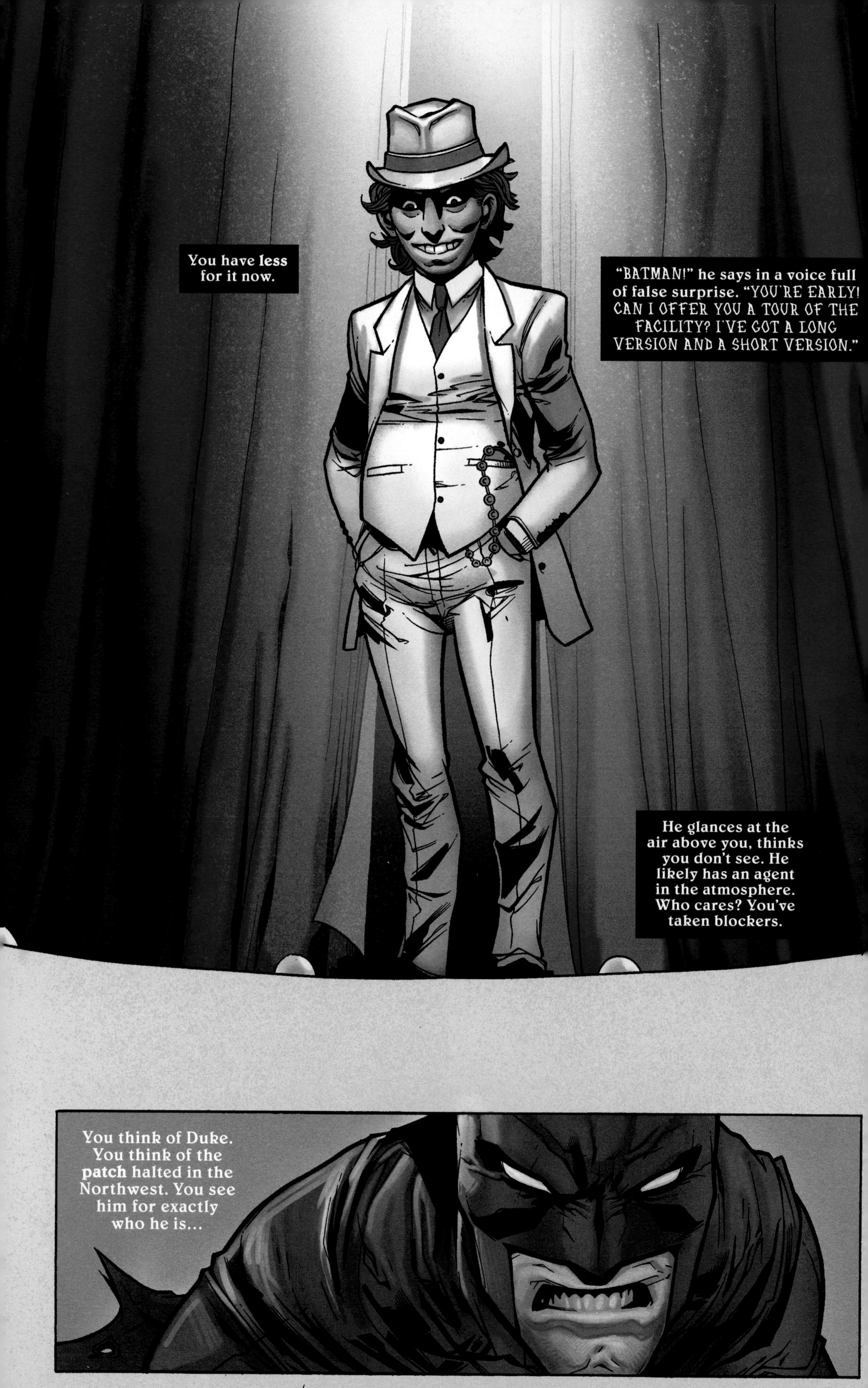
You have less for it now.
"BATMAN!" he says in a voice full of false surprise. "YOU'RE EARLY! CAN I OFFER YOU A TOUR OF THE FACILITY? I'VE GOT A LONG VERSION AND A SHORT VERSION."
He glances at the air above you, thinks you don't see. He likely has an agent in the atmosphere. Who cares? You've taken blockers.
You think of Duke. You think of the patch halted in the Northwest. You see him for exactly who he is...

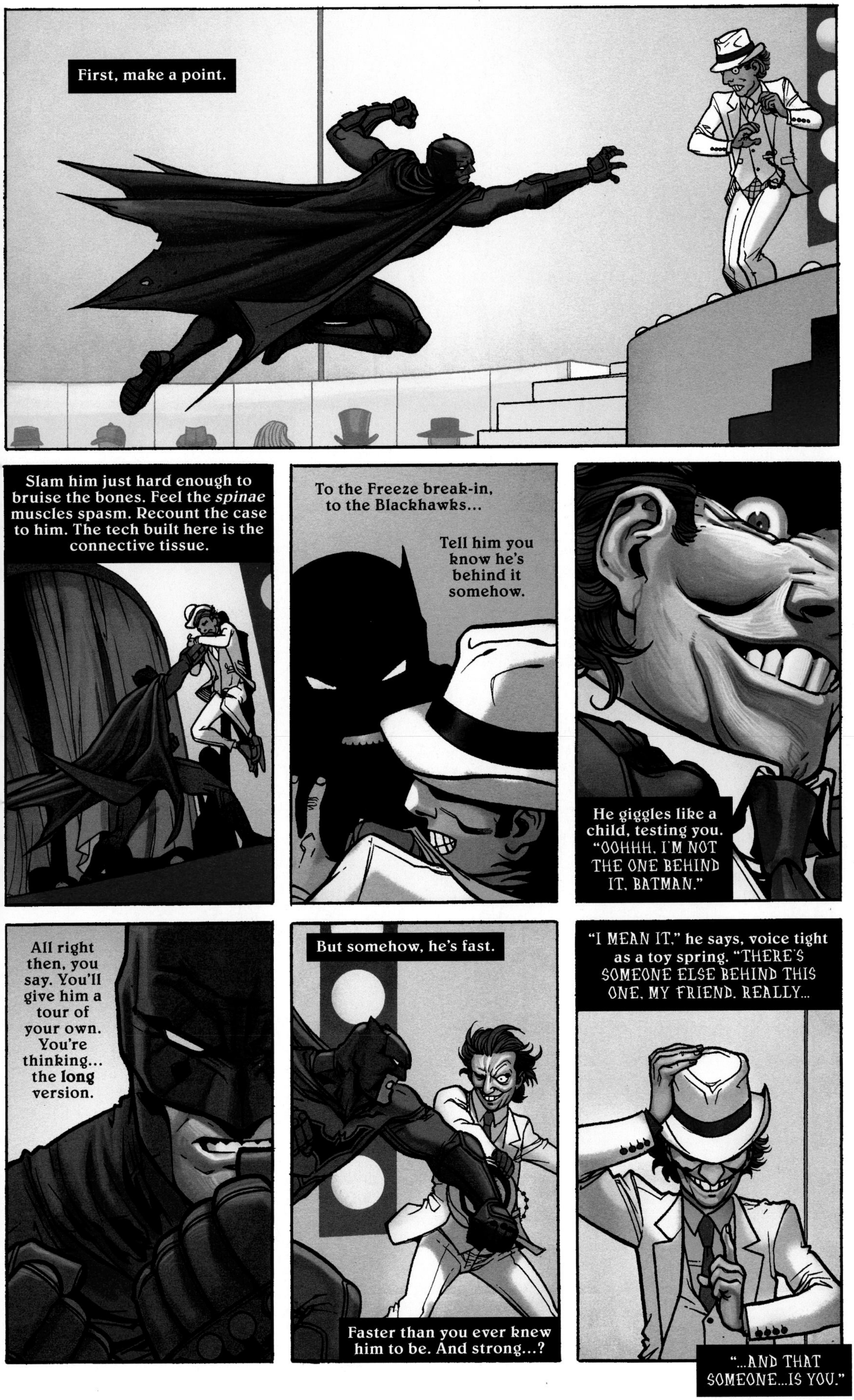
First, make a point.
Slam him just hard enough to bruise the bones. Feel the *spinae* muscles spasm. Recount the case to him. The tech built here is the connective tissue.
To the Freeze break-in, to the Blackhawks...
Tell him you know he's behind it somehow.
He giggles like a child, testing you. "OOHHH, I'M NOT THE ONE BEHIND IT, BATMAN."
All right then, you say. You'll give him a tour of your own. You're thinking... the **long** version.
But somehow, he's fast.
Faster than you ever knew him to be. And strong...?
"I MEAN IT," he says, voice tight as a toy spring. "THERE'S SOMEONE ELSE BEHIND THIS ONE, MY FRIEND. REALLY...
"...AND THAT SOMEONE...IS YOU."

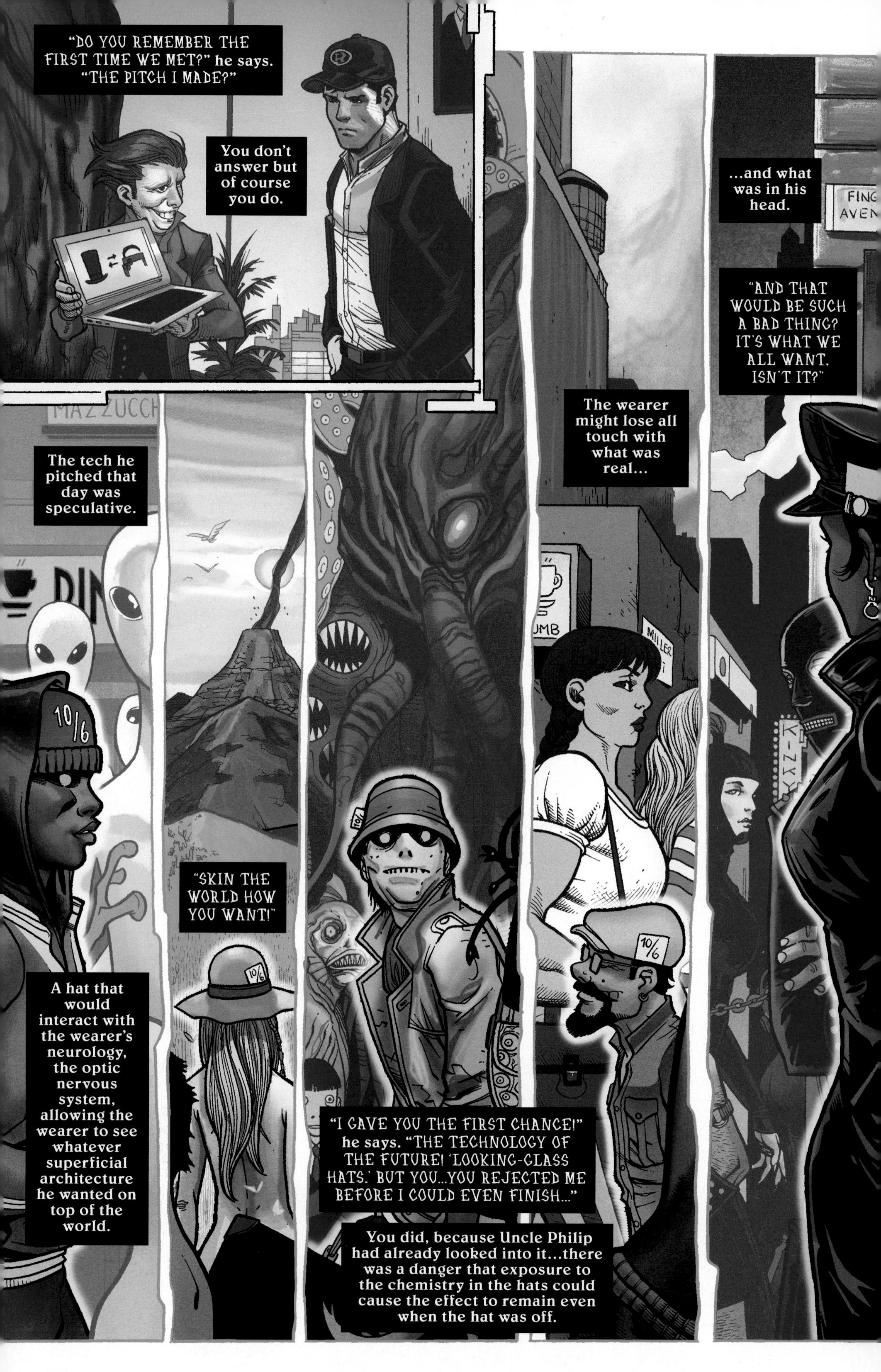
"DO YOU REMEMBER THE FIRST TIME WE MET?" he says. "THE PITCH I MADE?"
You don't answer but of course you do.
The tech he pitched that day was speculative.
A hat that would interact with the wearer's neurology, the optic nervous system, allowing the wearer to see whatever superficial architecture he wanted on top of the world.
"SKIN THE WORLD HOW YOU WANT!"
"I GAVE YOU THE FIRST CHANCE!" he says. "THE TECHNOLOGY OF THE FUTURE! 'LOOKING-GLASS HATS.' BUT YOU...YOU REJECTED ME BEFORE I COULD EVEN FINISH..."
You did, because Uncle Philip had already looked into it...there was a danger that exposure to the chemistry in the hats could cause the effect to remain even when the hat was off.
The wearer might lose all touch with what was real...
...and what was in his head.
"AND THAT WOULD BE SUCH A BAD THING? IT'S WHAT WE ALL WANT, ISN'T IT?"

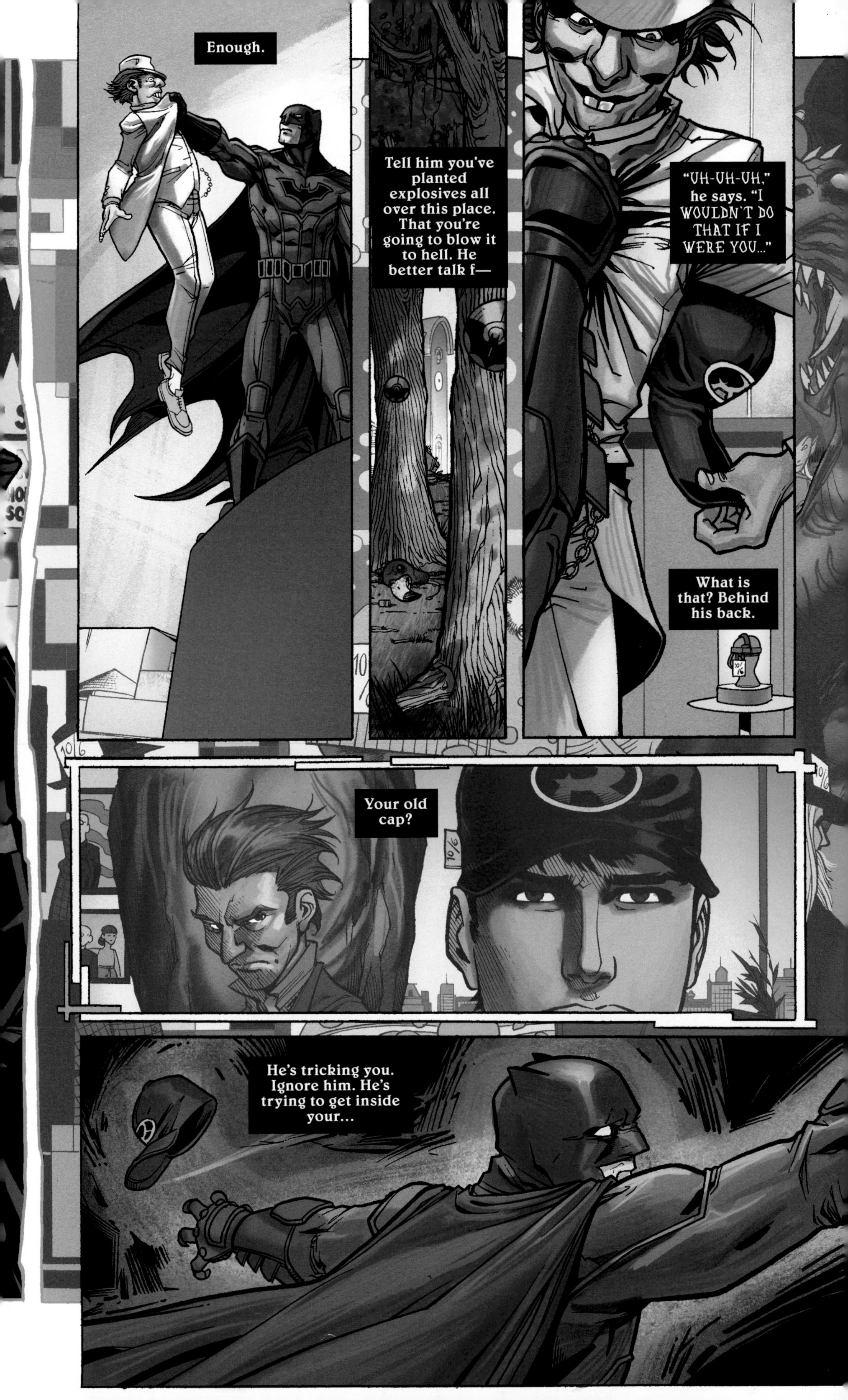
Enough.
Tell him you've planted explosives all over this place. That you're going to blow it to hell. He better talk f—
"UH-UH-UH," he says. "I WOULDN'T DO THAT IF I WERE YOU..."
What is that? Behind his back.
Your old cap?
He's tricking you. Ignore him. He's trying to get inside your...

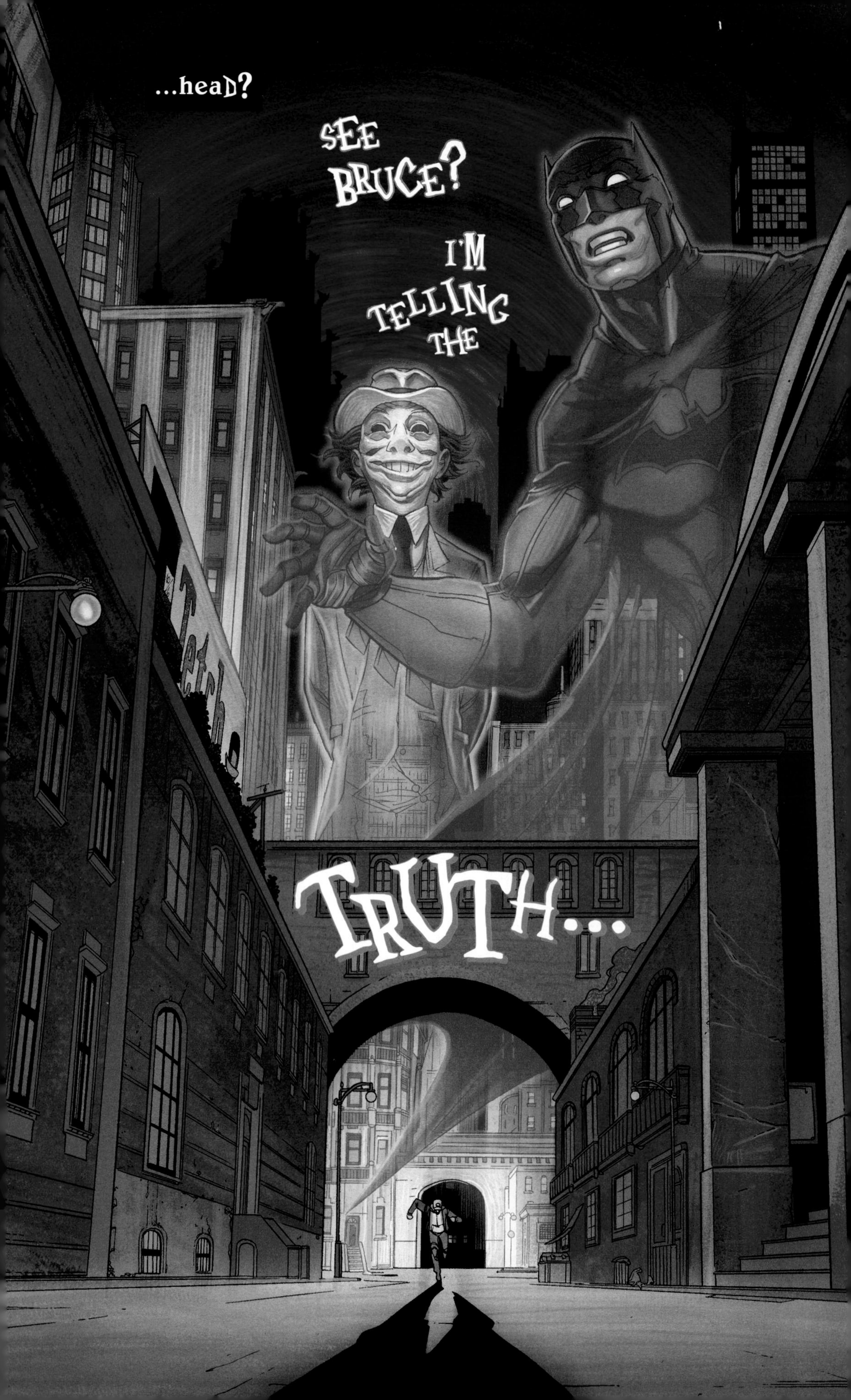
...heaD?
SEE BRUCE?
I'M TELLING THE
TRUTH...

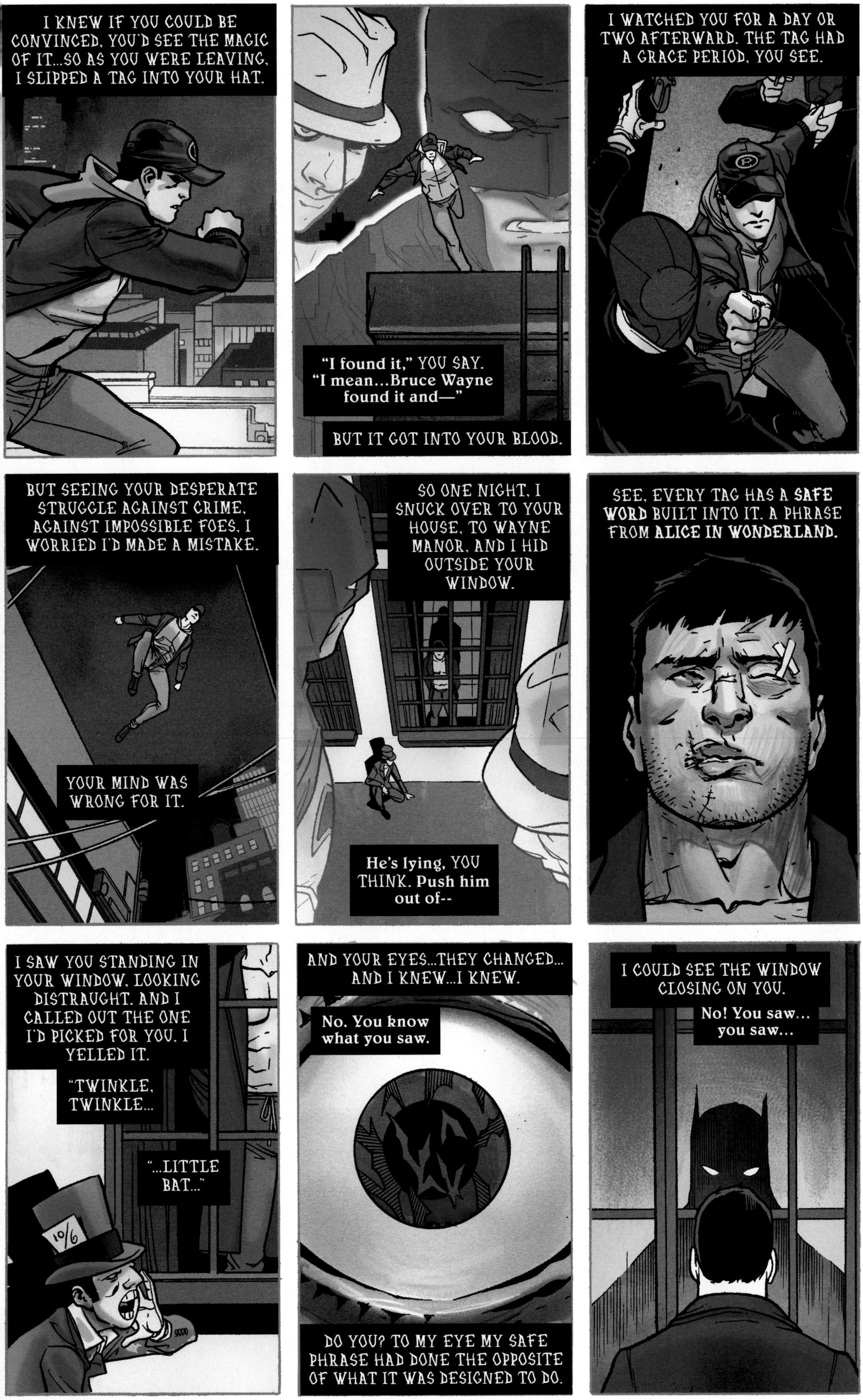
I KNEW IF YOU COULD BE CONVINCED, YOU'D SEE THE MAGIC OF IT...SO AS YOU WERE LEAVING, I SLIPPED A TAG INTO YOUR HAT.
"I found it," YOU SAY. "I mean...Bruce Wayne found it and—"
BUT IT GOT INTO YOUR BLOOD.
I WATCHED YOU FOR A DAY OR TWO AFTERWARD. THE TAG HAD A GRACE PERIOD, YOU SEE.
BUT SEEING YOUR DESPERATE STRUGGLE AGAINST CRIME, AGAINST IMPOSSIBLE FOES, I WORRIED I'D MADE A MISTAKE.
YOUR MIND WAS WRONG FOR IT.
SO ONE NIGHT, I SNUCK OVER TO YOUR HOUSE, TO WAYNE MANOR, AND I HID OUTSIDE YOUR WINDOW.
He's lying, YOU THINK. Push him out of--
SEE, EVERY TAG HAS A SAFE WORD BUILT INTO IT. A PHRASE FROM ALICE IN WONDERLAND.
I SAW YOU STANDING IN YOUR WINDOW, LOOKING DISTRAUGHT. AND I CALLED OUT THE ONE I'D PICKED FOR YOU. I YELLED IT.
"TWINKLE, TWINKLE...
"...LITTLE BAT..."
10/6
AND YOUR EYES...THEY CHANGED... AND I KNEW...I KNEW.
No. You know what you saw.
DO YOU? TO MY EYE MY SAFE PHRASE HAD DONE THE OPPOSITE OF WHAT IT WAS DESIGNED TO DO.
I COULD SEE THE WINDOW CLOSING ON YOU.
No! You saw... you saw...

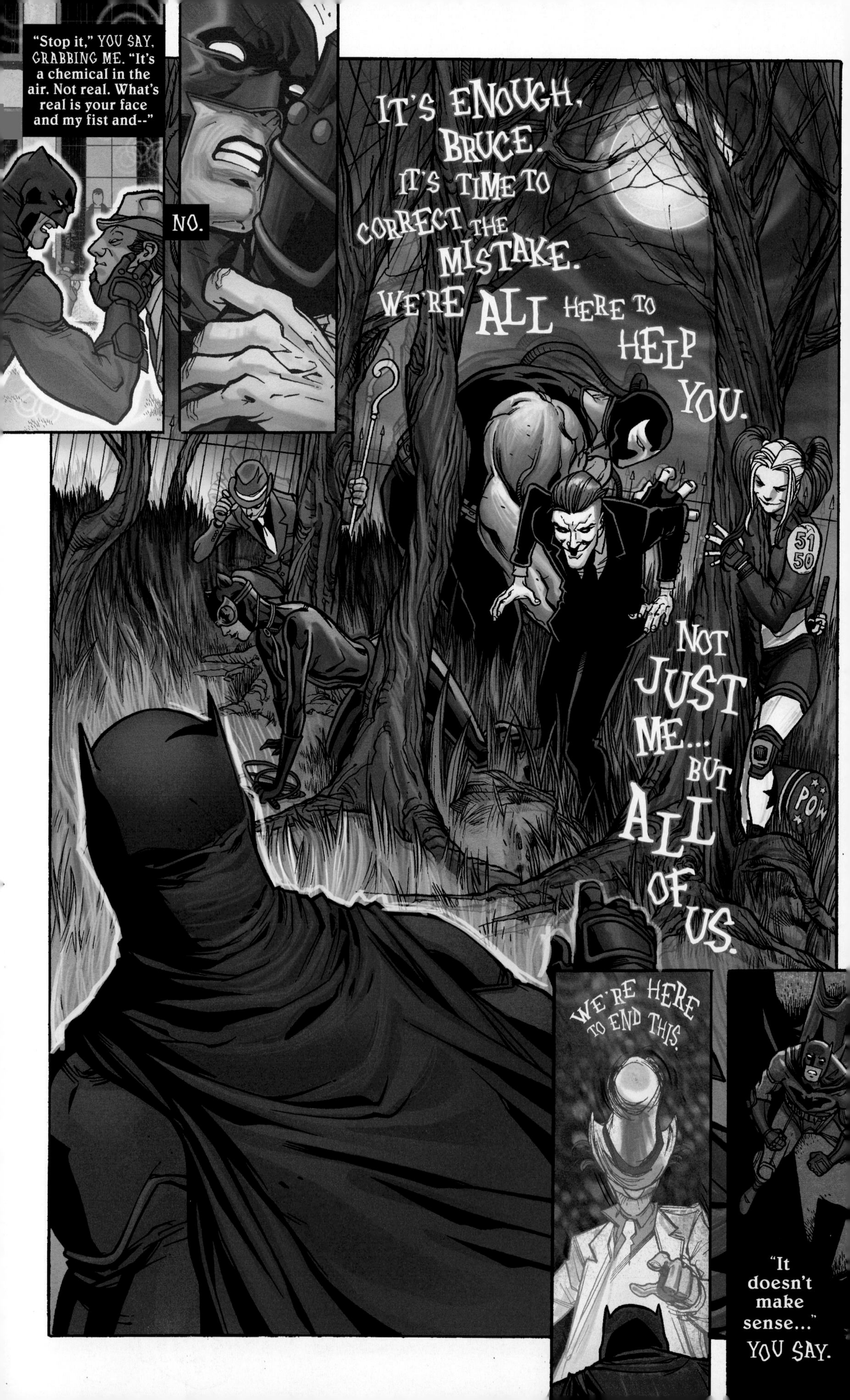

"Stop it," YOU SAY, GRABBING ME. "It's a chemical in the air. Not real. What's real is your face and my fist and--"
NO.
IT'S ENOUGH, BRUCE. IT'S TIME TO CORRECT THE MISTAKE. WE'RE ALL HERE TO HELP YOU.
51 50
NOT JUST ME... BUT ALL OF US.
POW
WE'RE HERE TO END THIS.
"It doesn't make sense..." YOU SAY.

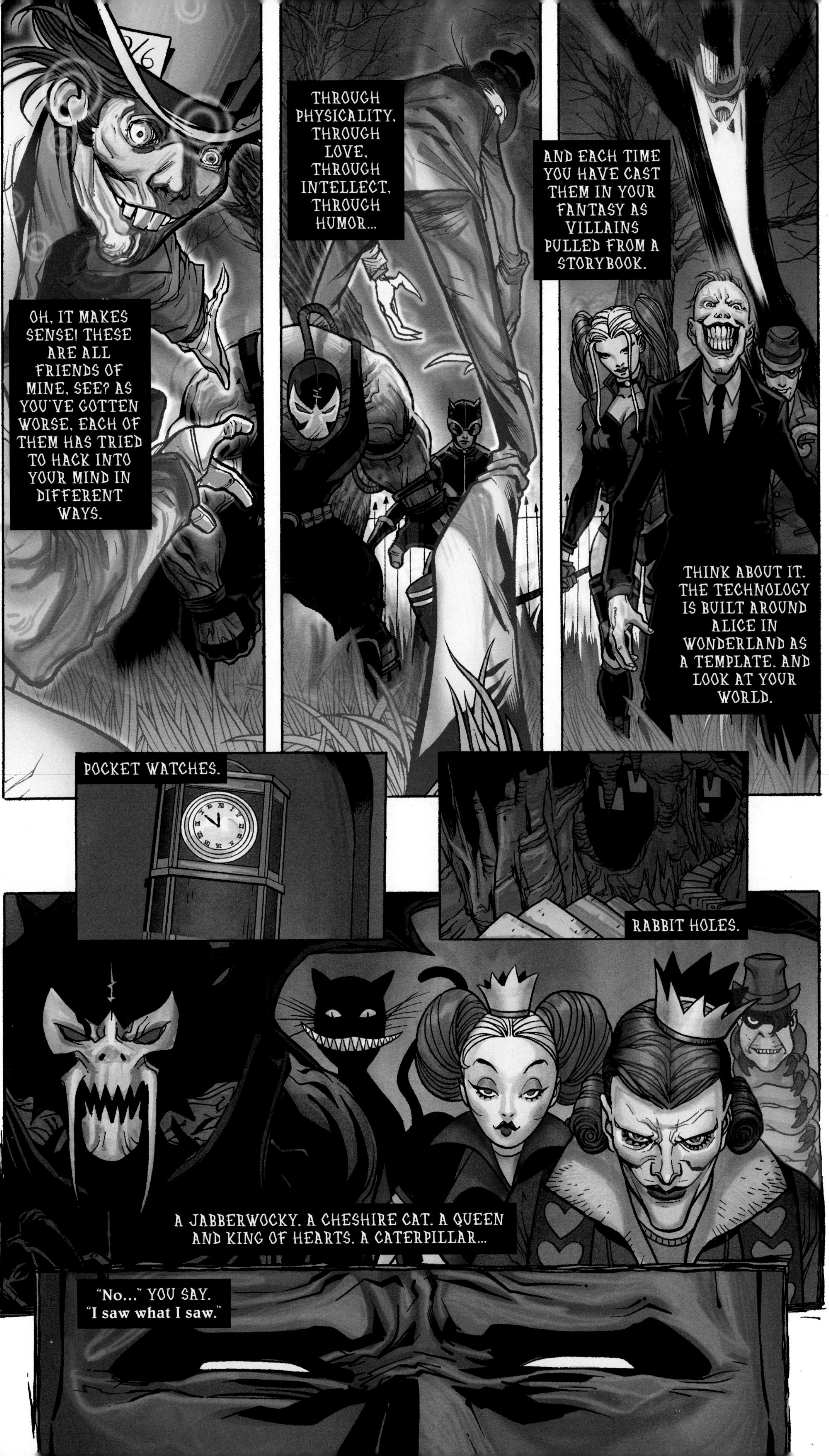
OH, IT MAKES SENSE! THESE ARE ALL FRIENDS OF MINE, SEE? AS YOU'VE GOTTEN WORSE, EACH OF THEM HAS TRIED TO HACK INTO YOUR MIND IN DIFFERENT WAYS.
THROUGH PHYSICALITY, THROUGH LOVE, THROUGH INTELLECT, THROUGH HUMOR...
AND EACH TIME YOU HAVE CAST THEM IN YOUR FANTASY AS VILLAINS PULLED FROM A STORYBOOK.
THINK ABOUT IT. THE TECHNOLOGY IS BUILT AROUND ALICE IN WONDERLAND AS A TEMPLATE. AND LOOK AT YOUR WORLD.
POCKET WATCHES.
RABBIT HOLES.
A JABBERWOCKY. A CHESHIRE CAT. A QUEEN AND KING OF HEARTS. A CATERPILLAR...
"No..." YOU SAY. "I saw what I saw."

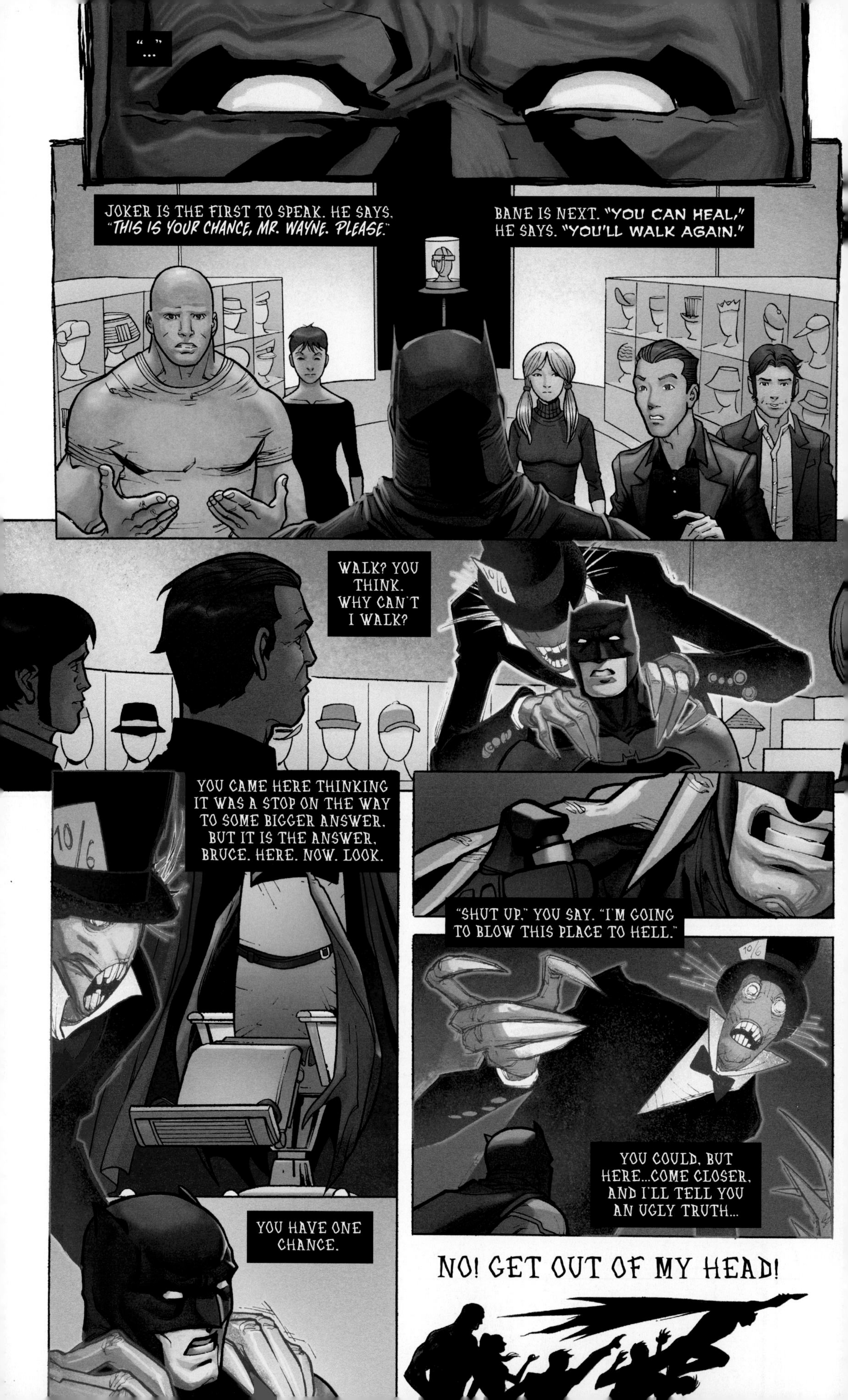
"..."
JOKER IS THE FIRST TO SPEAK. HE SAYS. "THIS IS YOUR CHANCE, MR. WAYNE. PLEASE."
BANE IS NEXT. "YOU CAN HEAL," HE SAYS. "YOU'LL WALK AGAIN."
WALK? YOU THINK. WHY CAN'T I WALK?
YOU CAME HERE THINKING IT WAS A STOP ON THE WAY TO SOME BIGGER ANSWER. BUT IT IS THE ANSWER, BRUCE. HERE. NOW. LOOK.
"SHUT UP," YOU SAY. "I'M GOING TO BLOW THIS PLACE TO HELL."
YOU COULD, BUT HERE...COME CLOSER, AND I'LL TELL YOU AN UGLY TRUTH...
YOU HAVE ONE CHANCE.
NO! GET OUT OF MY HEAD!

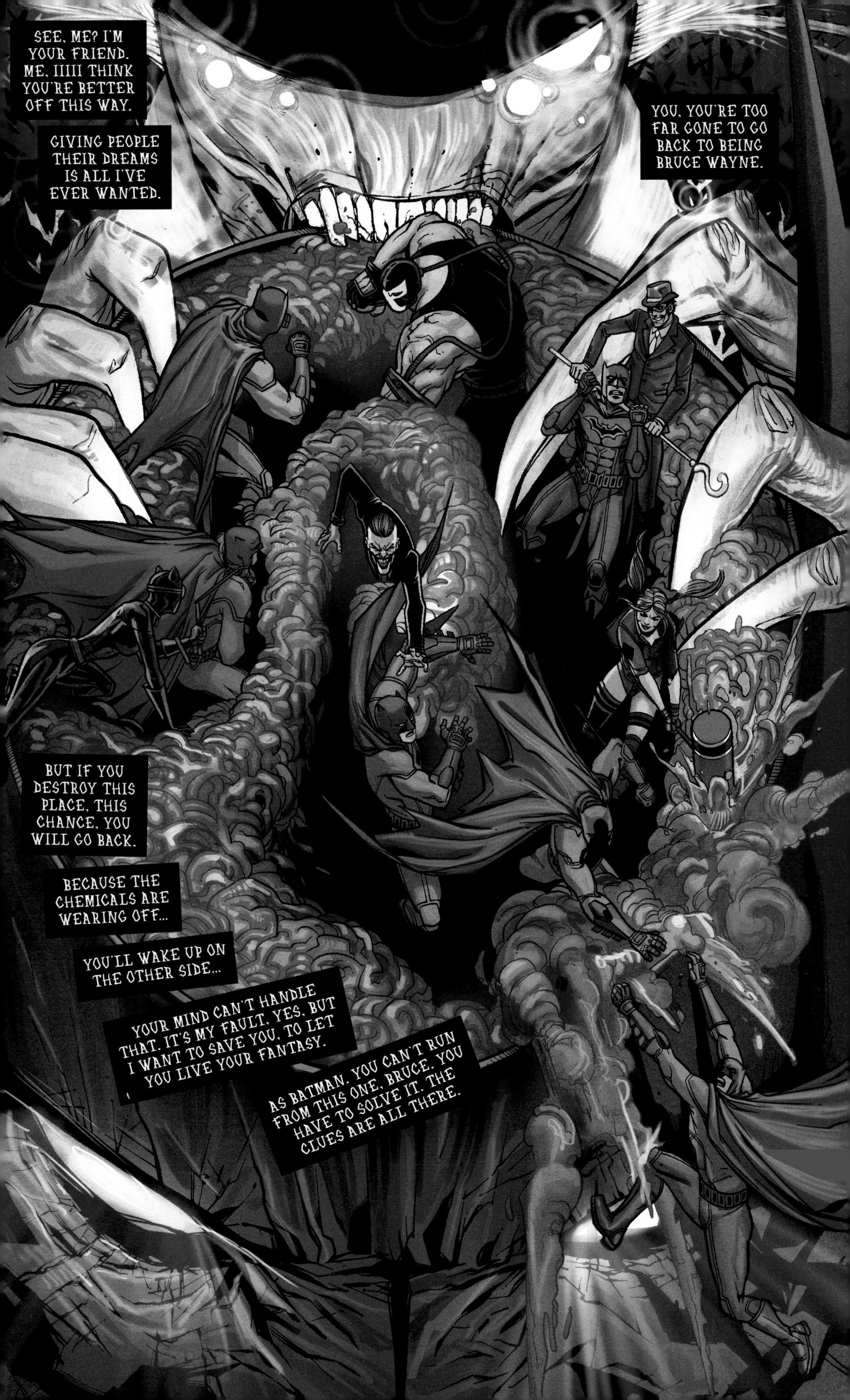
SEE, ME? I'M YOUR FRIEND. ME, IIIII THINK YOU'RE BETTER OFF THIS WAY.
GIVING PEOPLE THEIR DREAMS IS ALL I'VE EVER WANTED.
YOU, YOU'RE TOO FAR GONE TO GO BACK TO BEING BRUCE WAYNE.
BUT IF YOU DESTROY THIS PLACE, THIS CHANCE, YOU WILL GO BACK.
BECAUSE THE CHEMICALS ARE WEARING OFF...
YOU'LL WAKE UP ON THE OTHER SIDE...
YOUR MIND CAN'T HANDLE THAT. IT'S MY FAULT, YES, BUT I WANT TO SAVE YOU, TO LET YOU LIVE YOUR FANTASY.
AS BATMAN. YOU CAN'T RUN FROM THIS ONE, BRUCE. YOU HAVE TO SOLVE IT. THE CLUES ARE ALL THERE.

YOU JUST NEEEED TO SOLVE

THE MYSTERY

NO NO ONO NO NO NO NO NO NONONO NO NO NONO NO NO NO NO NO NO NO NO NO NO NO NO NO NO NO NO NO NO NO NO NO NO NO NO NO NO NO NO NO NO NO NO NO NO NO NO NO NO NO NO NO NO NO NO NO NO NO NO NO NO NO NO NO

YOU WANT TO SEE?!

YOU WANT TO SEE THE OTHER SIDE? BE MY GUEST!

not real. It's not real. It's real. It's not real. It's not It's not real. It's not real. real. It's not real. It's not real. It's not real. It's not real. It's not real. It's not real. It's not real. It's not real. It's not real. It's not real.

IT DOESN'T HAVE TO BE...

IF YOU JUST HAND ME THE REMOTE...

GIVE IT TO ME, BRUCE...

"NO," YOU SAY. "I'M GOING TO..."

YOU'RE GOING TO STAY RIGHT WHERE YOU ARE.

NOT THERE...HERE!

SAY IT WITH ME...YOU ARE AT THE WINDOW ONCE AGAIN...AND YOU SHALL BECOME A BAT...

...TWINKLE TWINKLE, BRUCE.

YES... YES, I SHALL... I...

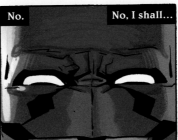

No. No, I shall...

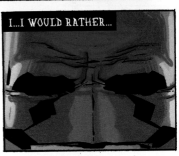

I...I WOULD RATHER...

...Know.

*Klik*

*"Noooooo!"*

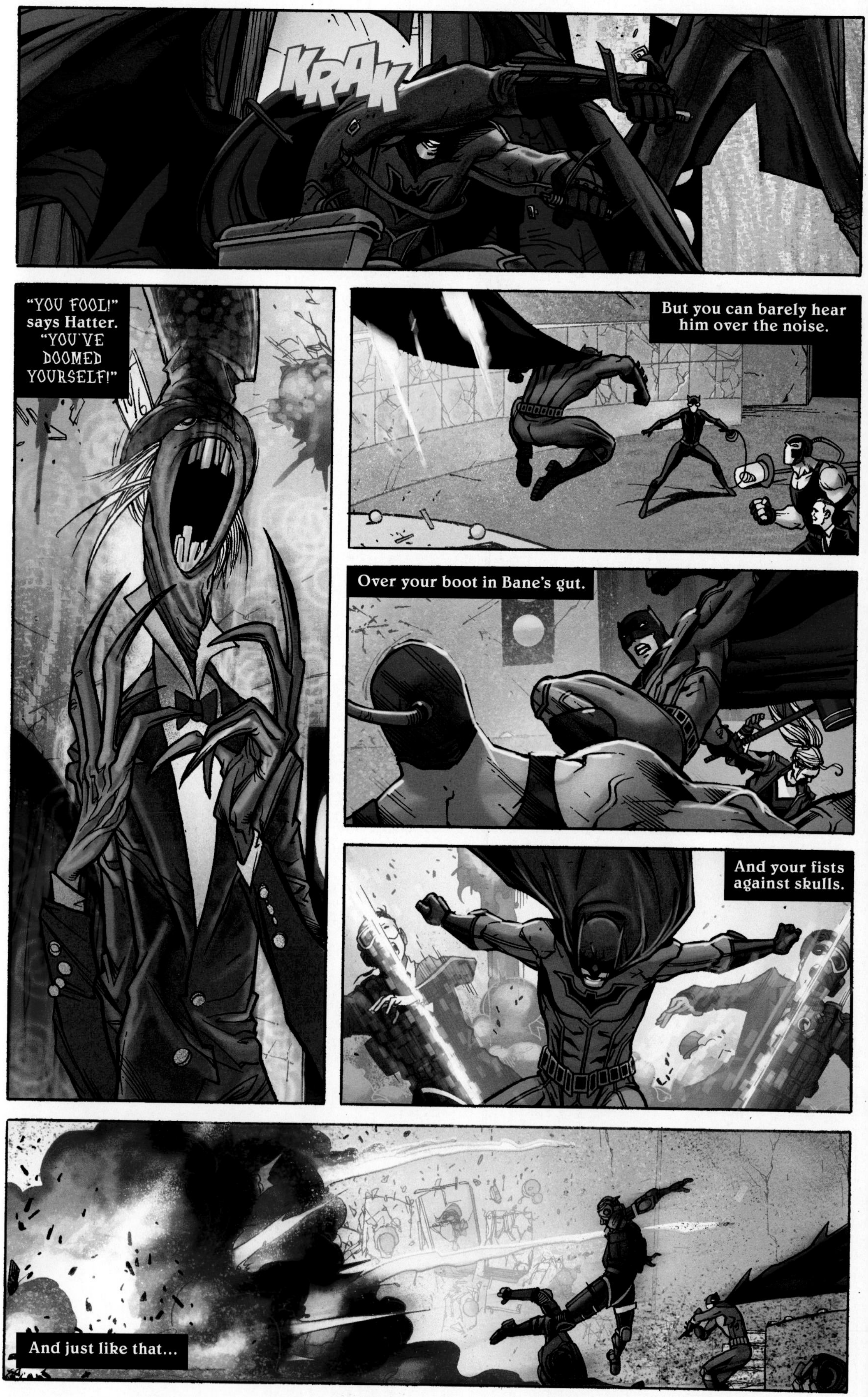
KRAK
"YOU FOOL!" says Hatter. "YOU'VE DOOMED YOURSELF!"
But you can barely hear him over the noise.
Over your boot in Bane's gut.
And your fists against skulls.
And just like that...

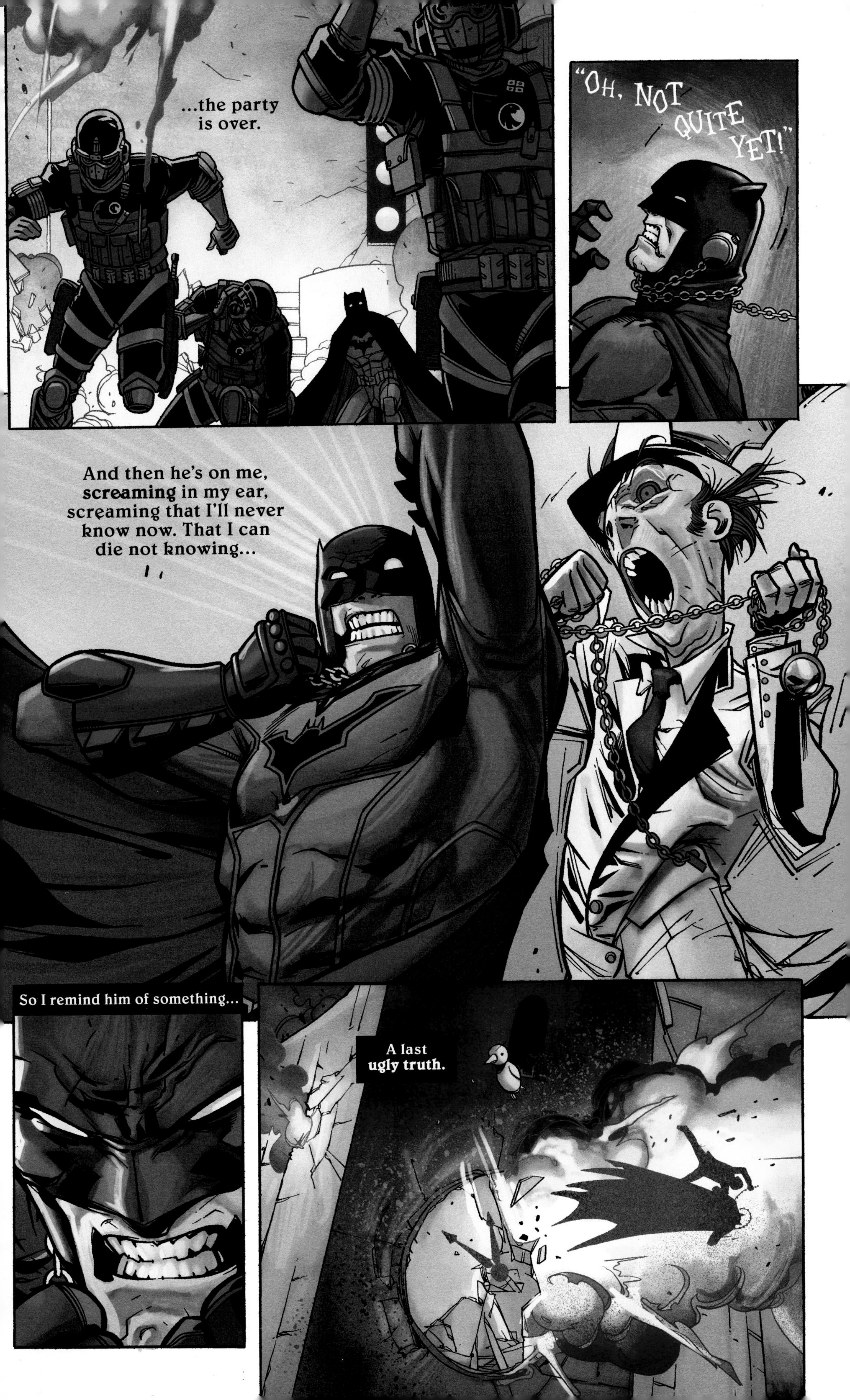
...the party is over.
"OH, NOT QUITE YET!"
And then he's on me, **screaming** in my ear, screaming that I'll never know now. That I can die not knowing...
So I remind him of something...
A last **ugly truth.**

I remind him that if this is all a dream, no one can really die. Which means...

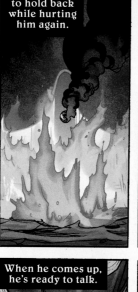

I never have to hold back while hurting him again.

Do I?

He tries one last time to worm his way in. His voice high and shrill.

I let him tell Aquaman.

SPLOOOSH

When he comes up, he's ready to talk.

It's right there in his eyes.

I lift my boot again, and he starts in. About who's behind this. The why, the where.

He's talking slowly, though, so I tell him to speed up. Go faster.

Before it gets too

late.

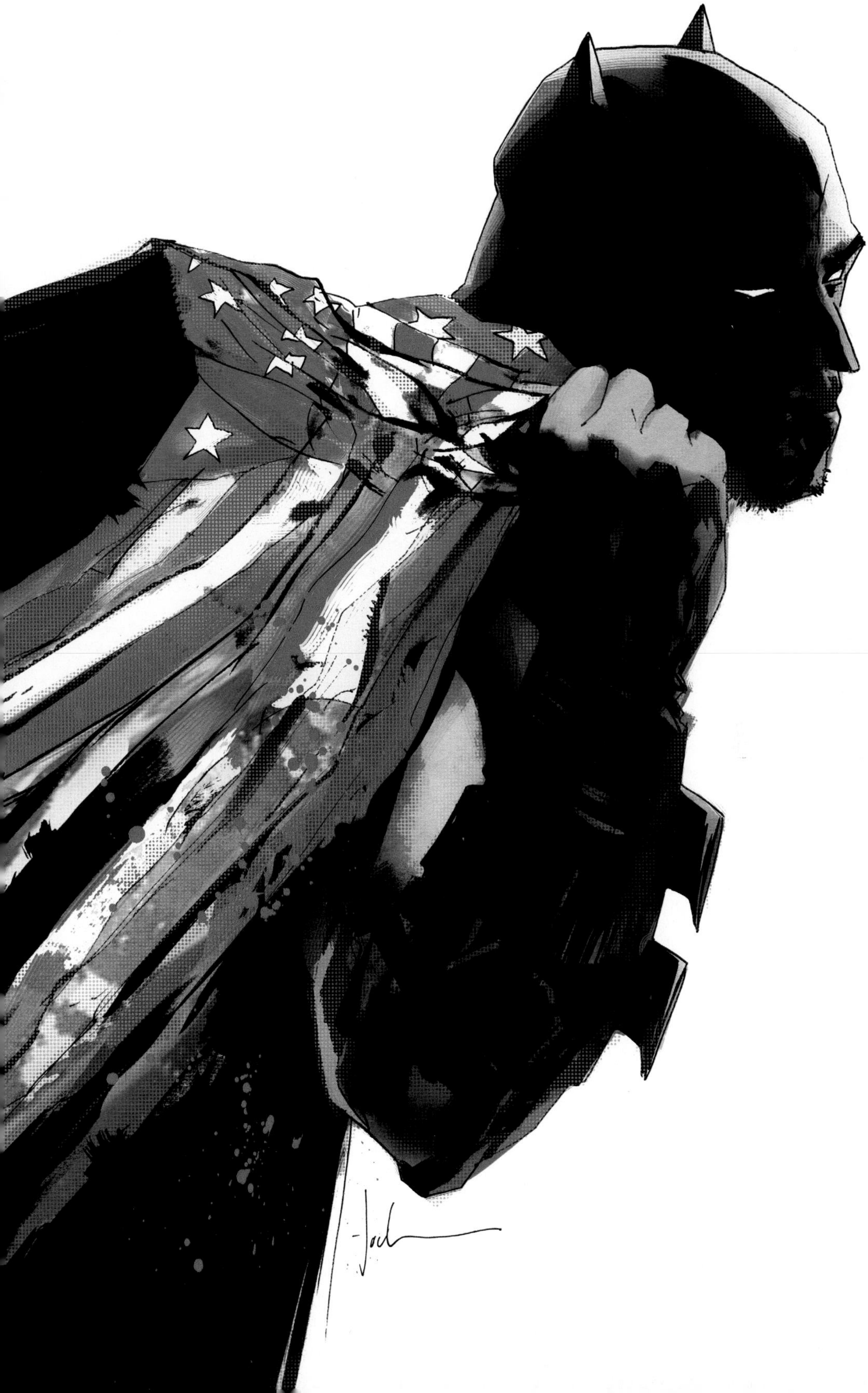

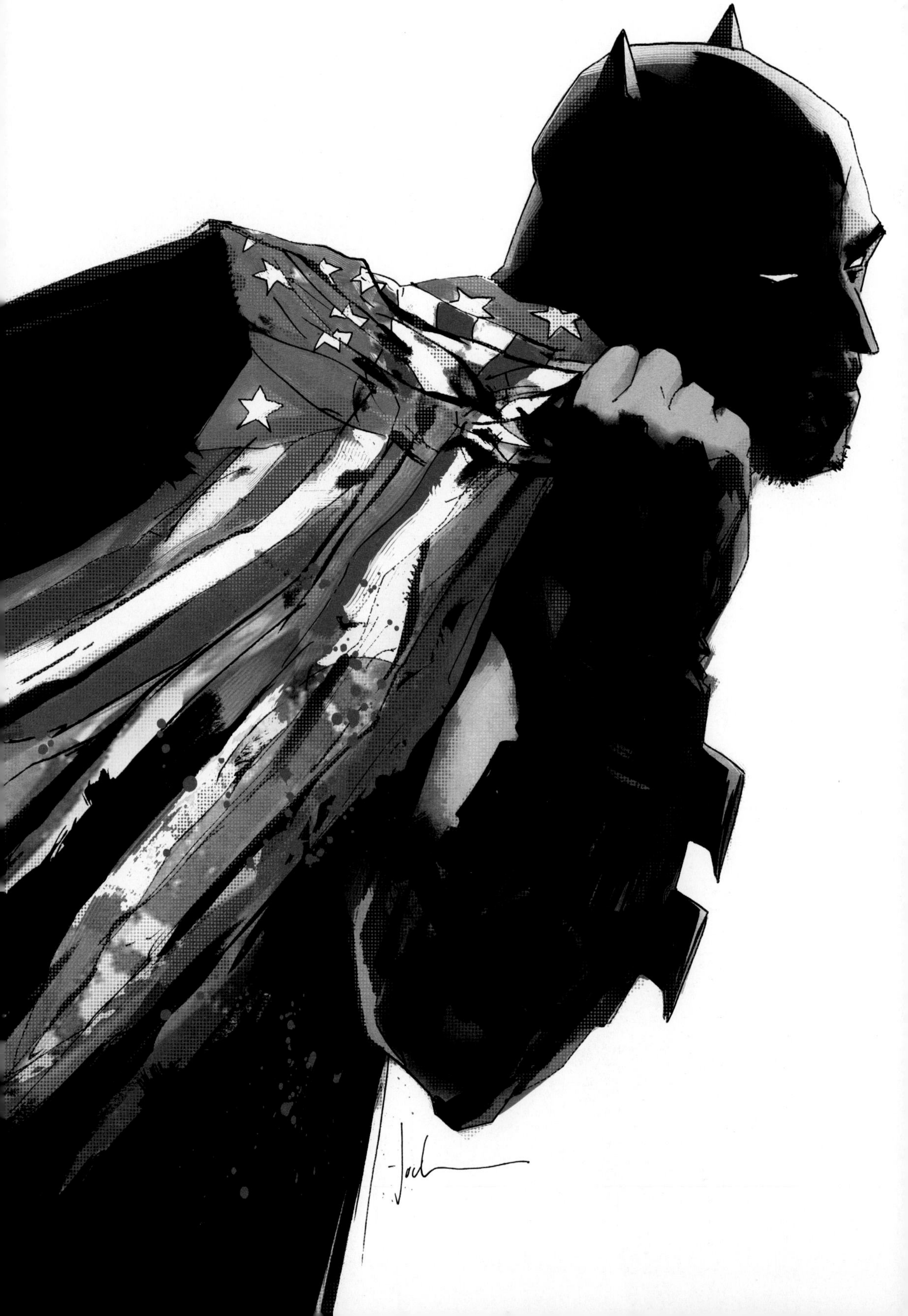

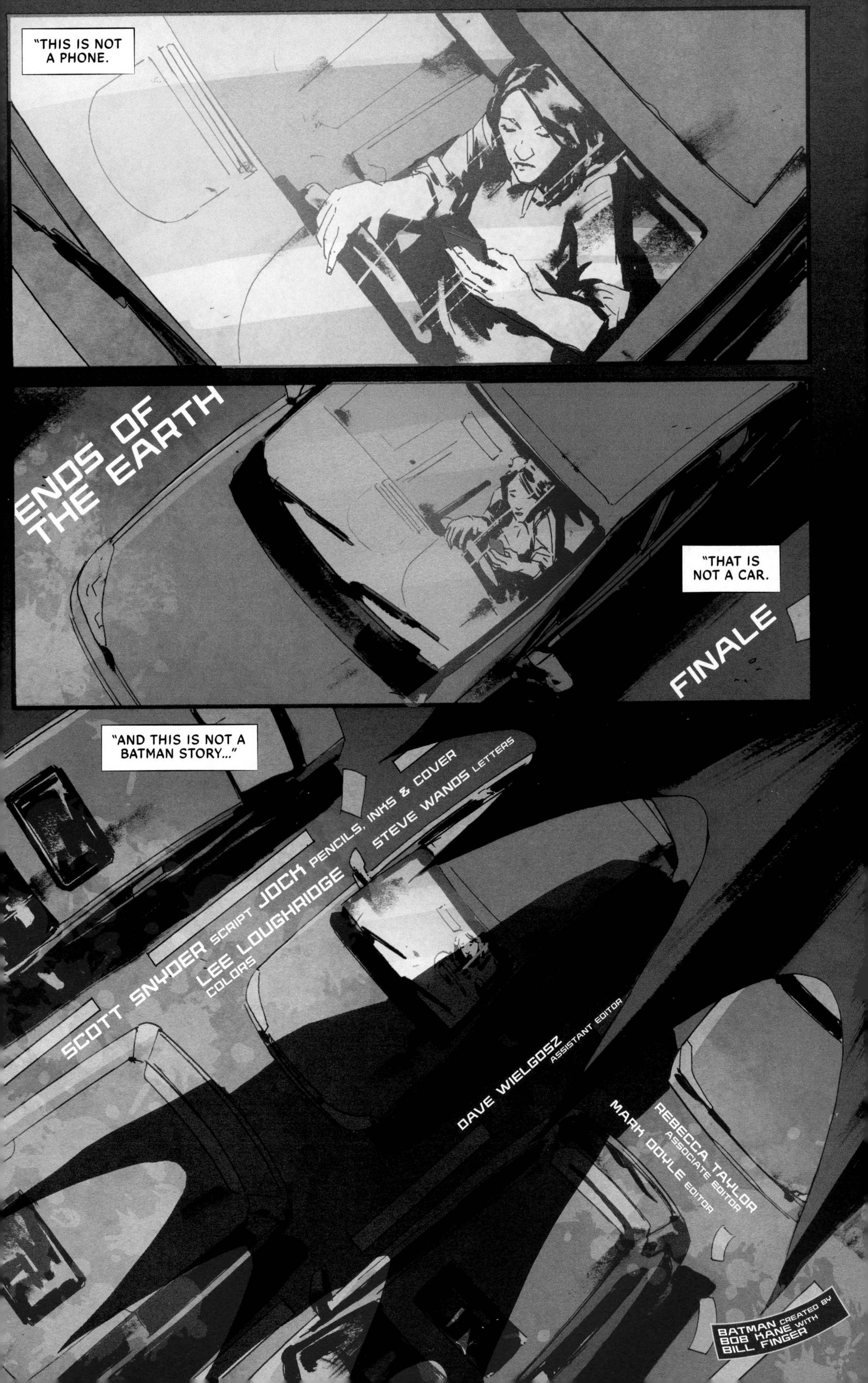
"THIS IS NOT A PHONE.
ENDS OF THE EARTH
"THAT IS NOT A CAR.
FINALE
"AND THIS IS NOT A BATMAN STORY..."
SCOTT SNYDER SCRIPT JOCK PENCILS, INKS & COVER
LEE LOUGHRIDGE COLORS
STEVE WANDS LETTERS
DAVE WIELGOSZ ASSISTANT EDITOR
REBECCA TAYLOR ASSOCIATE EDITOR
MARK DOYLE EDITOR
BATMAN CREATED BY BOB KANE WITH BILL FINGER

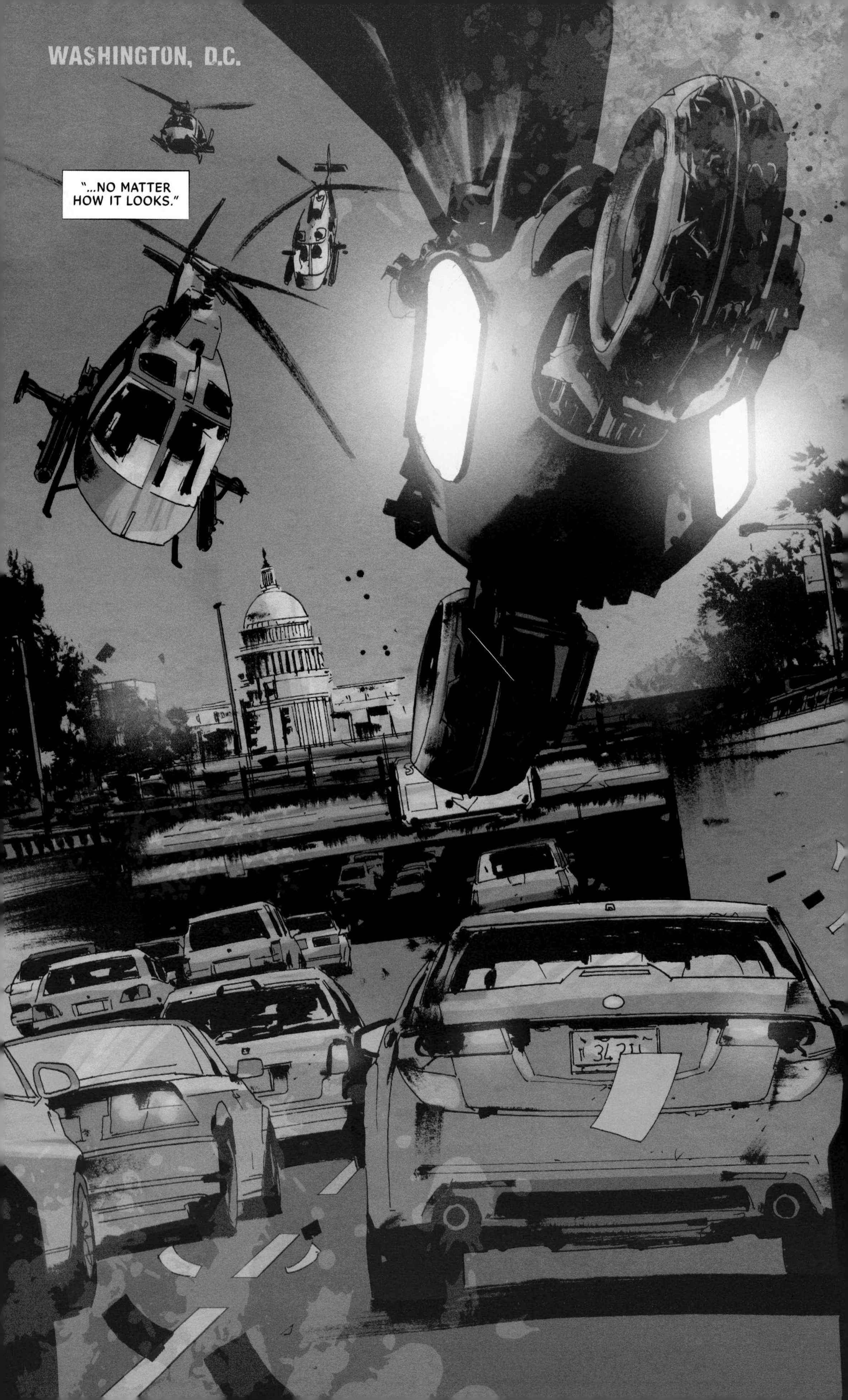
WASHINGTON, D.C.
"...NO MATTER HOW IT LOOKS."

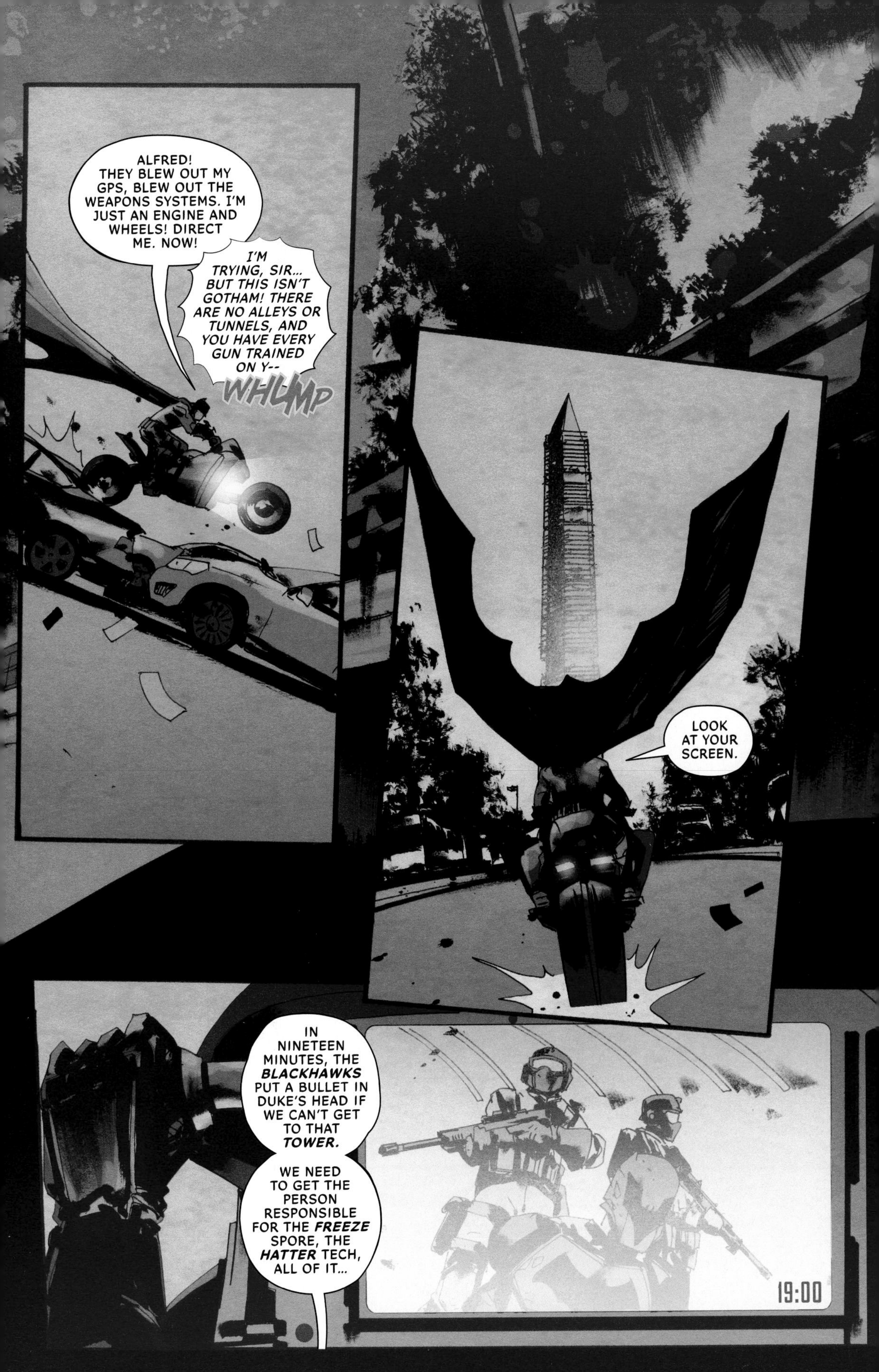
ALFRED! THEY BLEW OUT MY GPS, BLEW OUT THE WEAPONS SYSTEMS. I'M JUST AN ENGINE AND WHEELS! DIRECT ME. NOW!
I'M TRYING, SIR... BUT THIS ISN'T GOTHAM! THERE ARE NO ALLEYS OR TUNNELS, AND YOU HAVE EVERY GUN TRAINED ON Y--
WHUMP
LOOK AT YOUR SCREEN.
IN NINETEEN MINUTES, THE BLACKHAWKS PUT A BULLET IN DUKE'S HEAD IF WE CAN'T GET TO THAT TOWER.
WE NEED TO GET THE PERSON RESPONSIBLE FOR THE FREEZE SPORE, THE HATTER TECH, ALL OF IT...
19:00

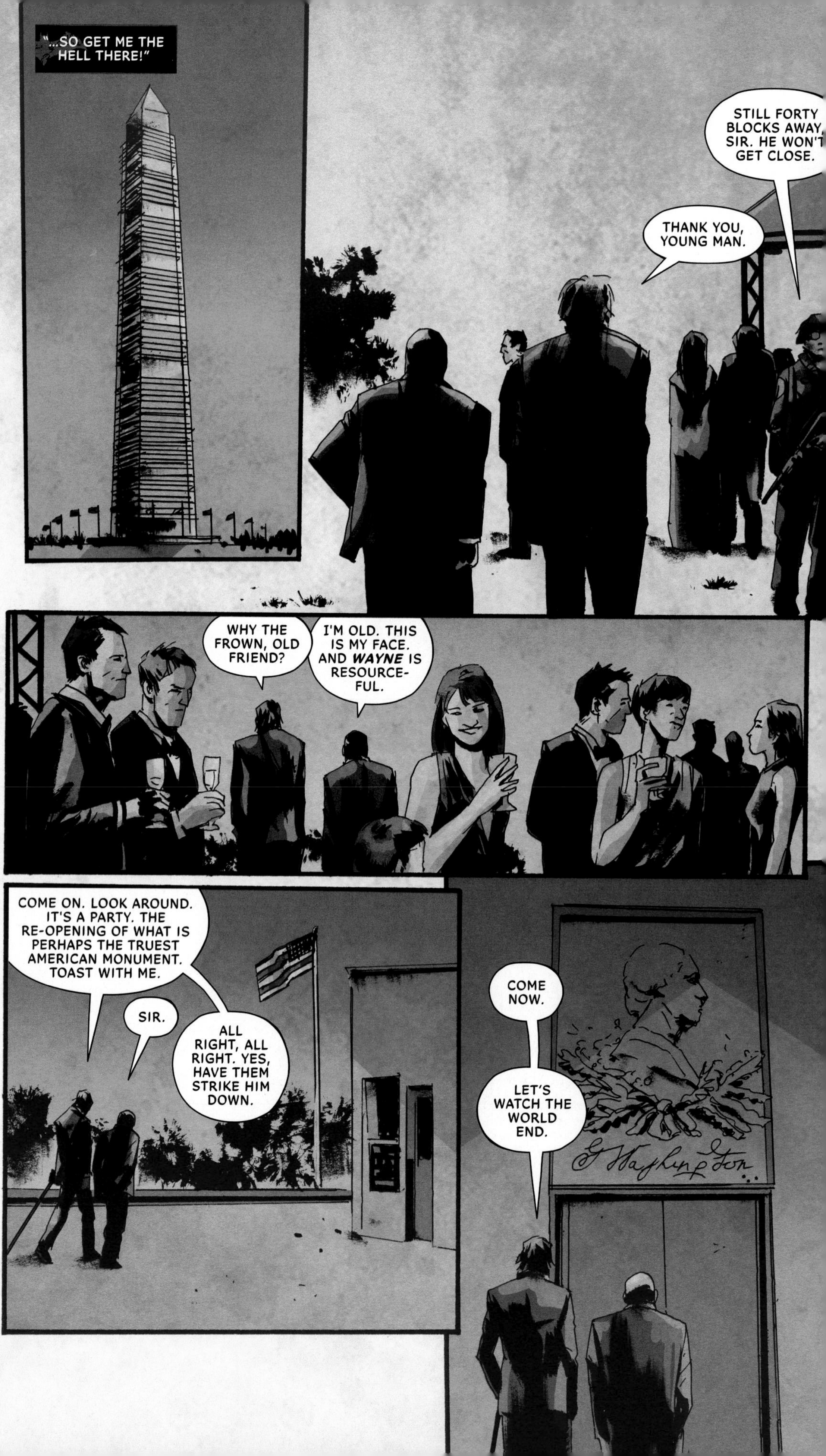
"...SO GET ME THE HELL THERE!"
STILL FORTY BLOCKS AWAY, SIR. HE WON'T GET CLOSE.
THANK YOU, YOUNG MAN.
WHY THE FROWN, OLD FRIEND?
I'M OLD. THIS IS MY FACE. AND WAYNE IS RESOURCE-FUL.
COME ON. LOOK AROUND. IT'S A PARTY. THE RE-OPENING OF WHAT IS PERHAPS THE TRUEST AMERICAN MONUMENT. TOAST WITH ME.
SIR.
ALL RIGHT, ALL RIGHT. YES, HAVE THEM STRIKE HIM DOWN.
COME NOW.
LET'S WATCH THE WORLD END.

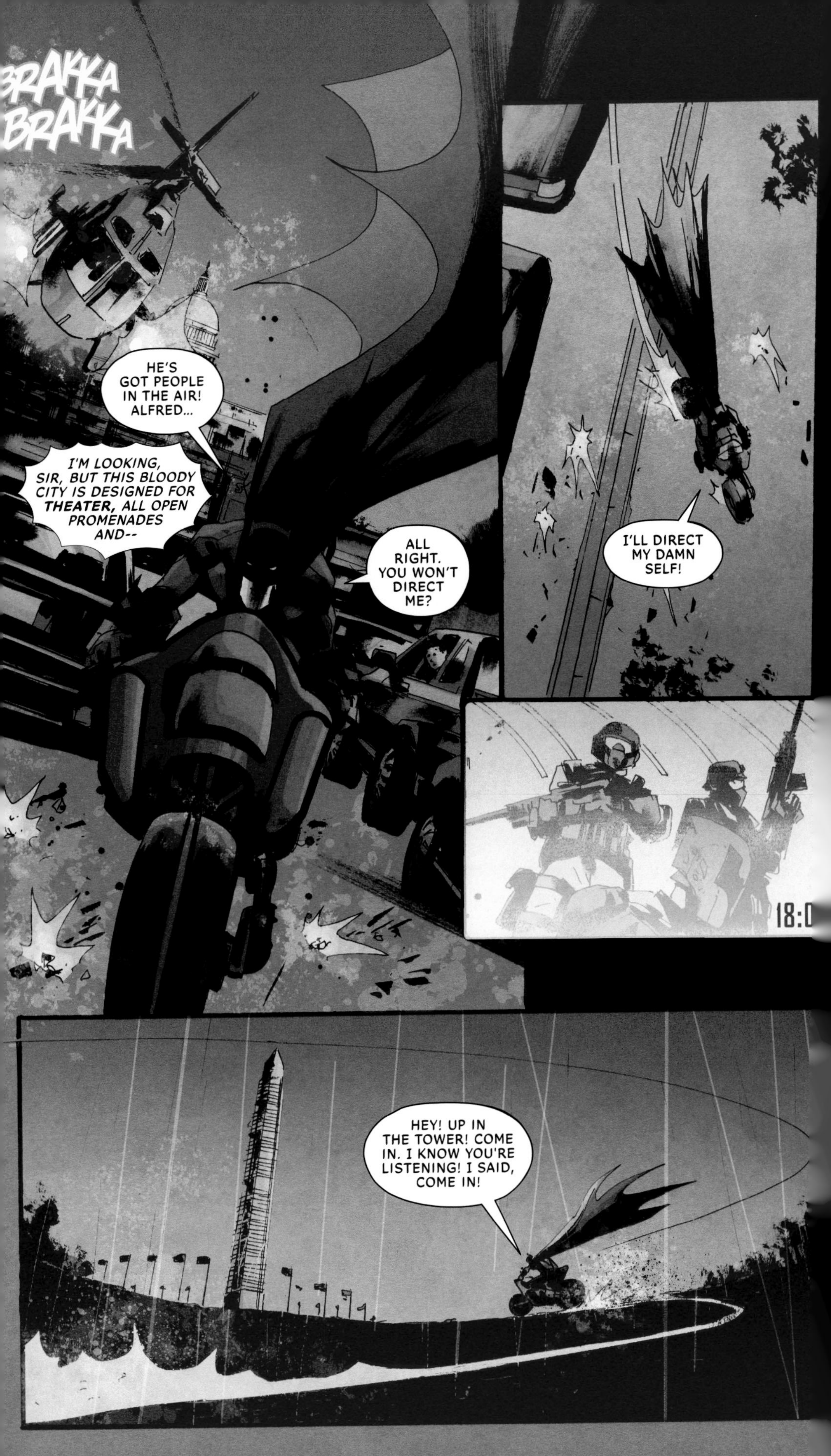
BRAKKA BRAKKA
HE'S GOT PEOPLE IN THE AIR! ALFRED...
I'M LOOKING, SIR, BUT THIS BLOODY CITY IS DESIGNED FOR **THEATER,** ALL OPEN PROMENADES AND--
ALL RIGHT. YOU WON'T DIRECT ME?
I'LL DIRECT MY DAMN SELF!
18:0
HEY! UP IN THE TOWER! COME IN. I KNOW YOU'RE LISTENING! I SAID, COME IN!

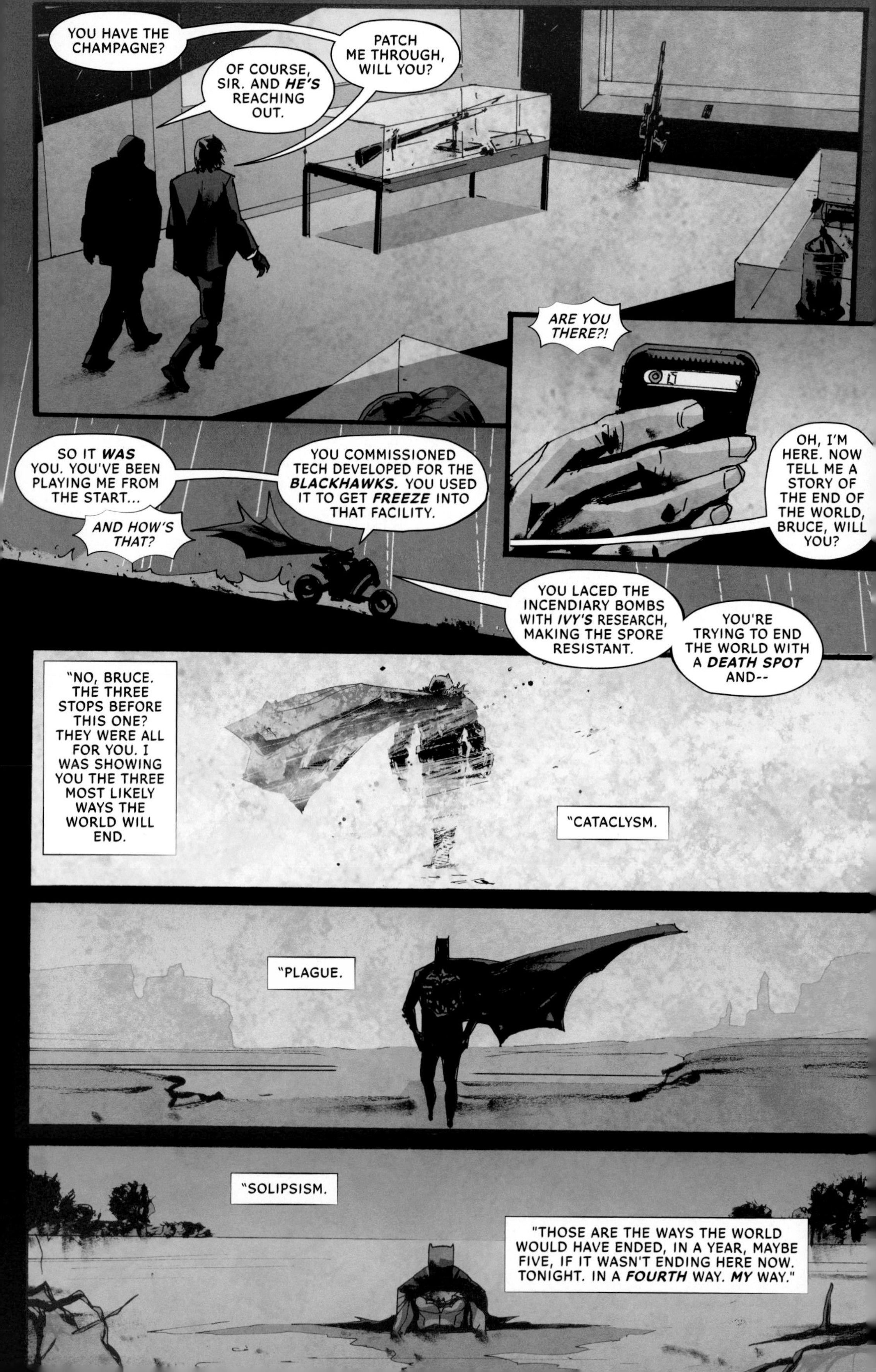
YOU HAVE THE CHAMPAGNE?
OF COURSE, SIR. AND *HE'S* REACHING OUT.
PATCH ME THROUGH, WILL YOU?
ARE YOU THERE?!
OH, I'M HERE. NOW TELL ME A STORY OF THE END OF THE WORLD, BRUCE, WILL YOU?
SO IT *WAS* YOU. YOU'VE BEEN PLAYING ME FROM THE START...
AND HOW'S THAT?
YOU COMMISSIONED TECH DEVELOPED FOR THE *BLACKHAWKS.* YOU USED IT TO GET *FREEZE* INTO THAT FACILITY.
YOU LACED THE INCENDIARY BOMBS WITH *IVY'S* RESEARCH, MAKING THE SPORE RESISTANT.
YOU'RE TRYING TO END THE WORLD WITH A *DEATH SPOT* AND--
"NO, BRUCE. THE THREE STOPS BEFORE THIS ONE? THEY WERE ALL FOR YOU. I WAS SHOWING YOU THE THREE MOST LIKELY WAYS THE WORLD WILL END.
"CATACLYSM.
"PLAGUE.
"SOLIPSISM.
"THOSE ARE THE WAYS THE WORLD WOULD HAVE ENDED, IN A YEAR, MAYBE FIVE, IF IT WASN'T ENDING HERE NOW. TONIGHT. IN A *FOURTH* WAY. *MY* WAY."

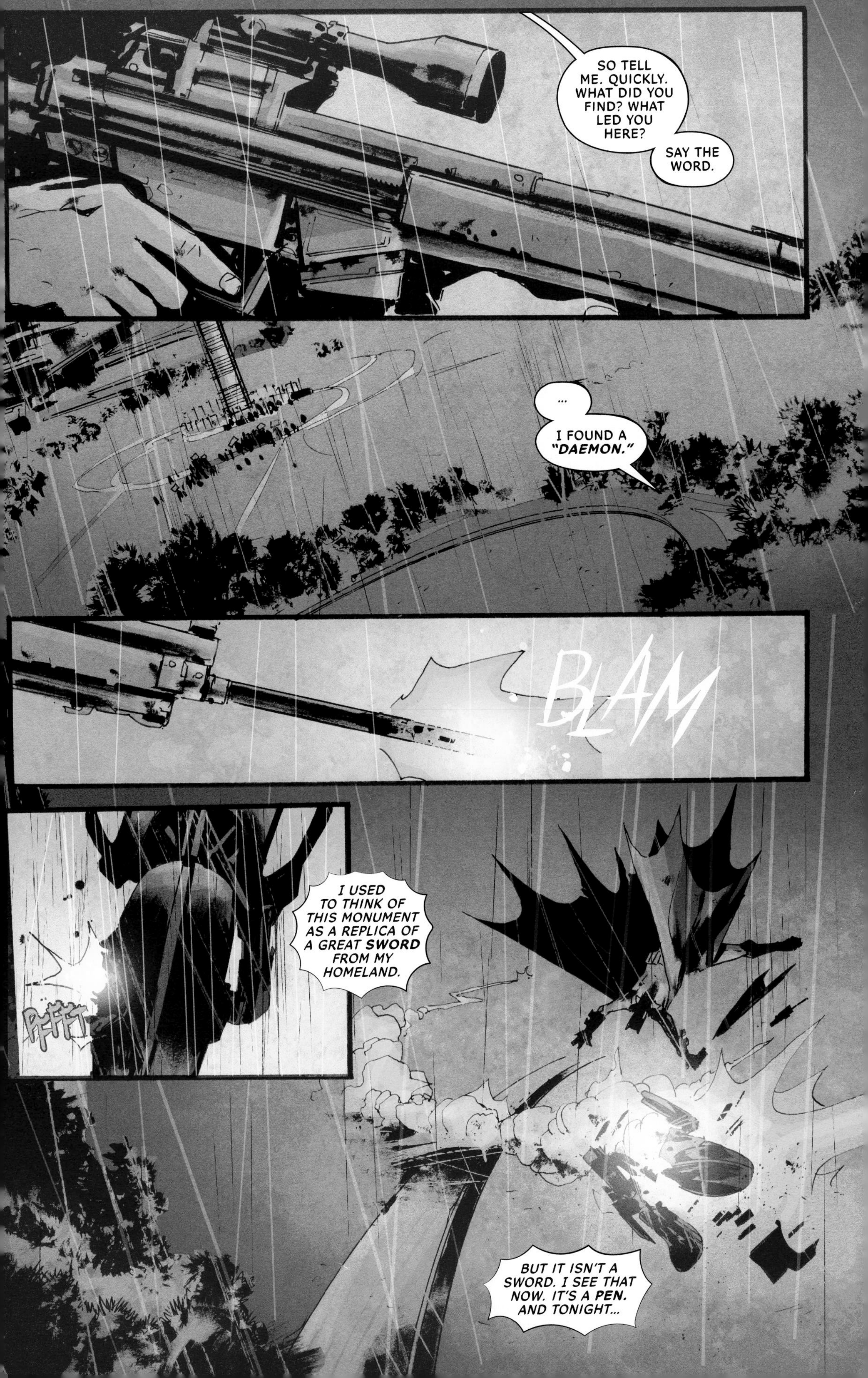
SO TELL ME. QUICKLY. WHAT DID YOU FIND? WHAT LED YOU HERE?
SAY THE WORD.
...
I FOUND A "DAEMON."
BLAM
I USED TO THINK OF THIS MONUMENT AS A REPLICA OF A GREAT SWORD FROM MY HOMELAND.
PFFFT
BUT IT ISN'T A SWORD. I SEE THAT NOW. IT'S A PEN. AND TONIGHT...

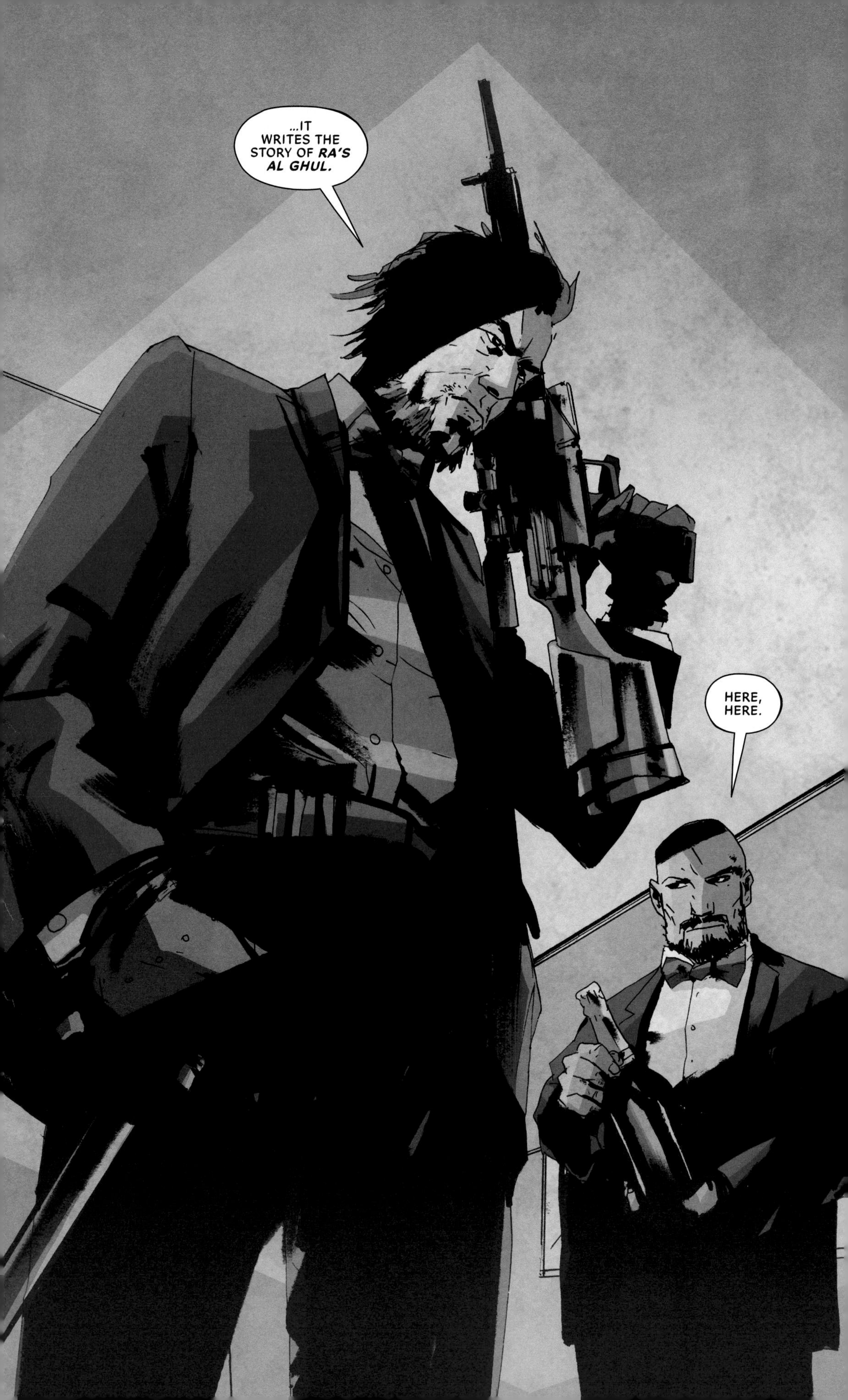
...IT WRITES THE STORY OF *RA'S AL GHUL.*
HERE, HERE.

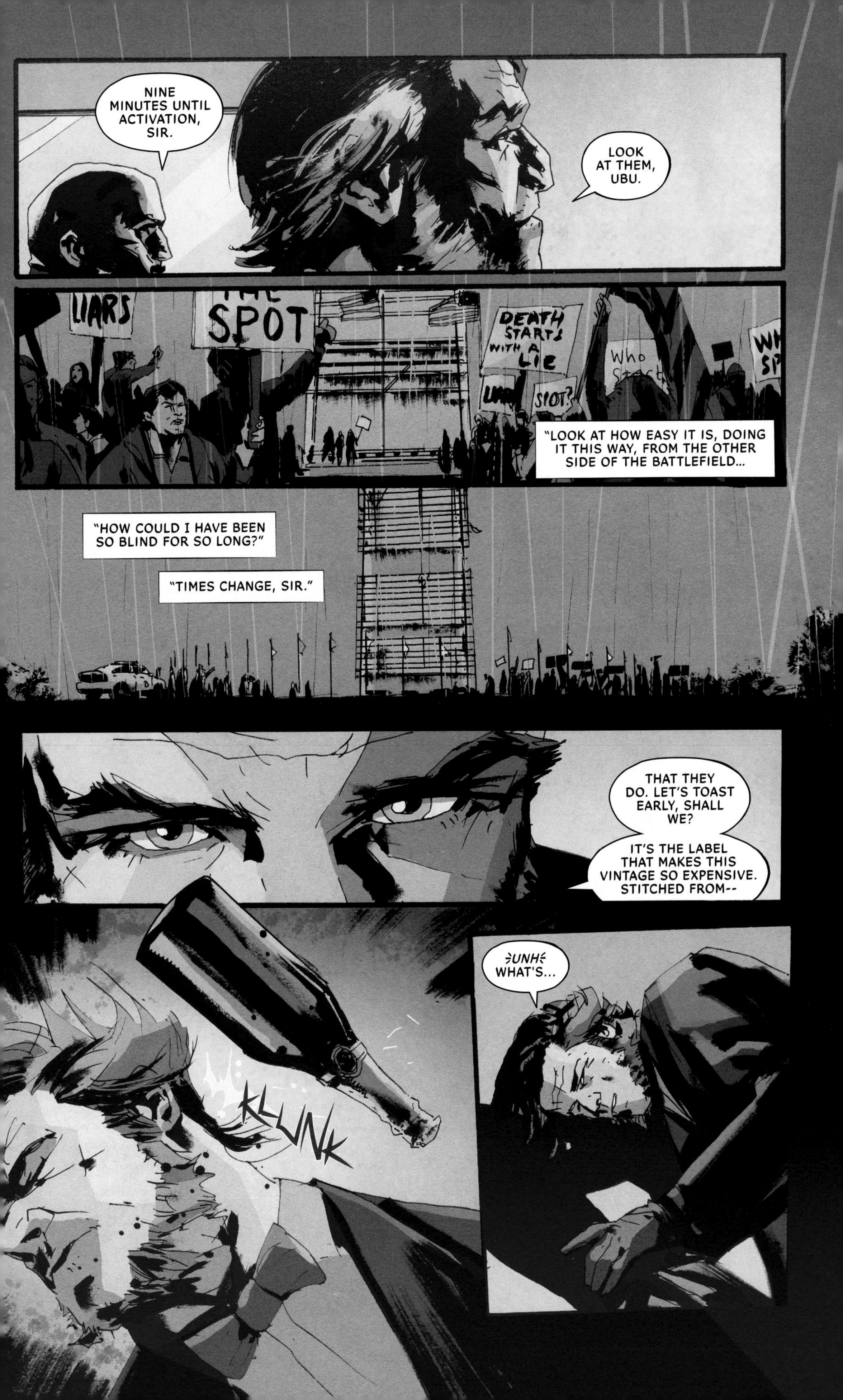
NINE MINUTES UNTIL ACTIVATION, SIR.
LOOK AT THEM, UBU.
LIARS
SPOT
DEATH STARTS WITH A LIE
Who Start
SPOT?
"LOOK AT HOW EASY IT IS, DOING IT THIS WAY, FROM THE OTHER SIDE OF THE BATTLEFIELD...
"HOW COULD I HAVE BEEN SO BLIND FOR SO LONG?"
"TIMES CHANGE, SIR."
THAT THEY DO. LET'S TOAST EARLY, SHALL WE?
IT'S THE LABEL THAT MAKES THIS VINTAGE SO EXPENSIVE. STITCHED FROM--
KLUNK
UNH WHAT'S...

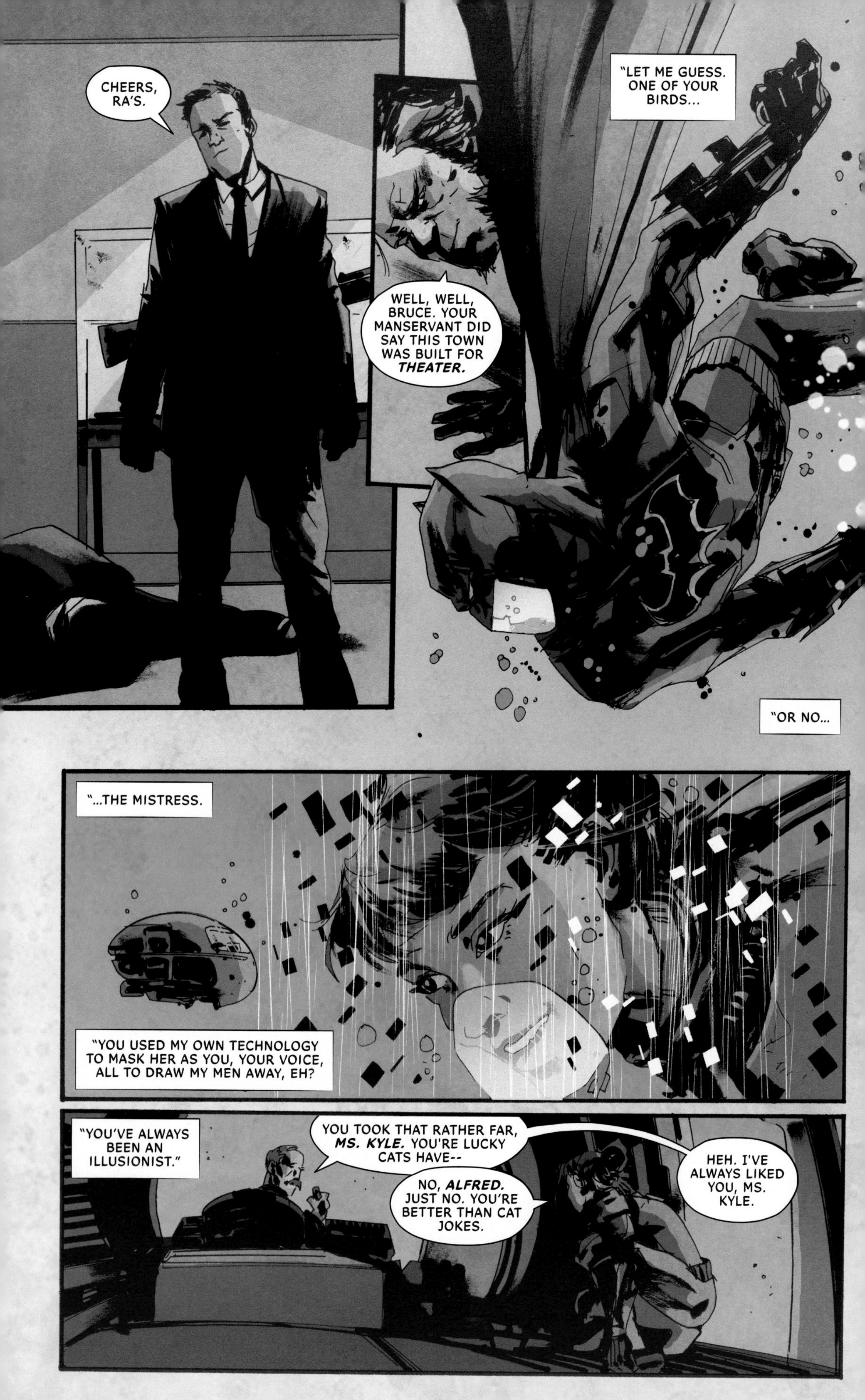
CHEERS, RA'S.
"LET ME GUESS. ONE OF YOUR BIRDS...
WELL, WELL, BRUCE. YOUR MANSERVANT DID SAY THIS TOWN WAS BUILT FOR *THEATER.*
"OR NO...
"...THE MISTRESS.
"YOU USED MY OWN TECHNOLOGY TO MASK HER AS YOU, YOUR VOICE, ALL TO DRAW MY MEN AWAY, EH?
"YOU'VE ALWAYS BEEN AN ILLUSIONIST."
YOU TOOK THAT RATHER FAR, *MS. KYLE.* YOU'RE LUCKY CATS HAVE--
NO, *ALFRED.* JUST NO. YOU'RE BETTER THAN CAT JOKES.
HEH. I'VE ALWAYS LIKED YOU, MS. KYLE.

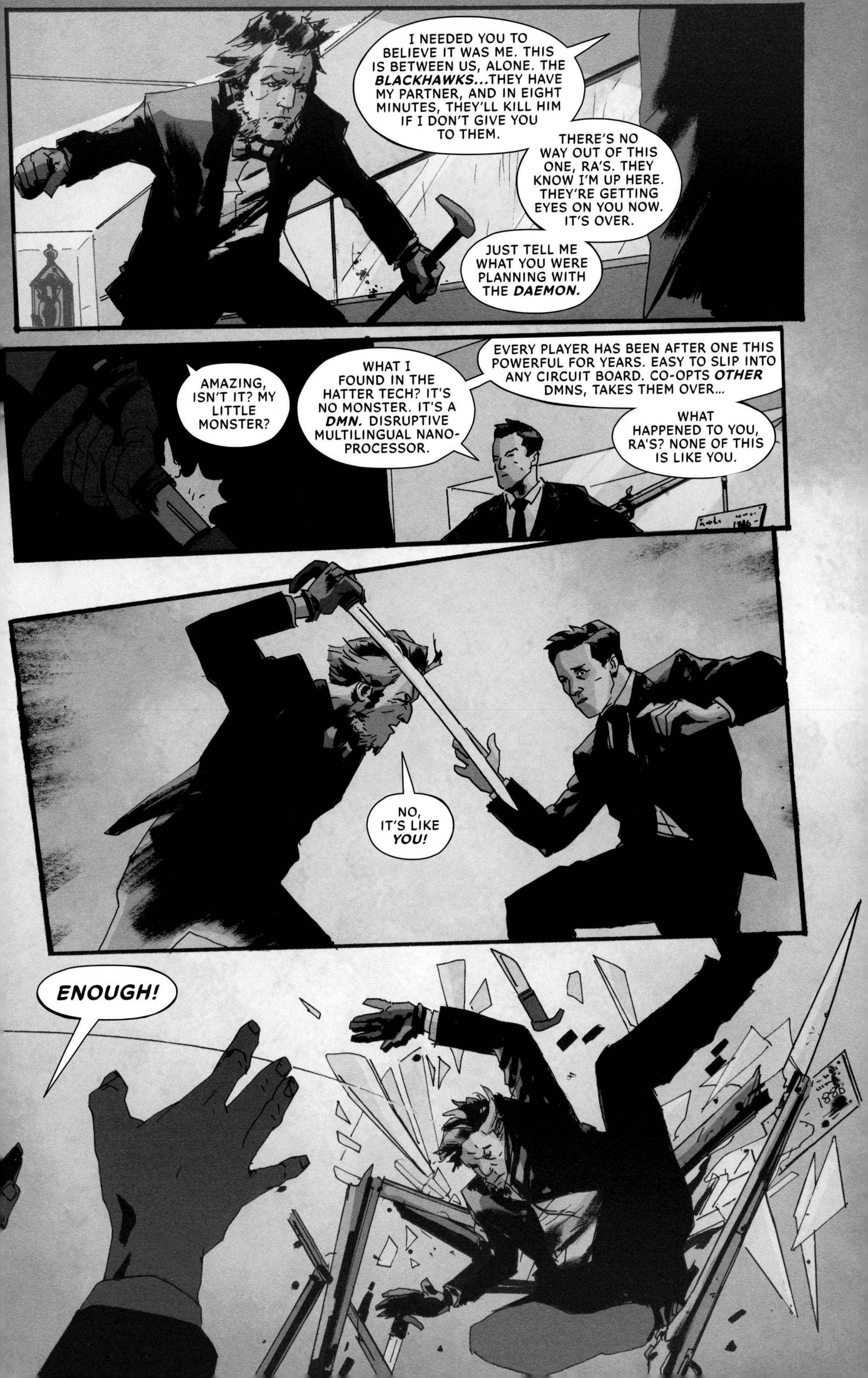
I NEEDED YOU TO BELIEVE IT WAS ME. THIS IS BETWEEN US, ALONE. THE BLACKHAWKS...THEY HAVE MY PARTNER, AND IN EIGHT MINUTES, THEY'LL KILL HIM IF I DON'T GIVE YOU TO THEM.
THERE'S NO WAY OUT OF THIS ONE, RA'S. THEY KNOW I'M UP HERE. THEY'RE GETTING EYES ON YOU NOW. IT'S OVER.
JUST TELL ME WHAT YOU WERE PLANNING WITH THE DAEMON.
AMAZING, ISN'T IT? MY LITTLE MONSTER?
WHAT I FOUND IN THE HATTER TECH? IT'S NO MONSTER. IT'S A DMN. DISRUPTIVE MULTILINGUAL NANO-PROCESSOR.
EVERY PLAYER HAS BEEN AFTER ONE THIS POWERFUL FOR YEARS. EASY TO SLIP INTO ANY CIRCUIT BOARD. CO-OPTS OTHER DMNS, TAKES THEM OVER...
WHAT HAPPENED TO YOU, RA'S? NONE OF THIS IS LIKE YOU.
NO, IT'S LIKE YOU!
ENOUGH!

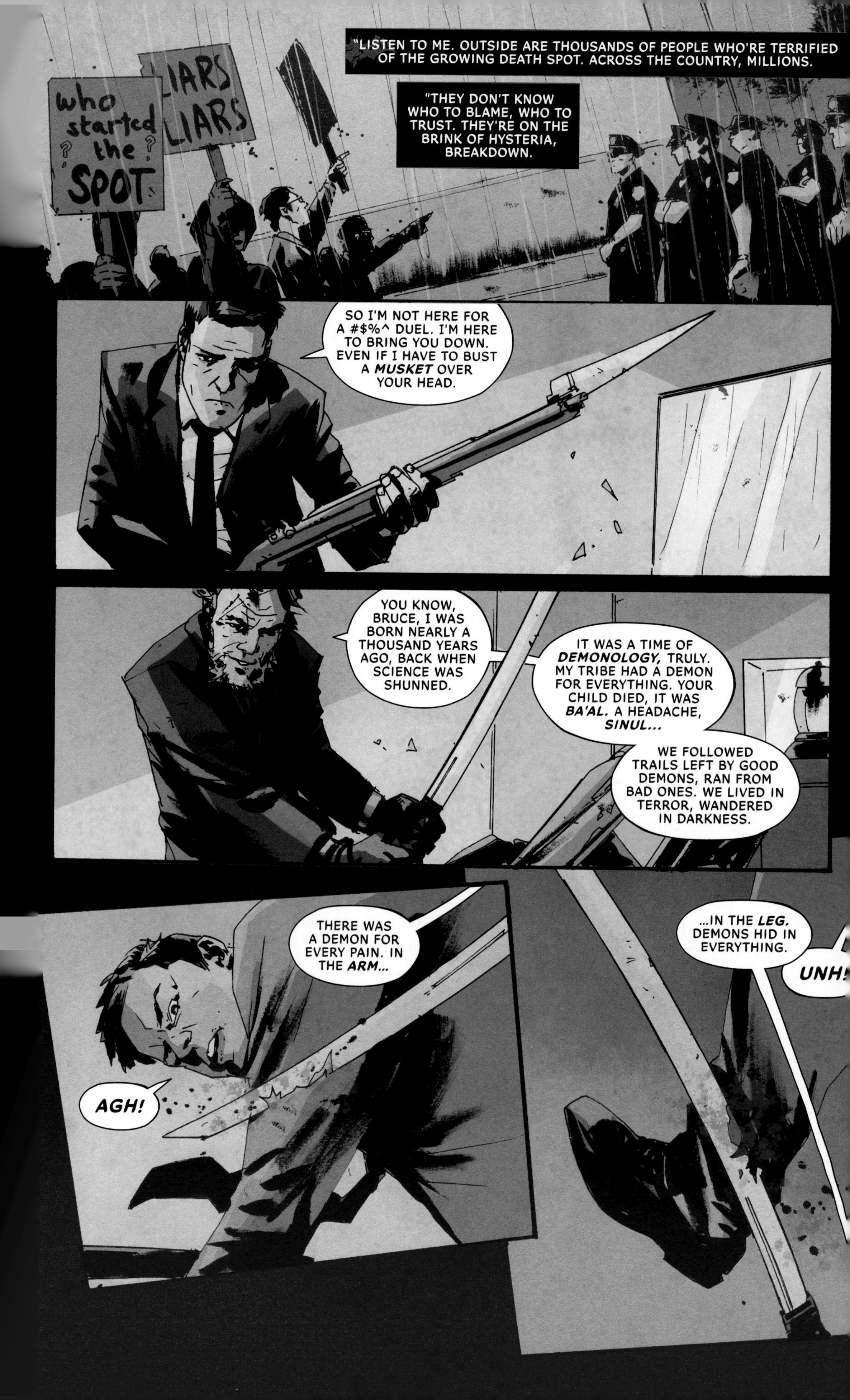

who started the ? SPOT ?
LIARS LIARS
"LISTEN TO ME. OUTSIDE ARE THOUSANDS OF PEOPLE WHO'RE TERRIFIED OF THE GROWING DEATH SPOT. ACROSS THE COUNTRY, MILLIONS.
"THEY DON'T KNOW WHO TO BLAME, WHO TO TRUST. THEY'RE ON THE BRINK OF HYSTERIA, BREAKDOWN.
SO I'M NOT HERE FOR A #$%^ DUEL. I'M HERE TO BRING YOU DOWN. EVEN IF I HAVE TO BUST A *MUSKET* OVER YOUR HEAD.
YOU KNOW, BRUCE, I WAS BORN NEARLY A THOUSAND YEARS AGO, BACK WHEN SCIENCE WAS SHUNNED.
IT WAS A TIME OF *DEMONOLOGY,* TRULY. MY TRIBE HAD A DEMON FOR EVERYTHING. YOUR CHILD DIED, IT WAS *BA'AL.* A HEADACHE, *SINUL...*
WE FOLLOWED TRAILS LEFT BY GOOD DEMONS, RAN FROM BAD ONES. WE LIVED IN TERROR, WANDERED IN DARKNESS.
THERE WAS A DEMON FOR EVERY PAIN. IN THE *ARM...*
*AGH!*
...IN THE *LEG.* DEMONS HID IN EVERYTHING.
*UNH!*

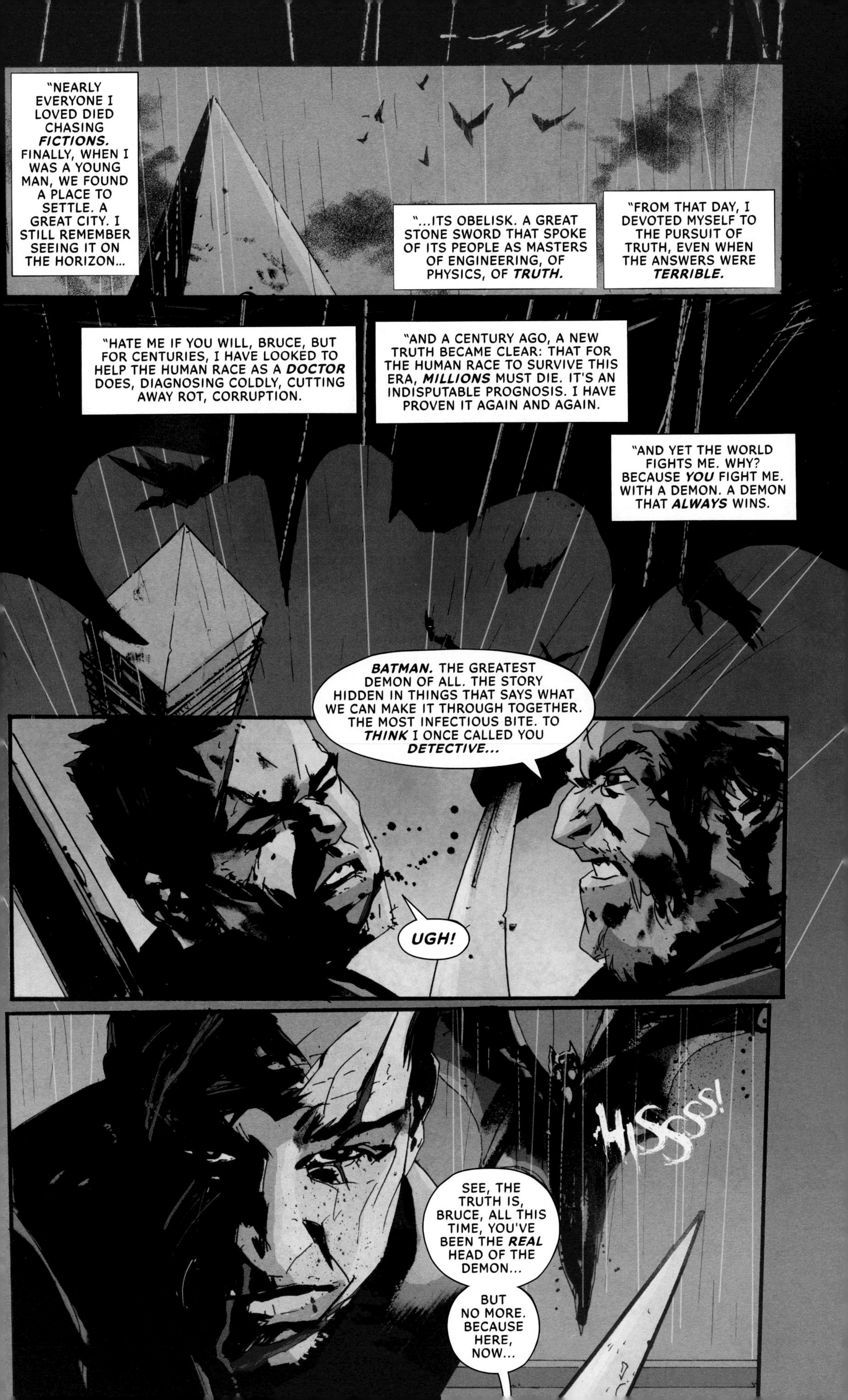
"NEARLY EVERYONE I LOVED DIED CHASING FICTIONS. FINALLY, WHEN I WAS A YOUNG MAN, WE FOUND A PLACE TO SETTLE. A GREAT CITY. I STILL REMEMBER SEEING IT ON THE HORIZON...
"...ITS OBELISK. A GREAT STONE SWORD THAT SPOKE OF ITS PEOPLE AS MASTERS OF ENGINEERING, OF PHYSICS, OF TRUTH.
"FROM THAT DAY, I DEVOTED MYSELF TO THE PURSUIT OF TRUTH, EVEN WHEN THE ANSWERS WERE TERRIBLE.
"HATE ME IF YOU WILL, BRUCE, BUT FOR CENTURIES, I HAVE LOOKED TO HELP THE HUMAN RACE AS A DOCTOR DOES, DIAGNOSING COLDLY, CUTTING AWAY ROT, CORRUPTION.
"AND A CENTURY AGO, A NEW TRUTH BECAME CLEAR: THAT FOR THE HUMAN RACE TO SURVIVE THIS ERA, MILLIONS MUST DIE. IT'S AN INDISPUTABLE PROGNOSIS. I HAVE PROVEN IT AGAIN AND AGAIN.
"AND YET THE WORLD FIGHTS ME. WHY? BECAUSE YOU FIGHT ME. WITH A DEMON. A DEMON THAT ALWAYS WINS.
BATMAN. THE GREATEST DEMON OF ALL. THE STORY HIDDEN IN THINGS THAT SAYS WHAT WE CAN MAKE IT THROUGH TOGETHER. THE MOST INFECTIOUS BITE. TO THINK I ONCE CALLED YOU DETECTIVE...
UGH!
HISSSS!
SEE, THE TRUTH IS, BRUCE, ALL THIS TIME, YOU'VE BEEN THE REAL HEAD OF THE DEMON...
BUT NO MORE. BECAUSE HERE, NOW...

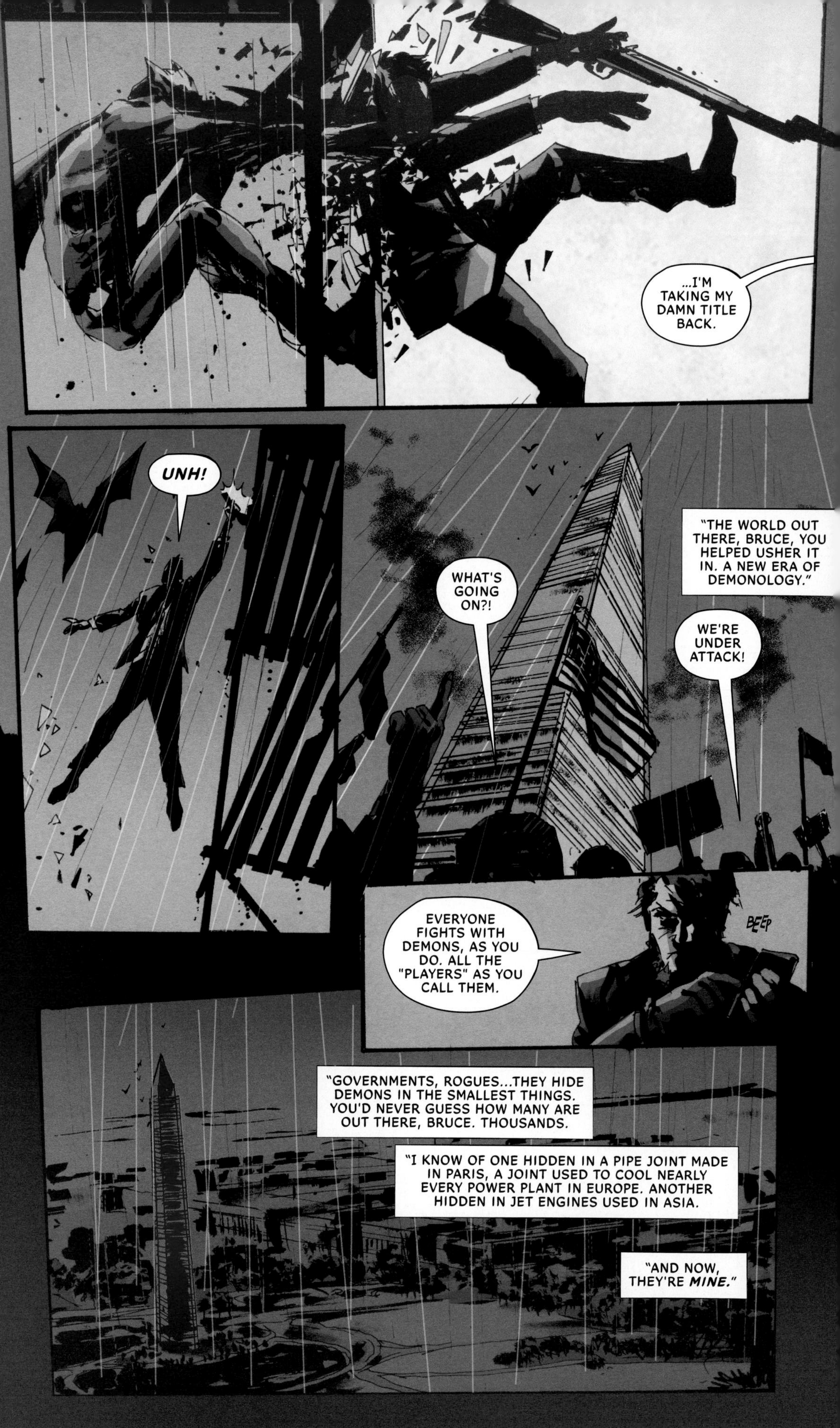
...I'M TAKING MY DAMN TITLE BACK.
UNH!
WHAT'S GOING ON?!
"THE WORLD OUT THERE, BRUCE, YOU HELPED USHER IT IN. A NEW ERA OF DEMONOLOGY."
WE'RE UNDER ATTACK!
BEEP
EVERYONE FIGHTS WITH DEMONS, AS YOU DO. ALL THE "PLAYERS" AS YOU CALL THEM.
"GOVERNMENTS, ROGUES...THEY HIDE DEMONS IN THE SMALLEST THINGS. YOU'D NEVER GUESS HOW MANY ARE OUT THERE, BRUCE. THOUSANDS.
"I KNOW OF ONE HIDDEN IN A PIPE JOINT MADE IN PARIS, A JOINT USED TO COOL NEARLY EVERY POWER PLANT IN EUROPE. ANOTHER HIDDEN IN JET ENGINES USED IN ASIA.
"AND NOW, THEY'RE *MINE.*"

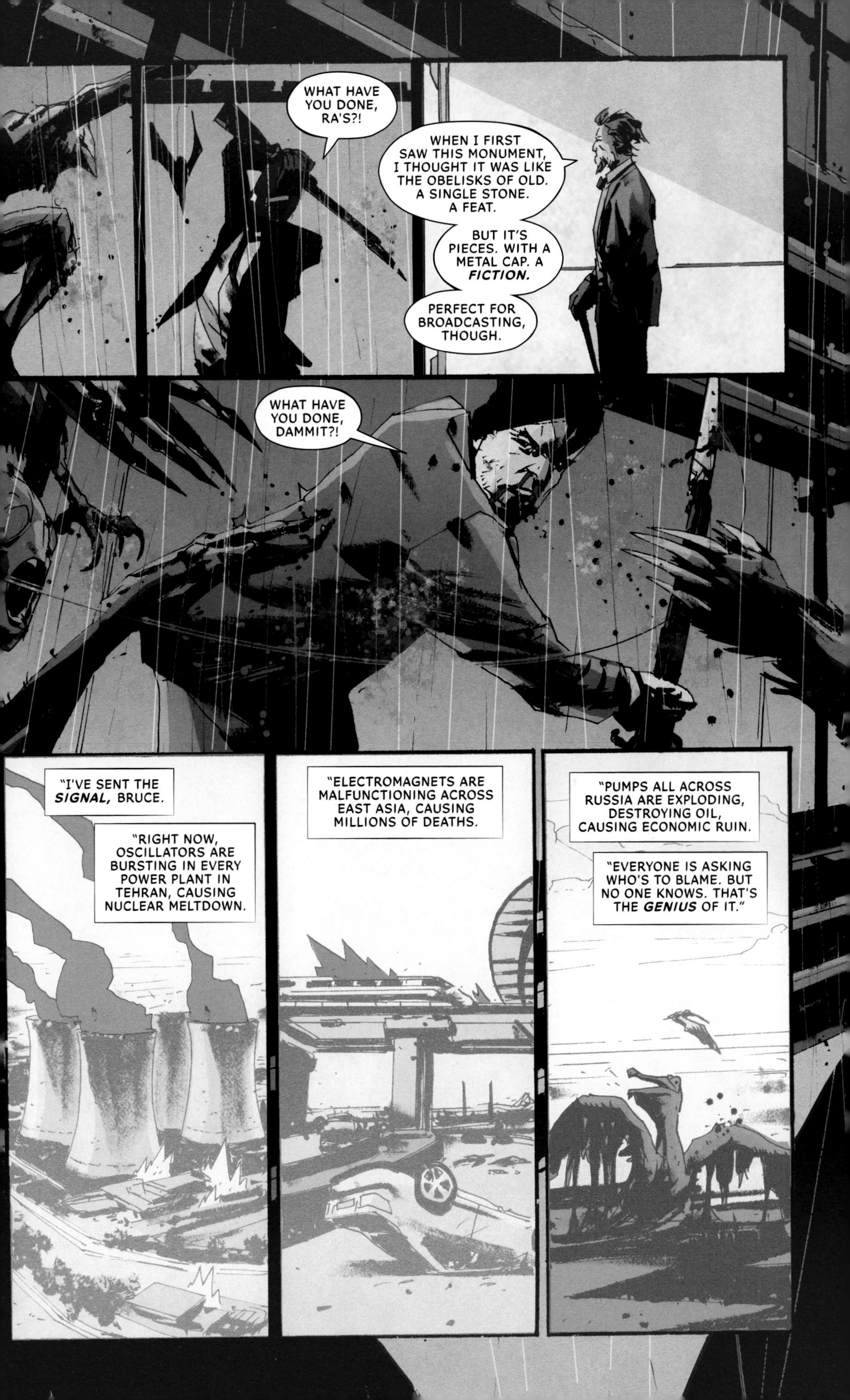
WHAT HAVE YOU DONE, RA'S?!
WHEN I FIRST SAW THIS MONUMENT, I THOUGHT IT WAS LIKE THE OBELISKS OF OLD. A SINGLE STONE. A FEAT.
BUT IT'S PIECES. WITH A METAL CAP. A *FICTION.*
PERFECT FOR BROADCASTING, THOUGH.
WHAT HAVE YOU DONE, DAMMIT?!
"I'VE SENT THE *SIGNAL,* BRUCE.
"RIGHT NOW, OSCILLATORS ARE BURSTING IN EVERY POWER PLANT IN TEHRAN, CAUSING NUCLEAR MELTDOWN.
"ELECTROMAGNETS ARE MALFUNCTIONING ACROSS EAST ASIA, CAUSING MILLIONS OF DEATHS.
"PUMPS ALL ACROSS RUSSIA ARE EXPLODING, DESTROYING OIL, CAUSING ECONOMIC RUIN.
"EVERYONE IS ASKING WHO'S TO BLAME. BUT NO ONE KNOWS. THAT'S THE *GENIUS* OF IT."

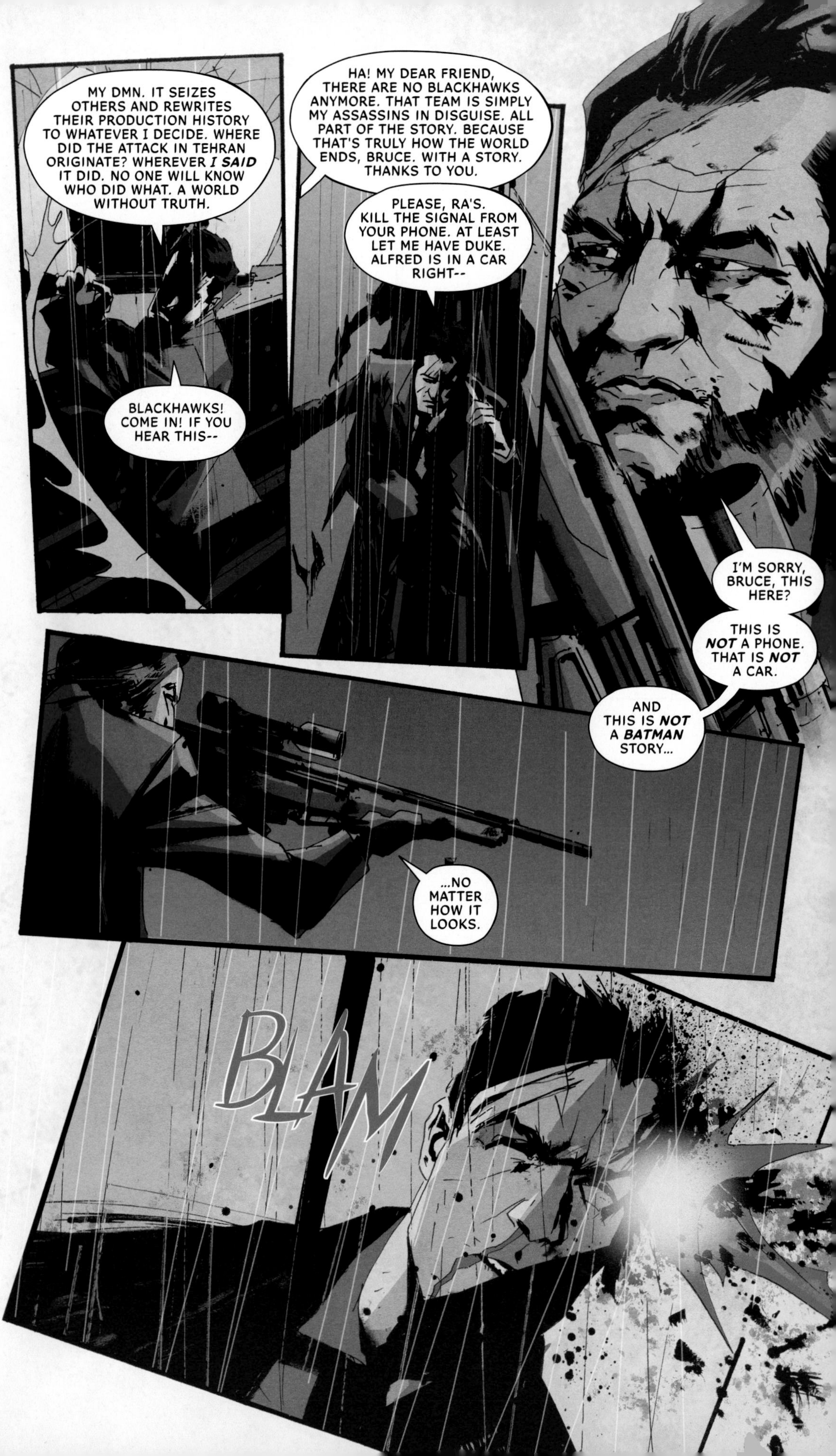
MY DMN. IT SEIZES OTHERS AND REWRITES THEIR PRODUCTION HISTORY TO WHATEVER I DECIDE. WHERE DID THE ATTACK IN TEHRAN ORIGINATE? WHEREVER *I SAID* IT DID. NO ONE WILL KNOW WHO DID WHAT. A WORLD WITHOUT TRUTH.
BLACKHAWKS! COME IN! IF YOU HEAR THIS--
HA! MY DEAR FRIEND, THERE ARE NO BLACKHAWKS ANYMORE. THAT TEAM IS SIMPLY MY ASSASSINS IN DISGUISE. ALL PART OF THE STORY. BECAUSE THAT'S TRULY HOW THE WORLD ENDS, BRUCE. WITH A STORY. THANKS TO YOU.
PLEASE, RA'S. KILL THE SIGNAL FROM YOUR PHONE. AT LEAST LET ME HAVE DUKE. ALFRED IS IN A CAR RIGHT--
I'M SORRY, BRUCE, THIS HERE?
THIS IS ***NOT*** A PHONE. THAT IS ***NOT*** A CAR.
AND THIS IS ***NOT*** A ***BATMAN*** STORY...
...NO MATTER HOW IT LOOKS.
BLAM

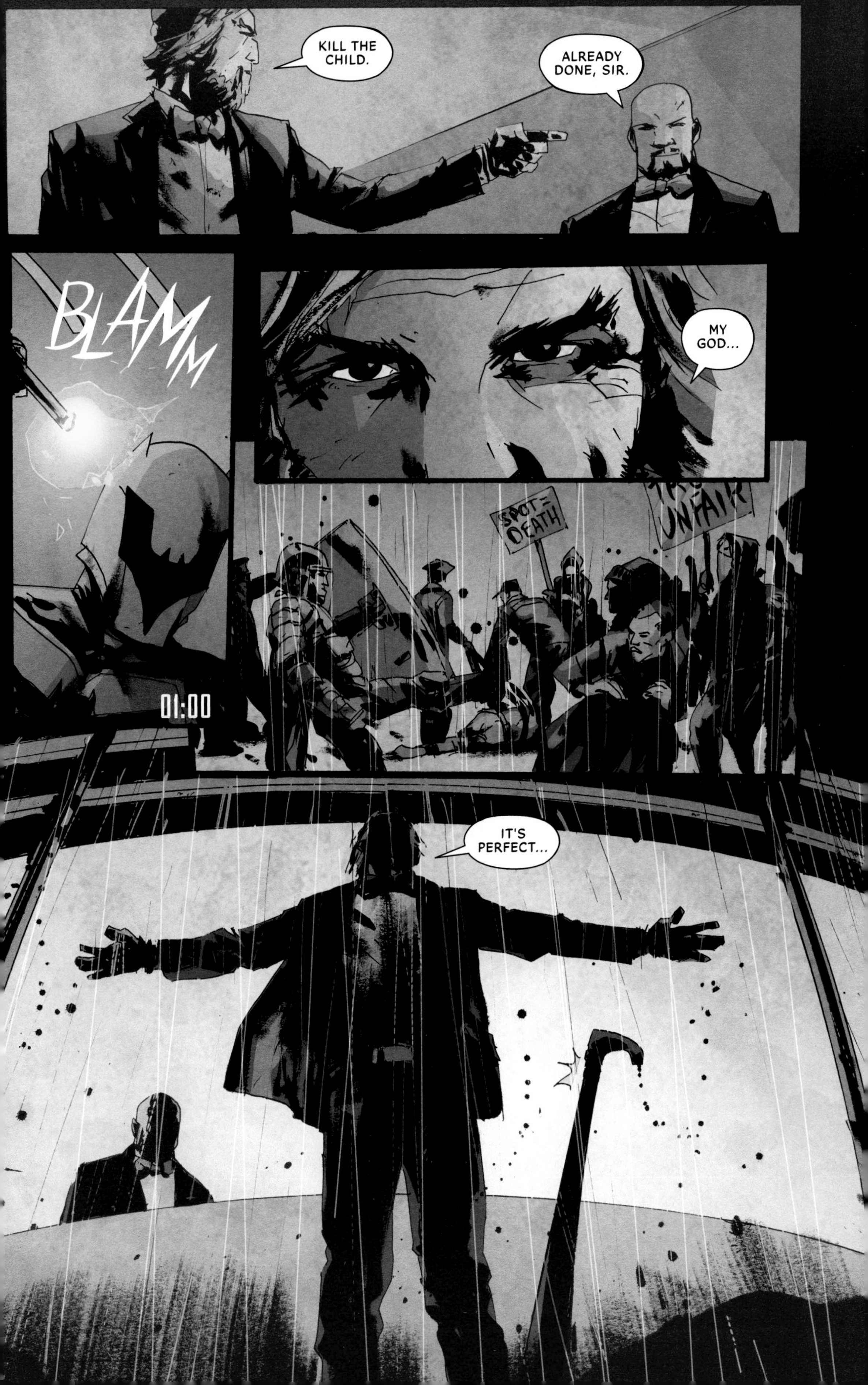
KILL THE CHILD.
ALREADY DONE, SIR.
BLAMM
MY GOD...
SPOT=DEATH
UNFAIR
01:00
IT'S PERFECT...

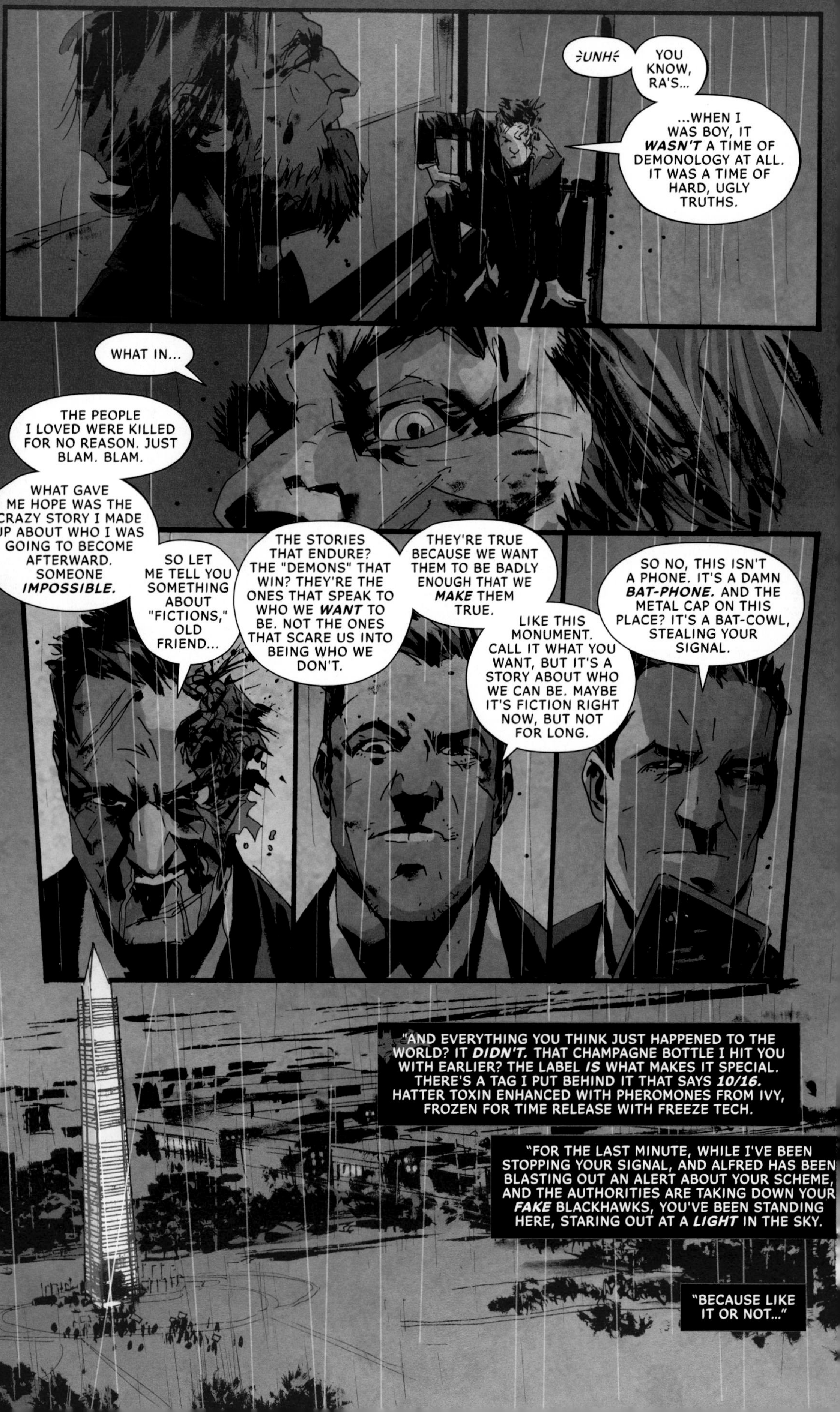
UNH
YOU KNOW, RA'S...
...WHEN I WAS BOY, IT WASN'T A TIME OF DEMONOLOGY AT ALL. IT WAS A TIME OF HARD, UGLY TRUTHS.
WHAT IN...
THE PEOPLE I LOVED WERE KILLED FOR NO REASON. JUST BLAM. BLAM.
WHAT GAVE ME HOPE WAS THE CRAZY STORY I MADE UP ABOUT WHO I WAS GOING TO BECOME AFTERWARD. SOMEONE IMPOSSIBLE.
SO LET ME TELL YOU SOMETHING ABOUT "FICTIONS," OLD FRIEND...
THE STORIES THAT ENDURE? THE "DEMONS" THAT WIN? THEY'RE THE ONES THAT SPEAK TO WHO WE WANT TO BE. NOT THE ONES THAT SCARE US INTO BEING WHO WE DON'T.
THEY'RE TRUE BECAUSE WE WANT THEM TO BE BADLY ENOUGH THAT WE MAKE THEM TRUE.
LIKE THIS MONUMENT. CALL IT WHAT YOU WANT, BUT IT'S A STORY ABOUT WHO WE CAN BE. MAYBE IT'S FICTION RIGHT NOW, BUT NOT FOR LONG.
SO NO, THIS ISN'T A PHONE. IT'S A DAMN BAT-PHONE. AND THE METAL CAP ON THIS PLACE? IT'S A BAT-COWL, STEALING YOUR SIGNAL.
"AND EVERYTHING YOU THINK JUST HAPPENED TO THE WORLD? IT DIDN'T. THAT CHAMPAGNE BOTTLE I HIT YOU WITH EARLIER? THE LABEL IS WHAT MAKES IT SPECIAL. THERE'S A TAG I PUT BEHIND IT THAT SAYS 10/16. HATTER TOXIN ENHANCED WITH PHEROMONES FROM IVY, FROZEN FOR TIME RELEASE WITH FREEZE TECH.
"FOR THE LAST MINUTE, WHILE I'VE BEEN STOPPING YOUR SIGNAL, AND ALFRED HAS BEEN BLASTING OUT AN ALERT ABOUT YOUR SCHEME, AND THE AUTHORITIES ARE TAKING DOWN YOUR FAKE BLACKHAWKS, YOU'VE BEEN STANDING HERE, STARING OUT AT A LIGHT IN THE SKY.
"BECAUSE LIKE IT OR NOT..."

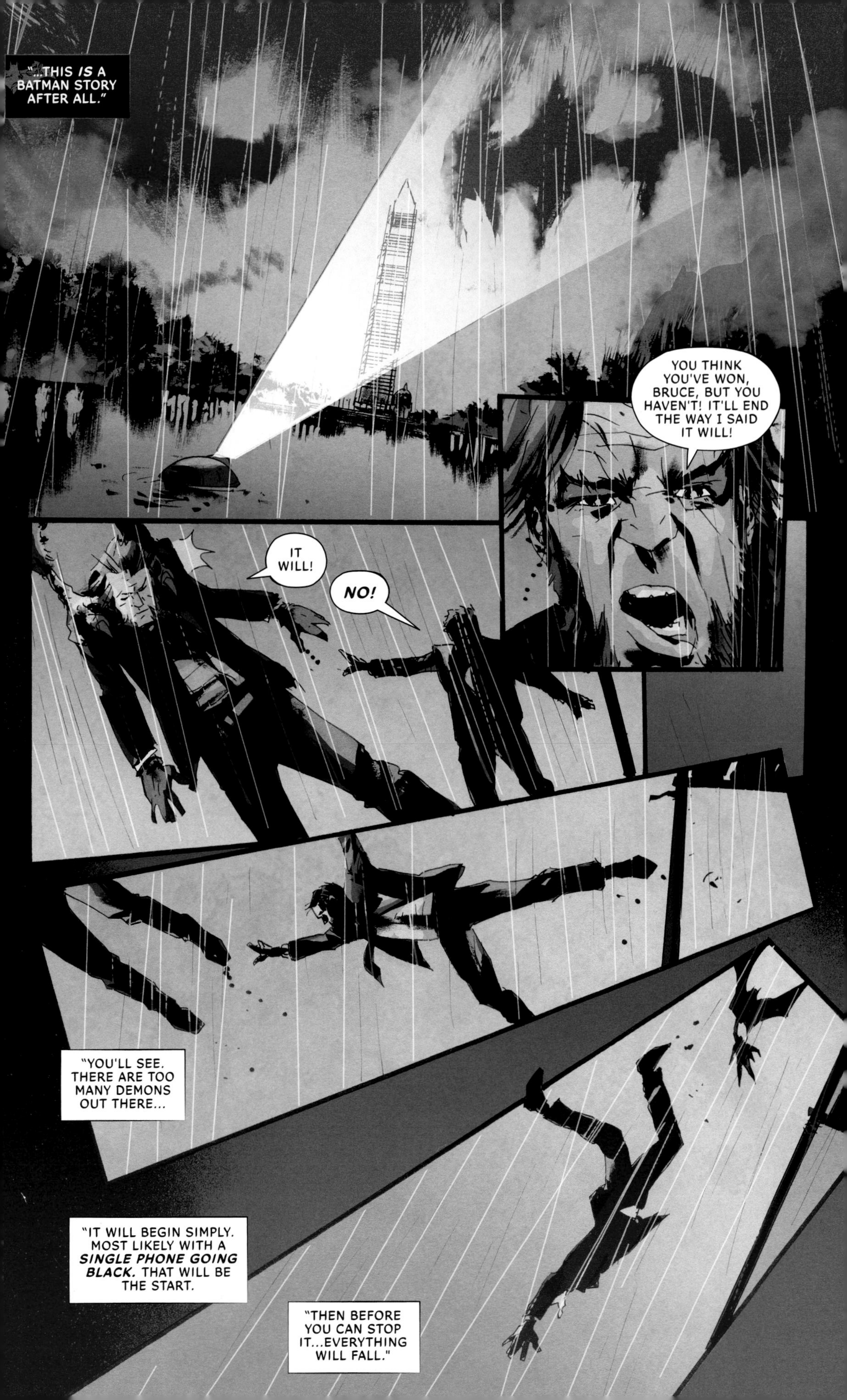
"...THIS IS A BATMAN STORY AFTER ALL."
YOU THINK YOU'VE WON, BRUCE, BUT YOU HAVEN'T! IT'LL END THE WAY I SAID IT WILL!
IT WILL!
NO!
"YOU'LL SEE. THERE ARE TOO MANY DEMONS OUT THERE...
"IT WILL BEGIN SIMPLY. MOST LIKELY WITH A SINGLE PHONE GOING BLACK. THAT WILL BE THE START.
"THEN BEFORE YOU CAN STOP IT...EVERYTHING WILL FALL."

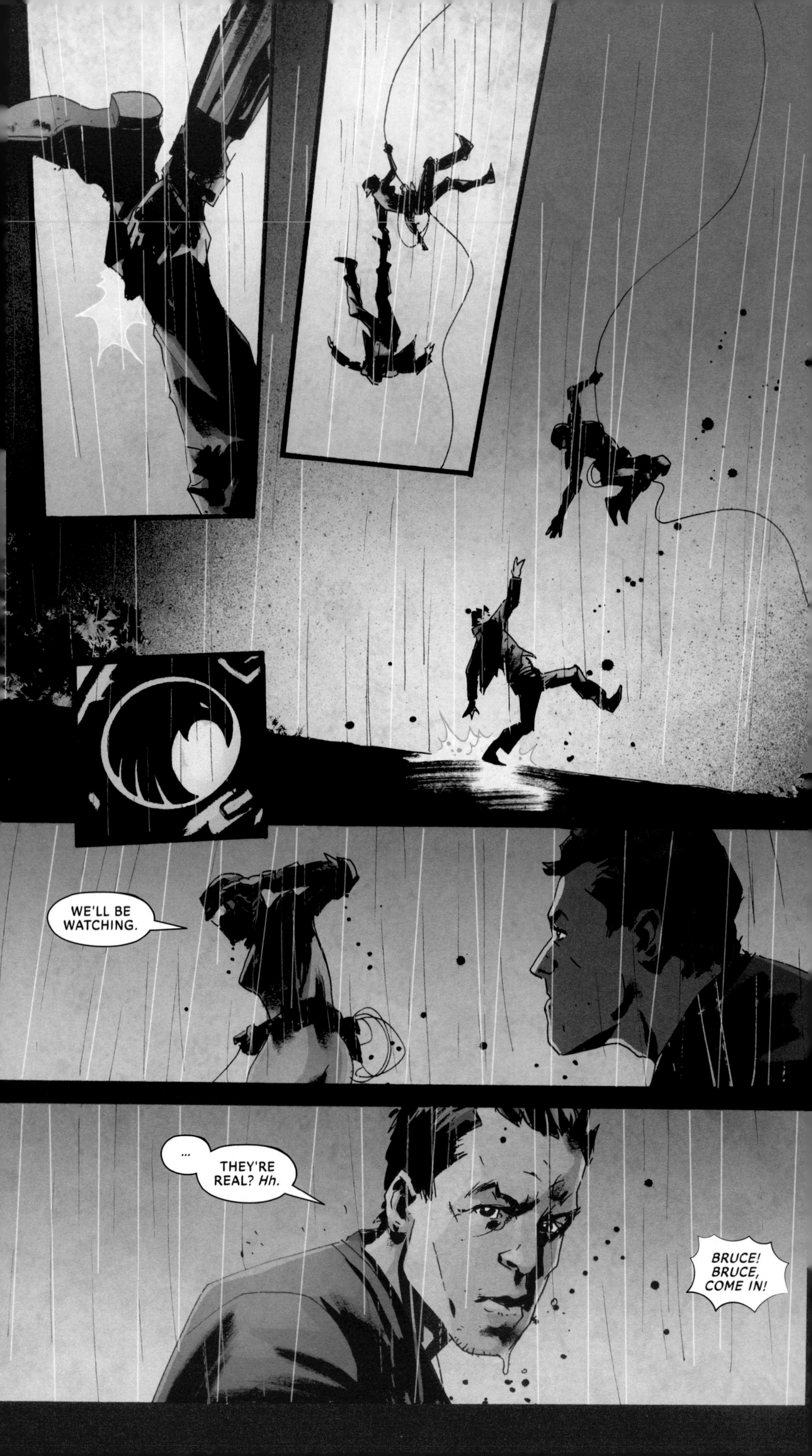

WE'LL BE WATCHING.
... THEY'RE REAL? *Hh.*
*BRUCE! BRUCE, COME IN!*

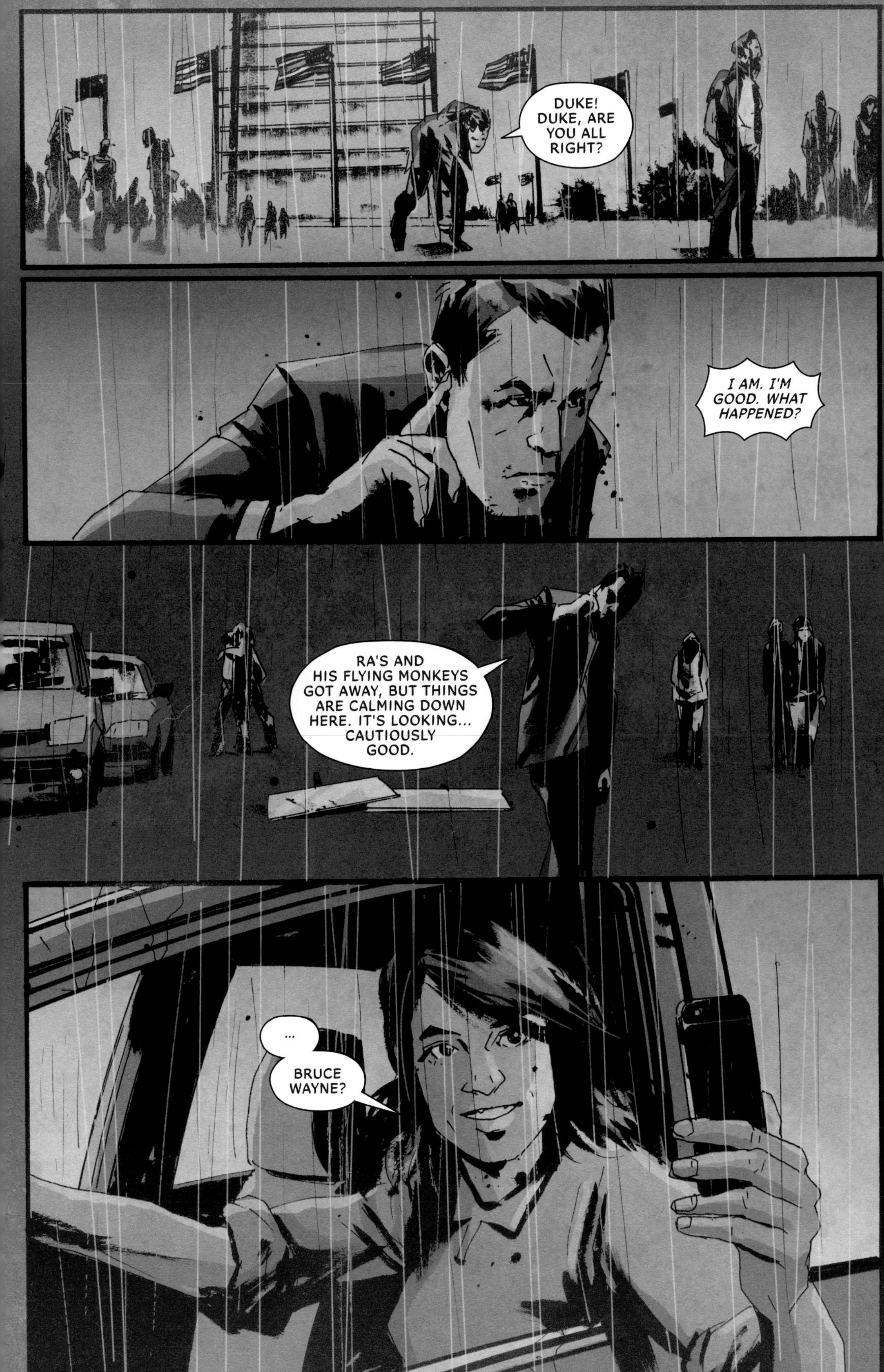
DUKE! DUKE, ARE YOU ALL RIGHT?
I AM. I'M GOOD. WHAT HAPPENED?
RA'S AND HIS FLYING MONKEYS GOT AWAY, BUT THINGS ARE CALMING DOWN HERE. IT'S LOOKING... CAUTIOUSLY GOOD.
...
BRUCE WAYNE?

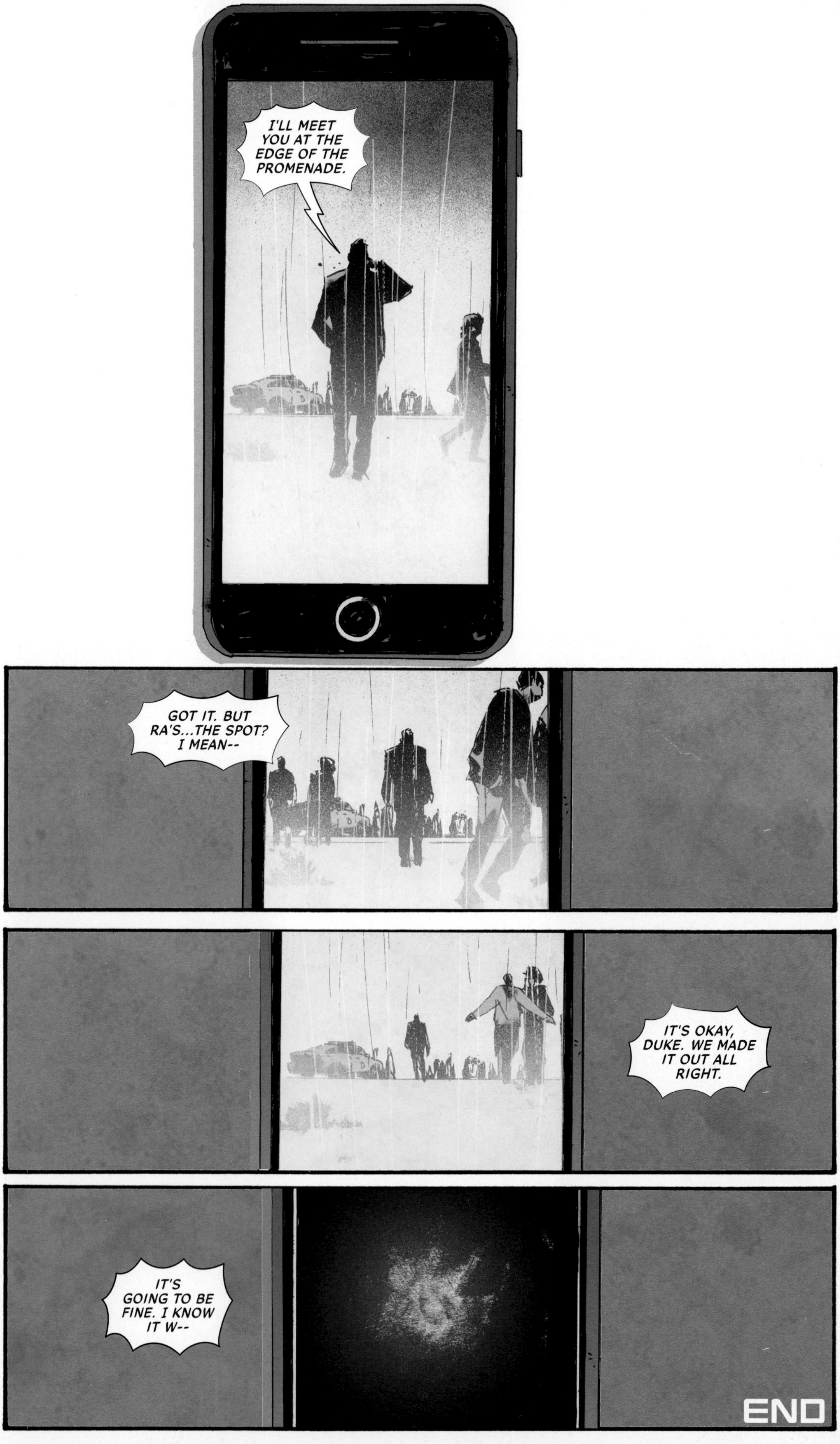
I'LL MEET YOU AT THE EDGE OF THE PROMENADE.
GOT IT. BUT RA'S...THE SPOT? I MEAN--
IT'S OKAY, DUKE. WE MADE IT OUT ALL RIGHT.
IT'S GOING TO BE FINE. I KNOW IT W--
END

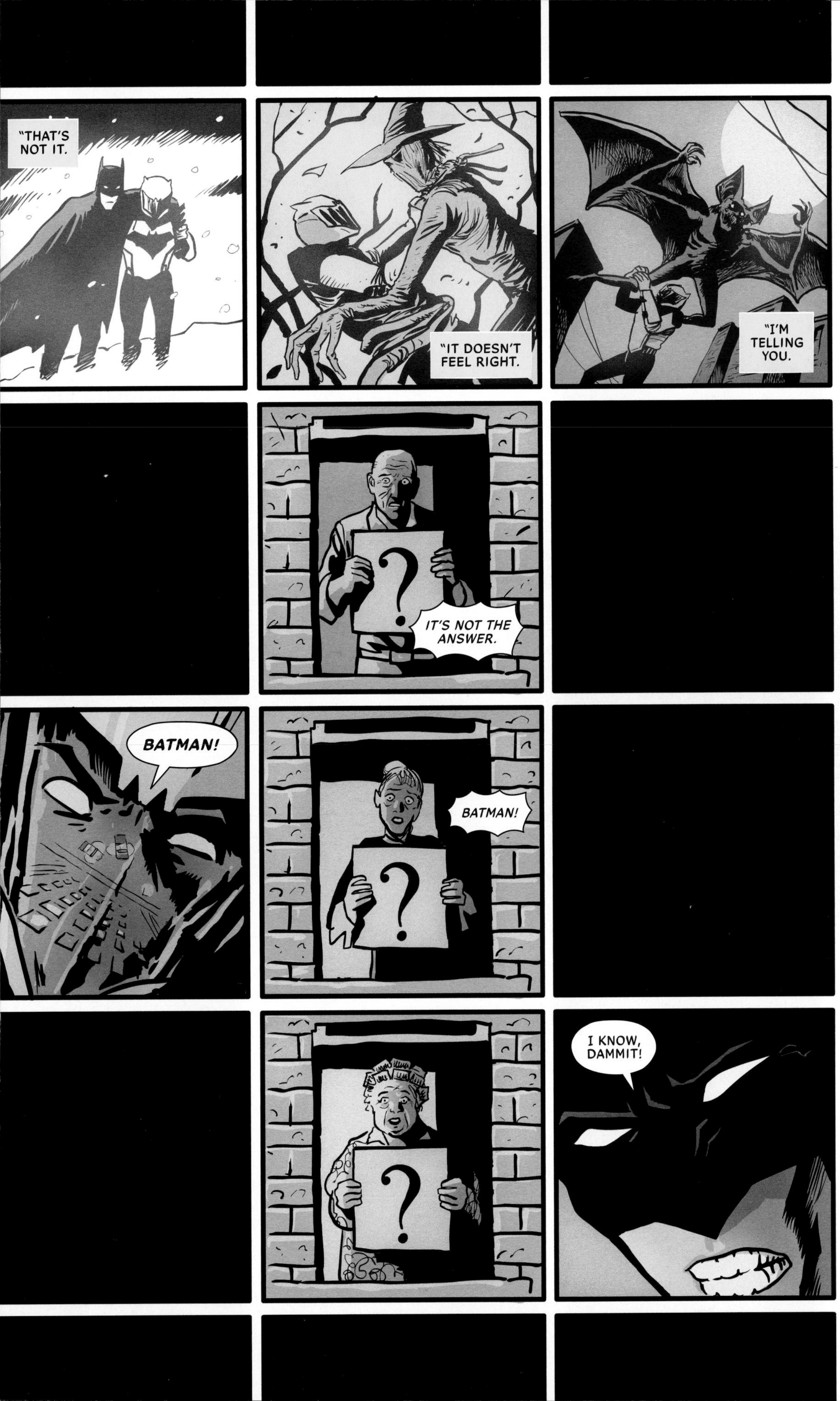
"THAT'S NOT IT.
"IT DOESN'T FEEL RIGHT.
"I'M TELLING YOU.
IT'S NOT THE ANSWER.
BATMAN!
BATMAN!
I KNOW, DAMMIT!

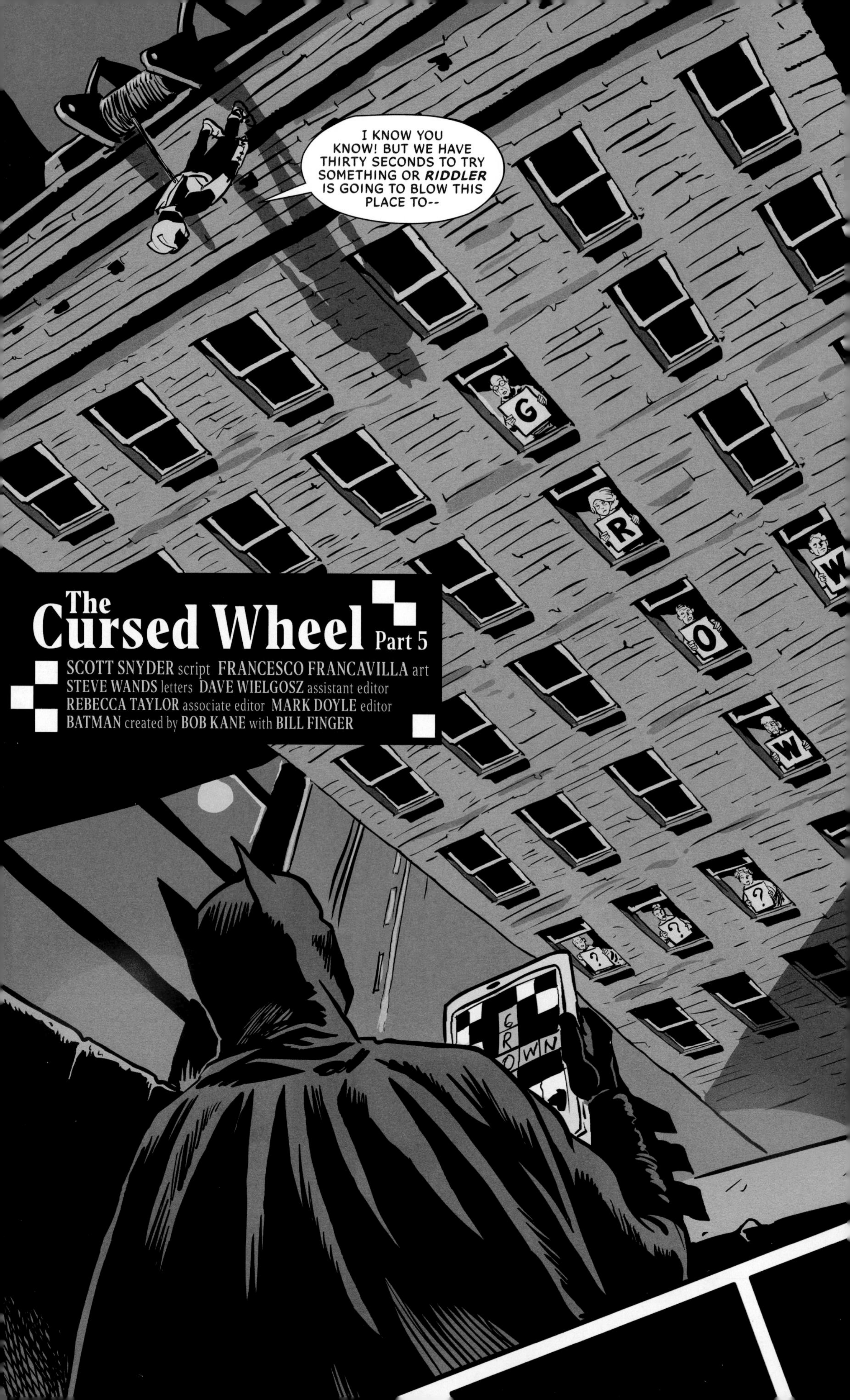
I KNOW YOU KNOW! BUT WE HAVE THIRTY SECONDS TO TRY SOMETHING OR *RIDDLER* IS GOING TO BLOW THIS PLACE TO--
The Cursed Wheel Part 5
SCOTT SNYDER script FRANCESCO FRANCAVILLA art
STEVE WANDS letters DAVE WIELGOSZ assistant editor
REBECCA TAYLOR associate editor MARK DOYLE editor
BATMAN created by BOB KANE with BILL FINGER

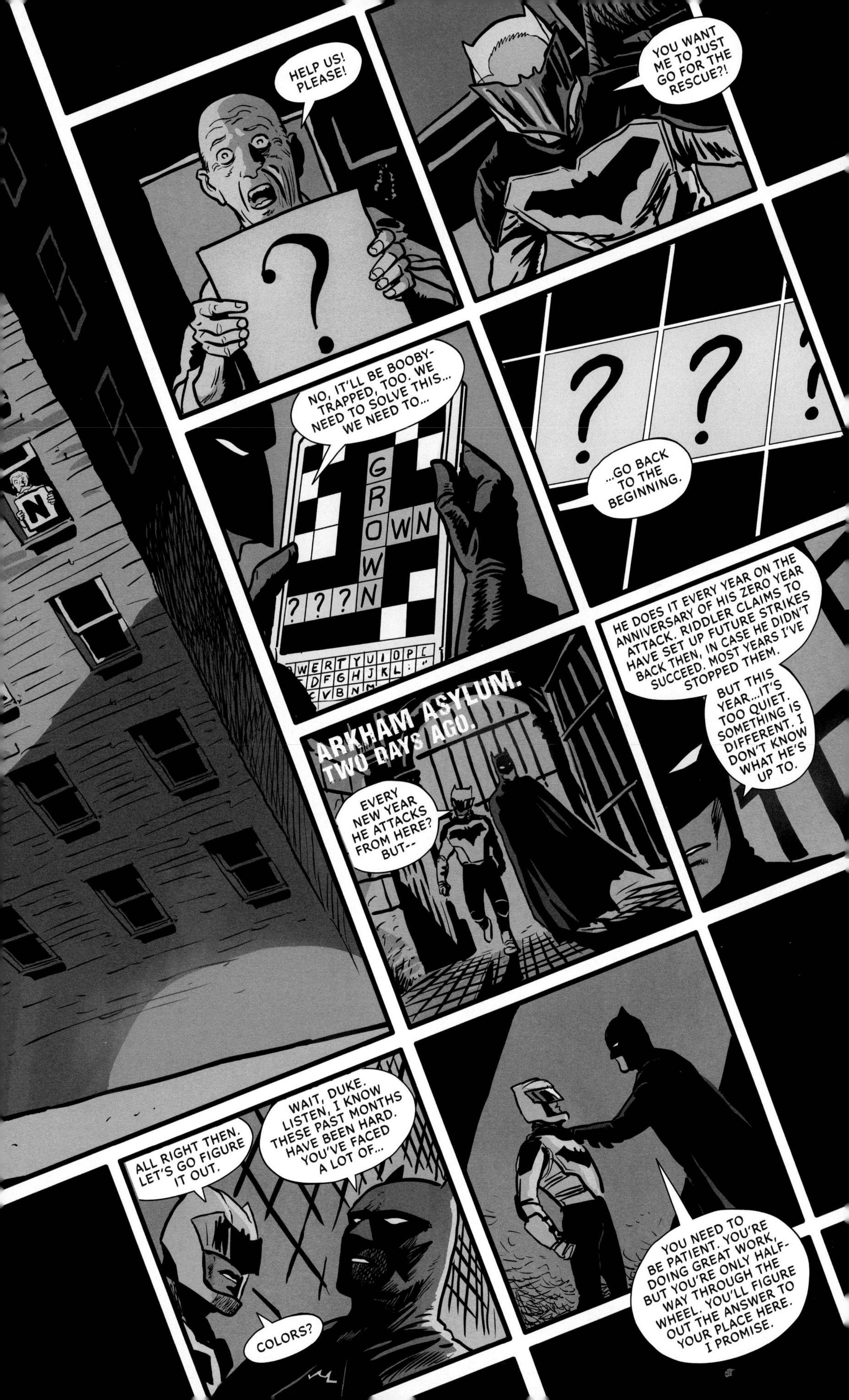
HELP US! PLEASE!
YOU WANT ME TO JUST GO FOR THE RESCUE?!
NO, IT'LL BE BOOBY-TRAPPED, TOO. WE NEED TO SOLVE THIS... WE NEED TO...
...GO BACK TO THE BEGINNING.
ARKHAM ASYLUM. TWO DAYS AGO.
EVERY NEW YEAR HE ATTACKS FROM HERE? BUT--
HE DOES IT EVERY YEAR ON THE ANNIVERSARY OF HIS ZERO YEAR ATTACK. RIDDLER CLAIMS TO HAVE SET UP FUTURE STRIKES BACK THEN, IN CASE HE DIDN'T SUCCEED. MOST YEARS I'VE STOPPED THEM.
BUT THIS YEAR...IT'S TOO QUIET. SOMETHING IS DIFFERENT. I DON'T KNOW WHAT HE'S UP TO.
YOU NEED TO BE PATIENT. YOU'RE DOING GREAT WORK, BUT YOU'RE ONLY HALF-WAY THROUGH THE WHEEL. YOU'LL FIGURE OUT THE ANSWER TO YOUR PLACE HERE. I PROMISE.
WAIT, DUKE. LISTEN, I KNOW THESE PAST MONTHS HAVE BEEN HARD. YOU'VE FACED A LOT OF...
ALL RIGHT THEN. LET'S GO FIGURE IT OUT.
COLORS?

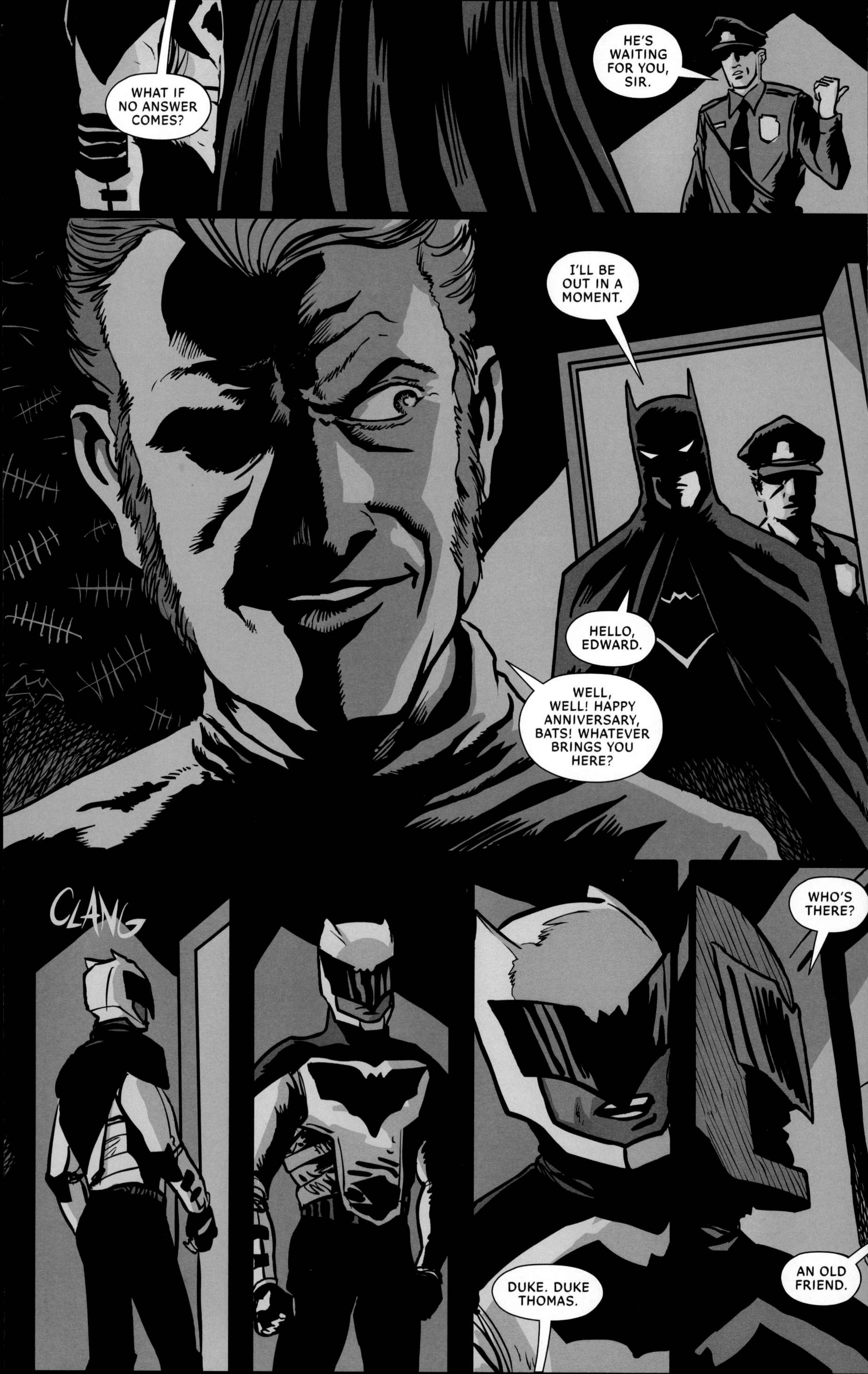
WHAT IF NO ANSWER COMES?
HE'S WAITING FOR YOU, SIR.
I'LL BE OUT IN A MOMENT.
HELLO, EDWARD.
WELL, WELL! HAPPY ANNIVERSARY, BATS! WHATEVER BRINGS YOU HERE?
CLANG
WHO'S THERE?
DUKE. DUKE THOMAS.
AN OLD FRIEND.

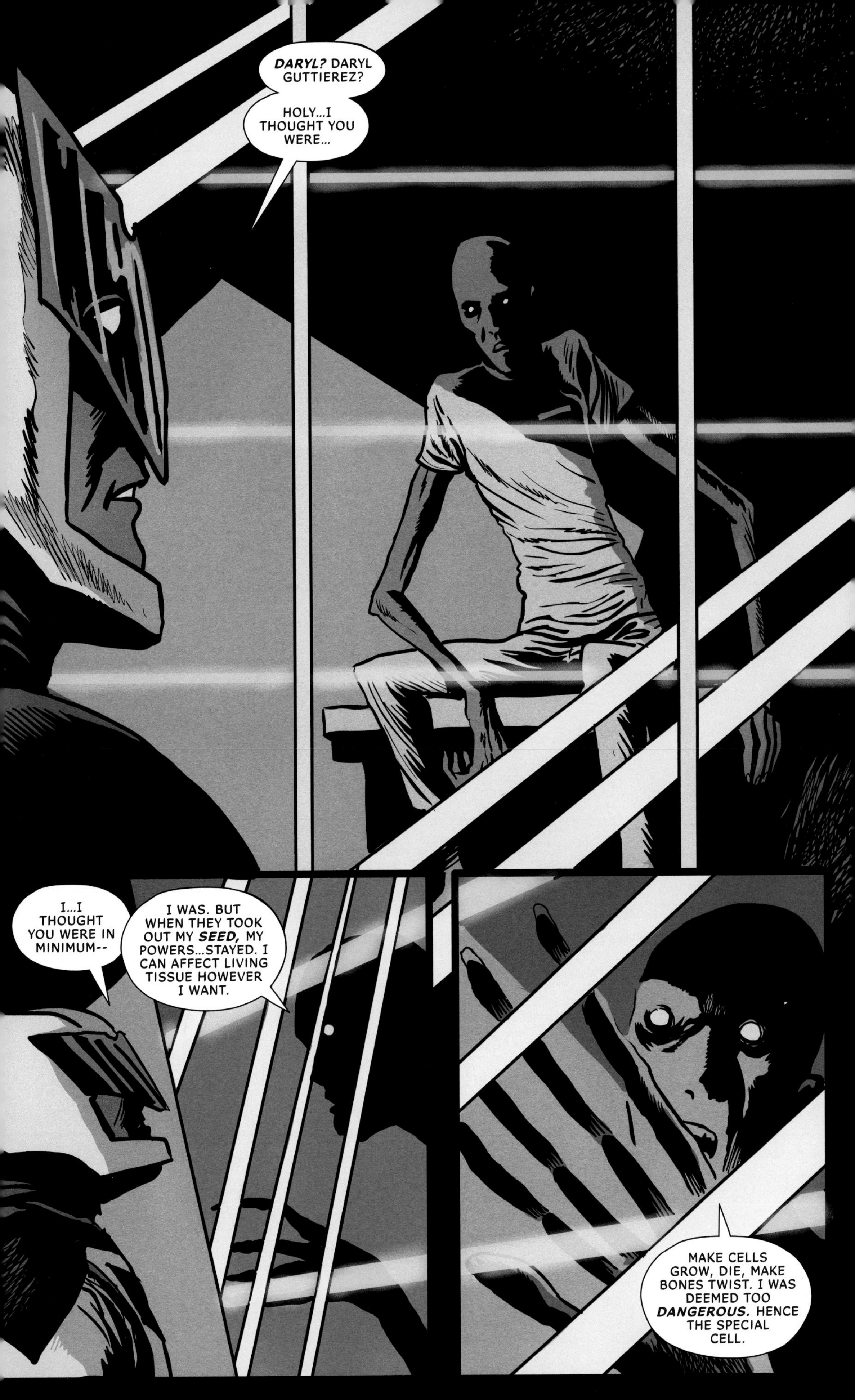
DARYL? DARYL GUTTIEREZ?
HOLY...I THOUGHT YOU WERE...
I...I THOUGHT YOU WERE IN MINIMUM--
I WAS. BUT WHEN THEY TOOK OUT MY SEED, MY POWERS...STAYED. I CAN AFFECT LIVING TISSUE HOWEVER I WANT.
MAKE CELLS GROW, DIE, MAKE BONES TWIST. I WAS DEEMED TOO DANGEROUS. HENCE THE SPECIAL CELL.

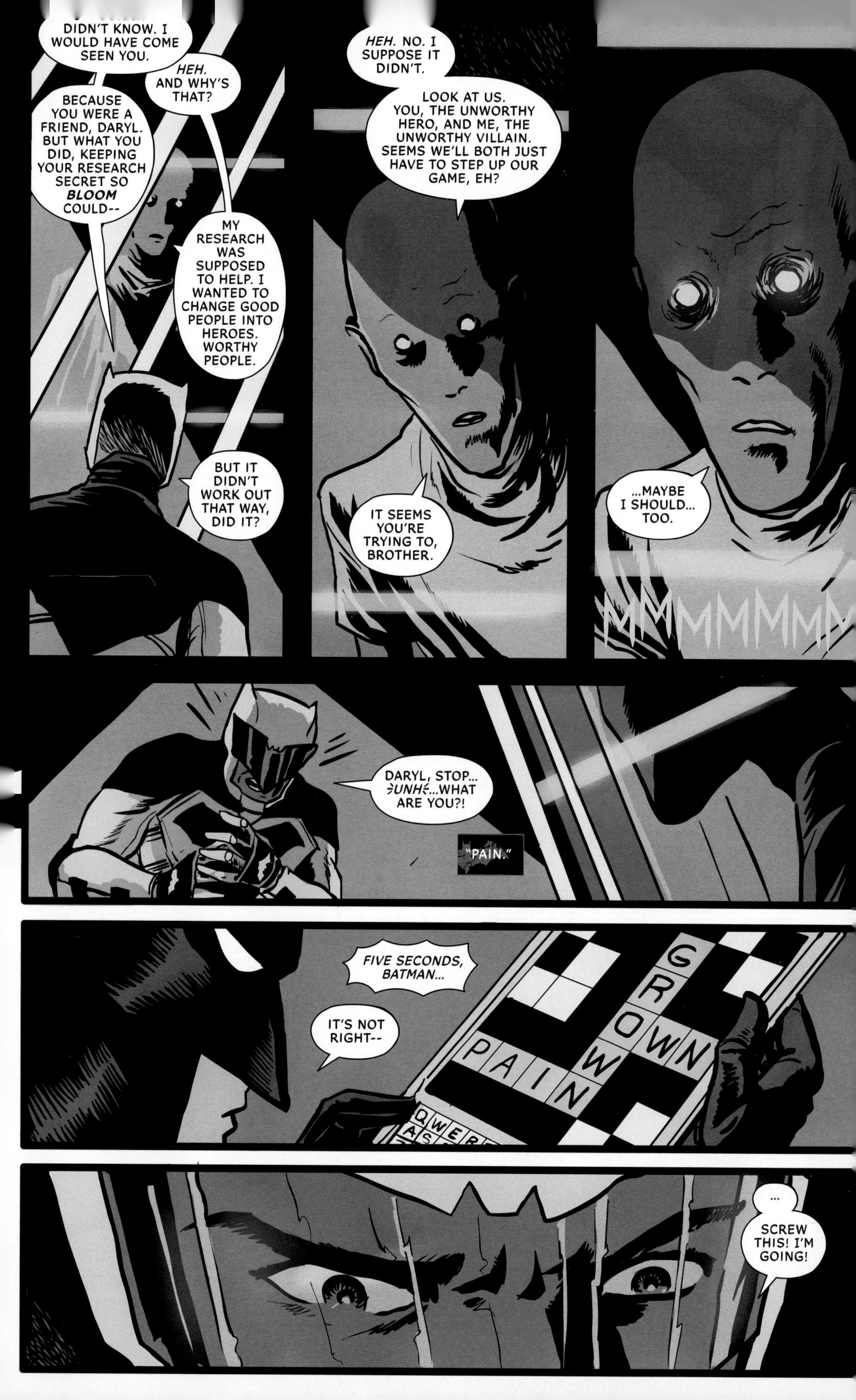
DIDN'T KNOW. I WOULD HAVE COME SEEN YOU.
HEH. AND WHY'S THAT?
BECAUSE YOU WERE A FRIEND, DARYL. BUT WHAT YOU DID, KEEPING YOUR RESEARCH SECRET SO BLOOM COULD--
MY RESEARCH WAS SUPPOSED TO HELP. I WANTED TO CHANGE GOOD PEOPLE INTO HEROES. WORTHY PEOPLE.
BUT IT DIDN'T WORK OUT THAT WAY, DID IT?
HEH. NO. I SUPPOSE IT DIDN'T.
LOOK AT US. YOU, THE UNWORTHY HERO, AND ME, THE UNWORTHY VILLAIN. SEEMS WE'LL BOTH JUST HAVE TO STEP UP OUR GAME, EH?
IT SEEMS YOU'RE TRYING TO, BROTHER.
...MAYBE I SHOULD... TOO.
MMMMMMM
DARYL, STOP... UNH...WHAT ARE YOU?!
"PAIN."
FIVE SECONDS, BATMAN...
IT'S NOT RIGHT--
GROWN
PAIN
...
SCREW THIS! I'M GOING!

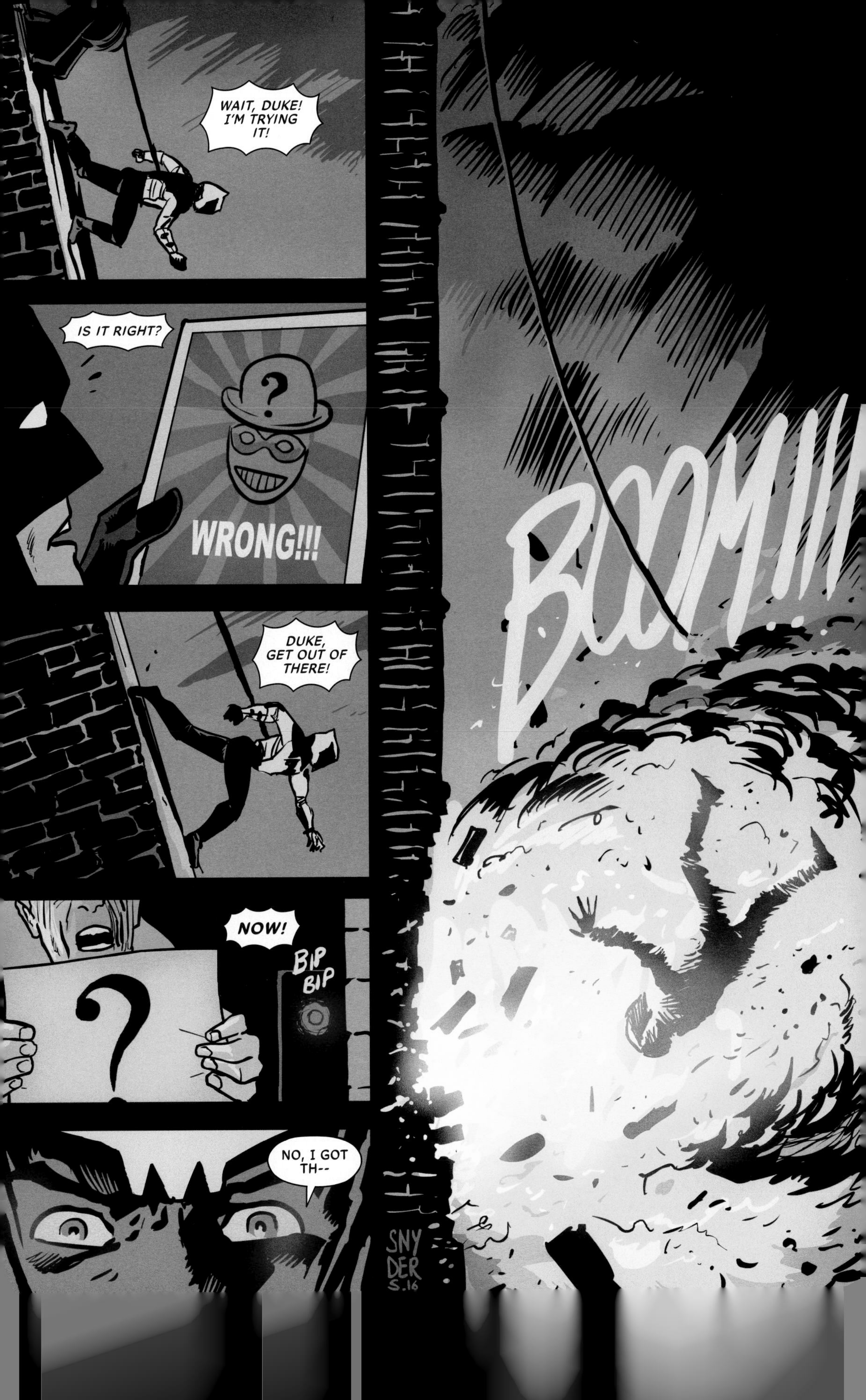
WAIT, DUKE! I'M TRYING IT!
IS IT RIGHT?
WRONG!!!
DUKE, GET OUT OF THERE!
NOW!
BIP BIP
NO, I GOT TH--
BOOM!!!
SNYDER S.16

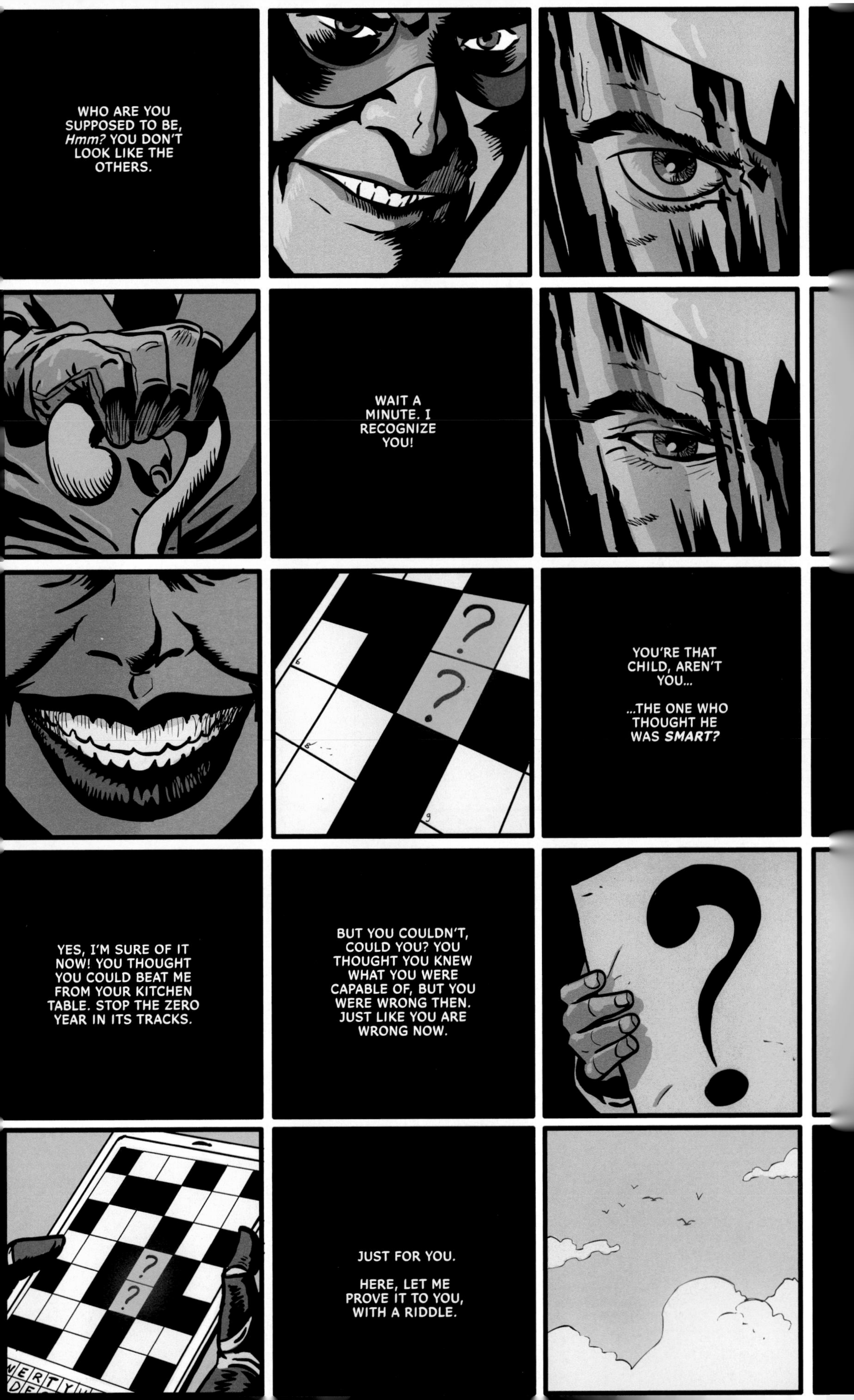
WHO ARE YOU SUPPOSED TO BE, *Hmm?* YOU DON'T LOOK LIKE THE OTHERS.
WAIT A MINUTE. I RECOGNIZE YOU!
YOU'RE THAT CHILD, AREN'T YOU...
...THE ONE WHO THOUGHT HE WAS *SMART?*
YES, I'M SURE OF IT NOW! YOU THOUGHT YOU COULD BEAT ME FROM YOUR KITCHEN TABLE. STOP THE ZERO YEAR IN ITS TRACKS.
BUT YOU COULDN'T, COULD YOU? YOU THOUGHT YOU KNEW WHAT YOU WERE CAPABLE OF, BUT YOU WERE WRONG THEN. JUST LIKE YOU ARE WRONG NOW.
JUST FOR YOU.
HERE, LET ME PROVE IT TO YOU, WITH A RIDDLE.

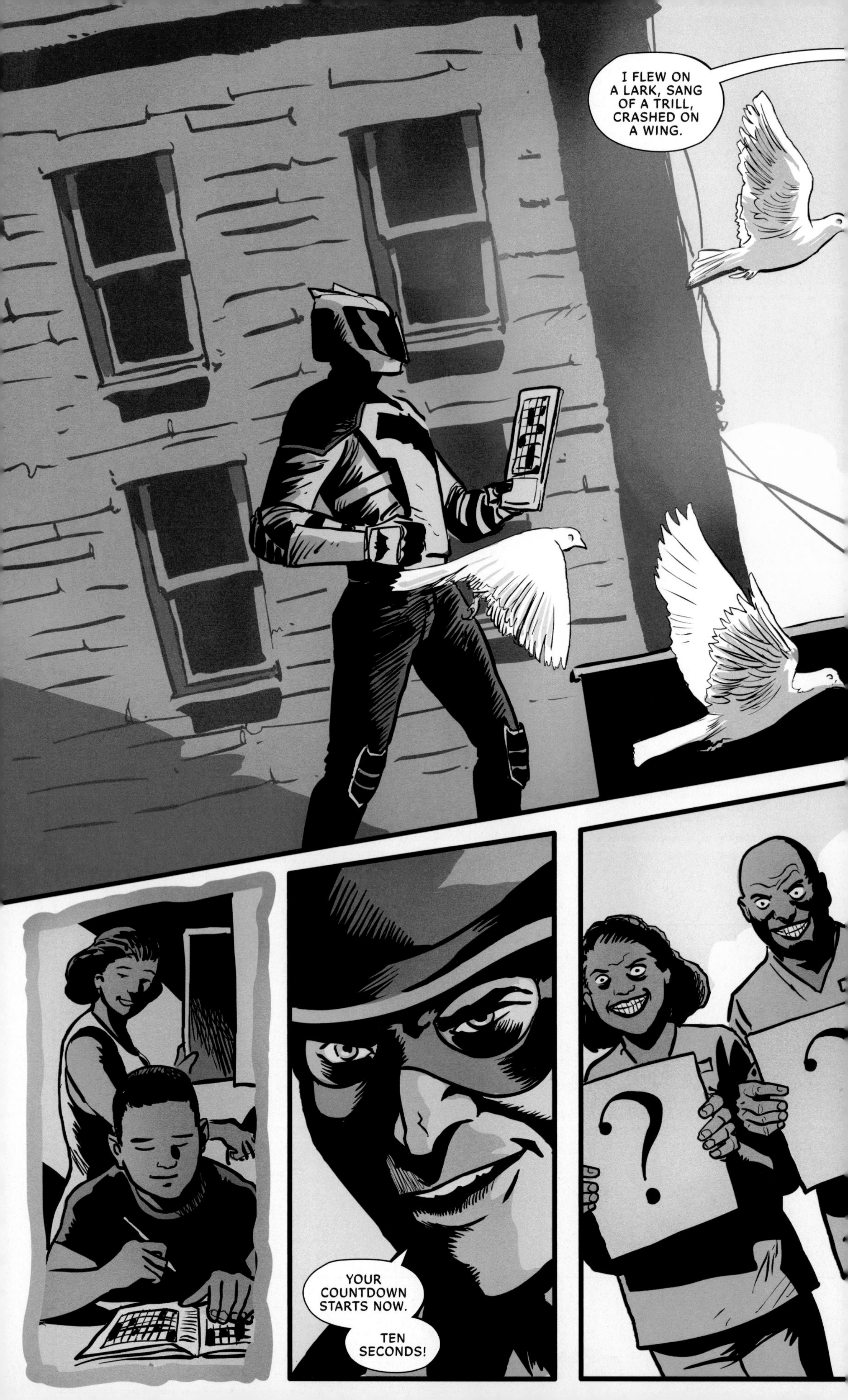

I FLEW ON A LARK, SANG OF A TRILL, CRASHED ON A WING.
YOUR COUNTDOWN STARTS NOW.
TEN SECONDS!

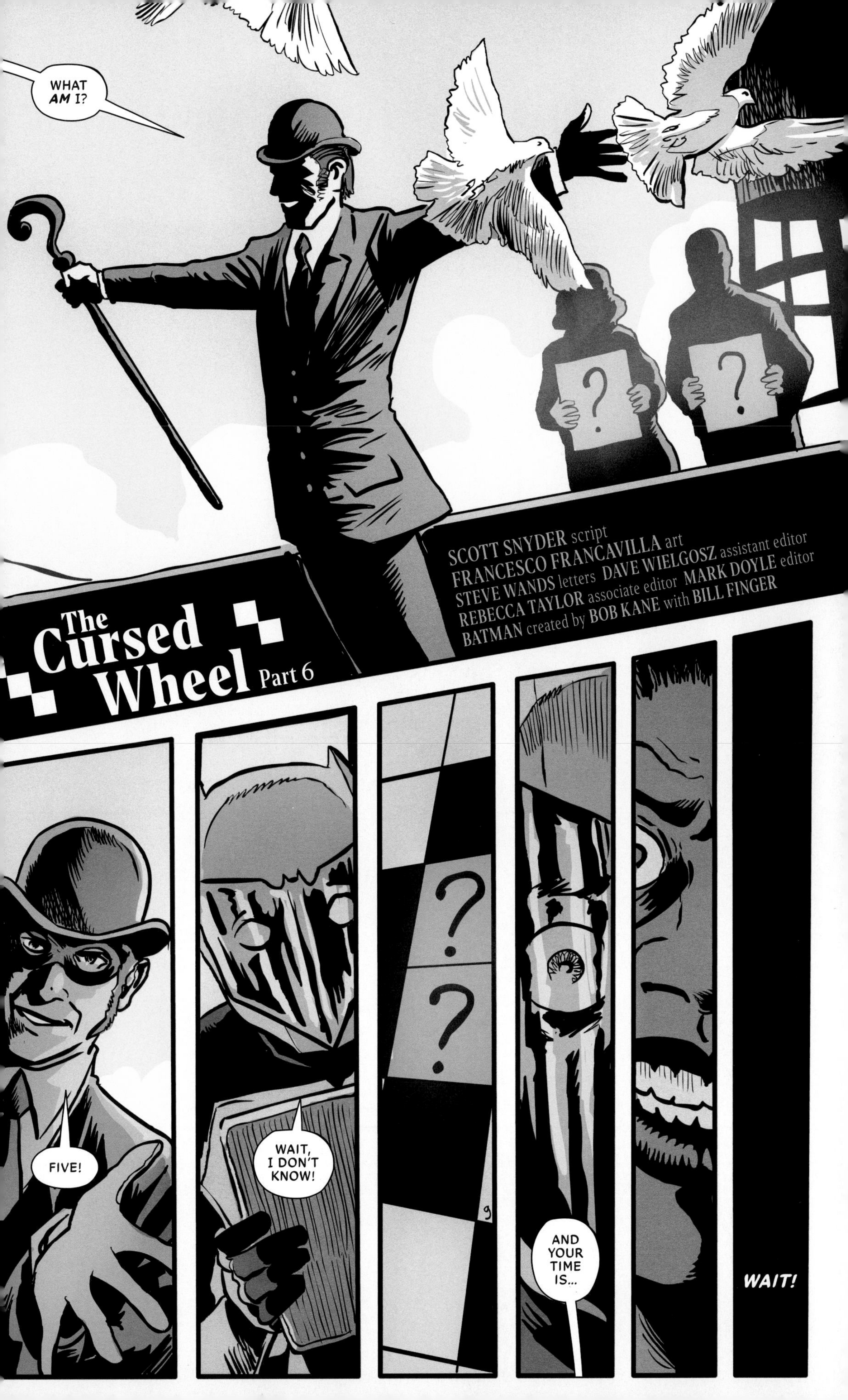
WHAT AM I?
The Cursed Wheel Part 6
SCOTT SNYDER script
FRANCESCO FRANCAVILLA art
STEVE WANDS letters DAVE WIELGOSZ assistant editor
REBECCA TAYLOR associate editor MARK DOYLE editor
BATMAN created by BOB KANE with BILL FINGER
FIVE!
WAIT, I DON'T KNOW!
AND YOUR TIME IS...
WAIT!

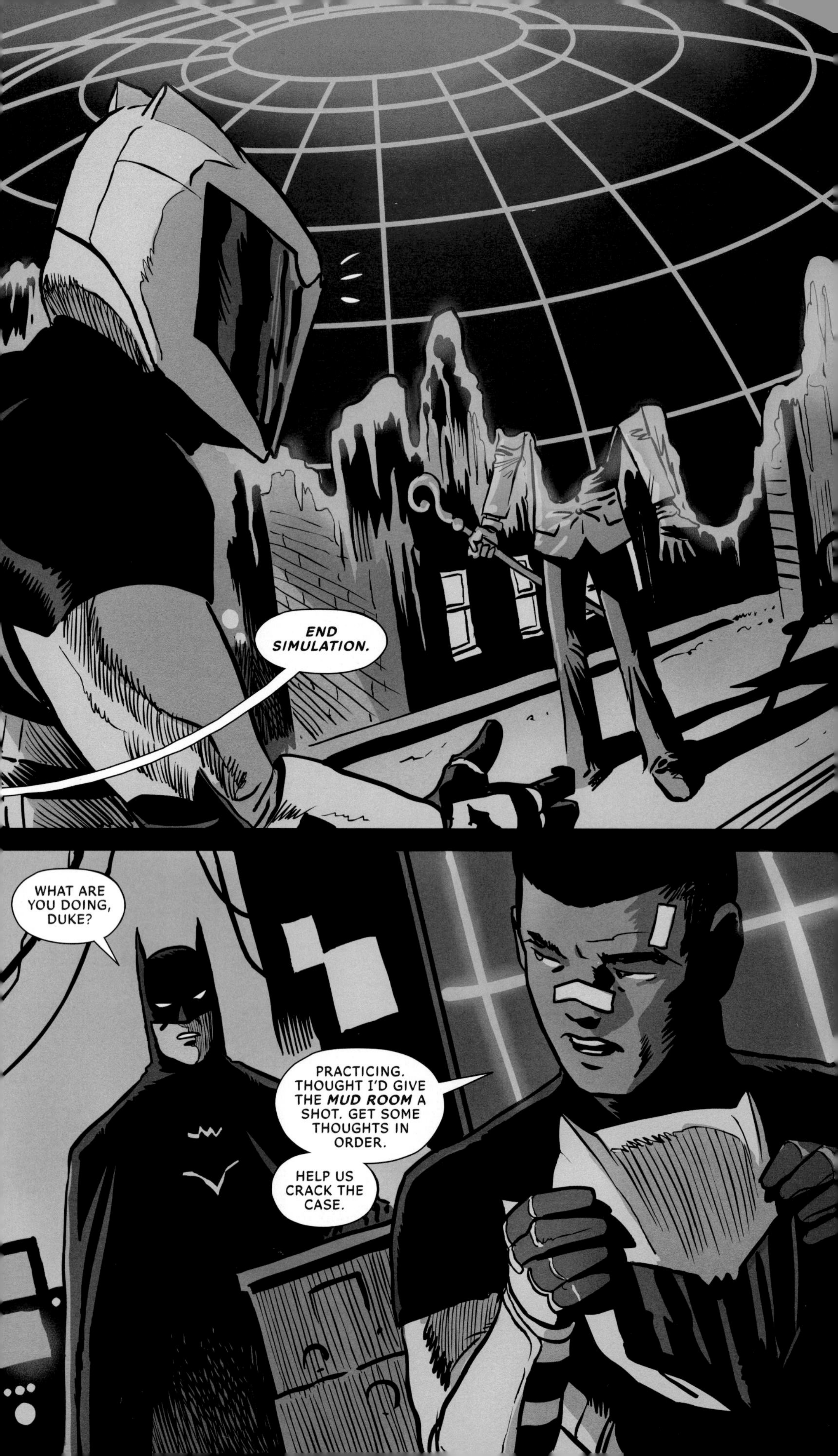
END SIMULATION.
WHAT ARE YOU DOING, DUKE?
PRACTICING. THOUGHT I'D GIVE THE MUD ROOM A SHOT. GET SOME THOUGHTS IN ORDER.
HELP US CRACK THE CASE.

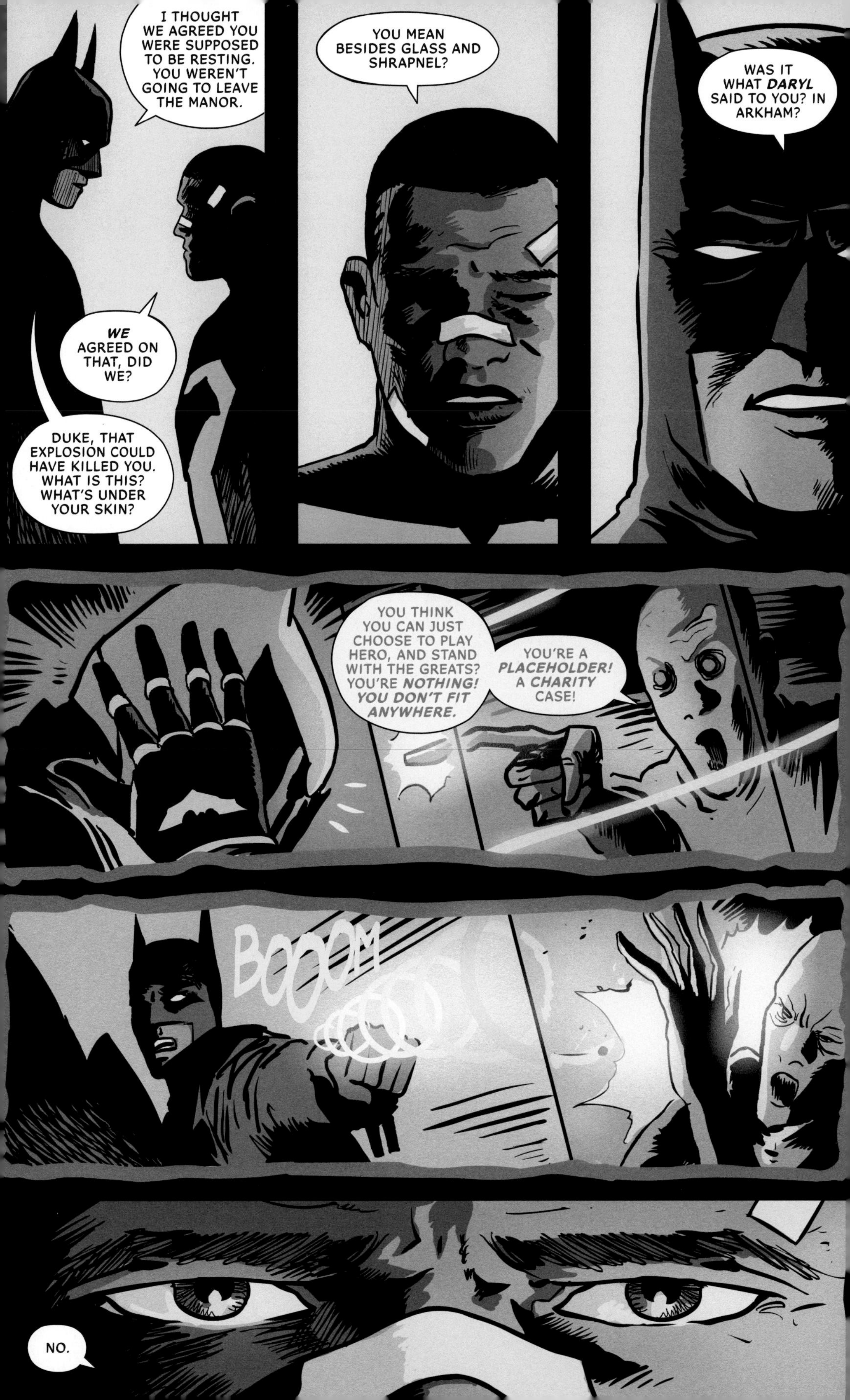
I THOUGHT WE AGREED YOU WERE SUPPOSED TO BE RESTING. YOU WEREN'T GOING TO LEAVE THE MANOR.
*WE* AGREED ON THAT, DID WE?
DUKE, THAT EXPLOSION COULD HAVE KILLED YOU. WHAT IS THIS? WHAT'S UNDER YOUR SKIN?
YOU MEAN BESIDES GLASS AND SHRAPNEL?
WAS IT WHAT *DARYL* SAID TO YOU? IN ARKHAM?
YOU THINK YOU CAN JUST CHOOSE TO PLAY HERO, AND STAND WITH THE GREATS? YOU'RE *NOTHING! YOU DON'T FIT ANYWHERE.*
YOU'RE A *PLACEHOLDER!* A *CHARITY* CASE!
BOOOM
NO.

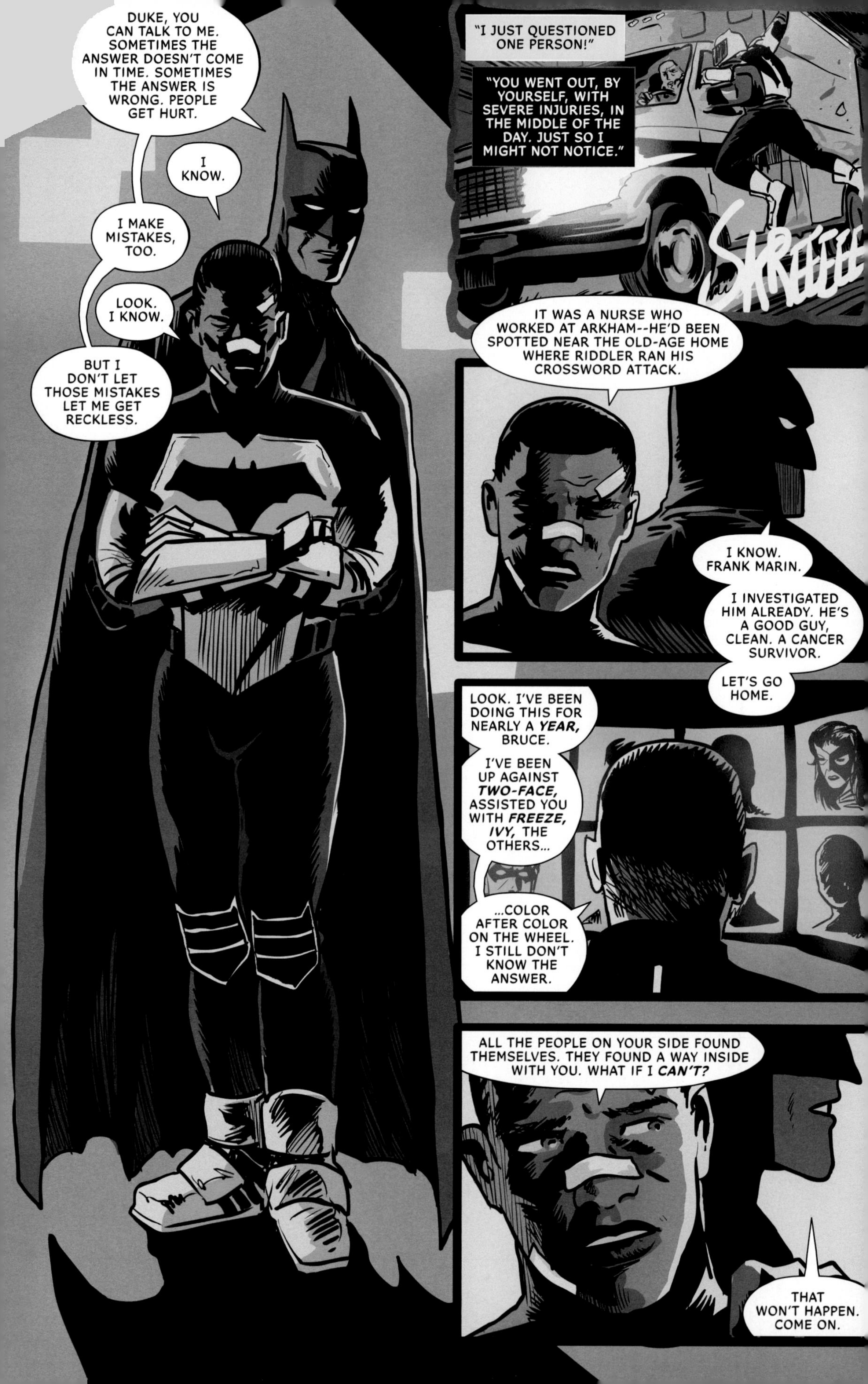
DUKE, YOU CAN TALK TO ME. SOMETIMES THE ANSWER DOESN'T COME IN TIME. SOMETIMES THE ANSWER IS WRONG. PEOPLE GET HURT.
I KNOW.
I MAKE MISTAKES, TOO.
LOOK. I KNOW.
BUT I DON'T LET THOSE MISTAKES LET ME GET RECKLESS.
"I JUST QUESTIONED ONE PERSON!"
"YOU WENT OUT, BY YOURSELF, WITH SEVERE INJURIES, IN THE MIDDLE OF THE DAY. JUST SO I MIGHT NOT NOTICE."
SKREEEEE
IT WAS A NURSE WHO WORKED AT ARKHAM--HE'D BEEN SPOTTED NEAR THE OLD-AGE HOME WHERE RIDDLER RAN HIS CROSSWORD ATTACK.
I KNOW. FRANK MARIN.
I INVESTIGATED HIM ALREADY. HE'S A GOOD GUY, CLEAN. A CANCER SURVIVOR.
LET'S GO HOME.
LOOK. I'VE BEEN DOING THIS FOR NEARLY A *YEAR,* BRUCE.
I'VE BEEN UP AGAINST *TWO-FACE,* ASSISTED YOU WITH *FREEZE, IVY,* THE OTHERS...
...COLOR AFTER COLOR ON THE WHEEL. I STILL DON'T KNOW THE ANSWER.
ALL THE PEOPLE ON YOUR SIDE FOUND THEMSELVES. THEY FOUND A WAY INSIDE WITH YOU. WHAT IF I *CAN'T?*
THAT WON'T HAPPEN. COME ON.

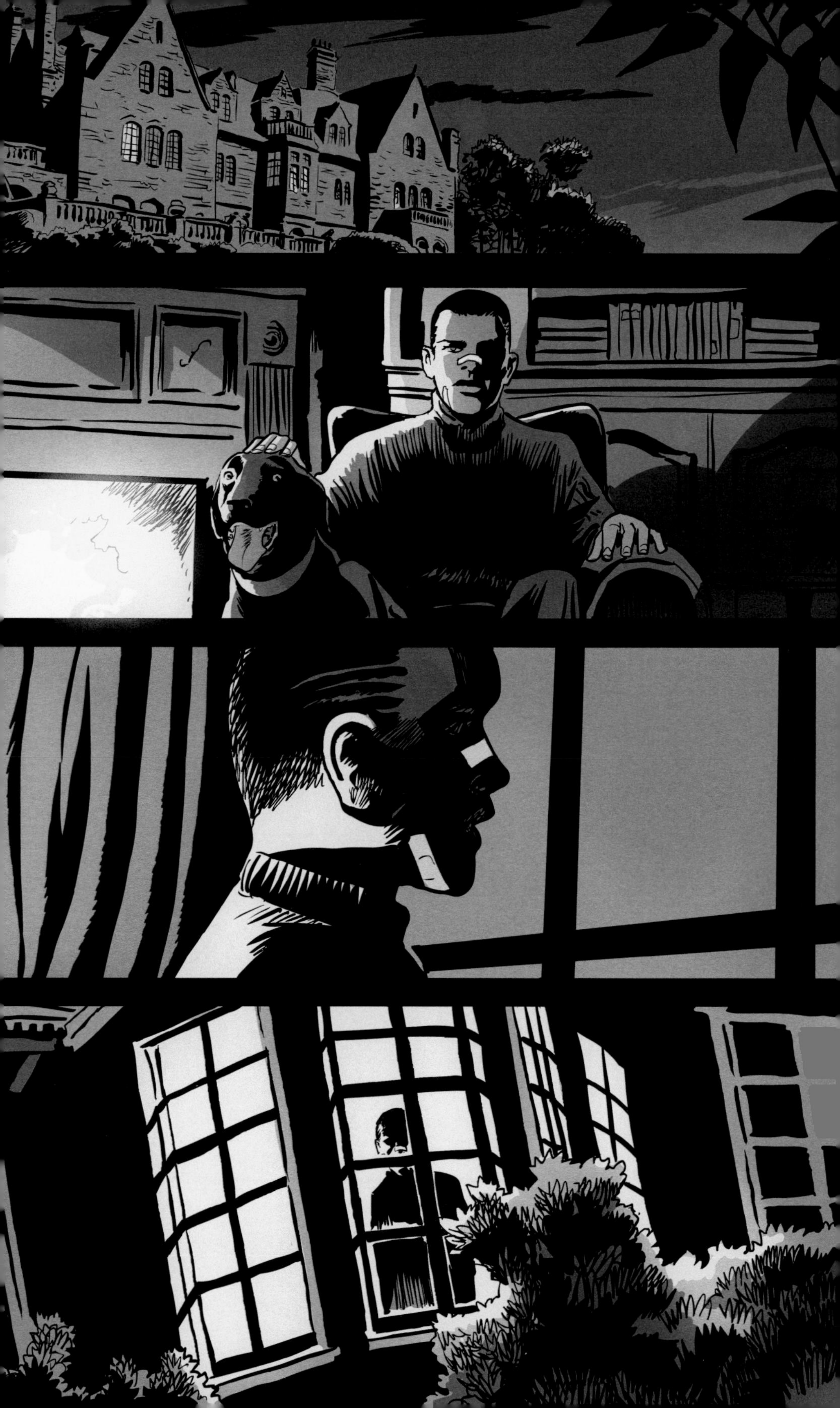

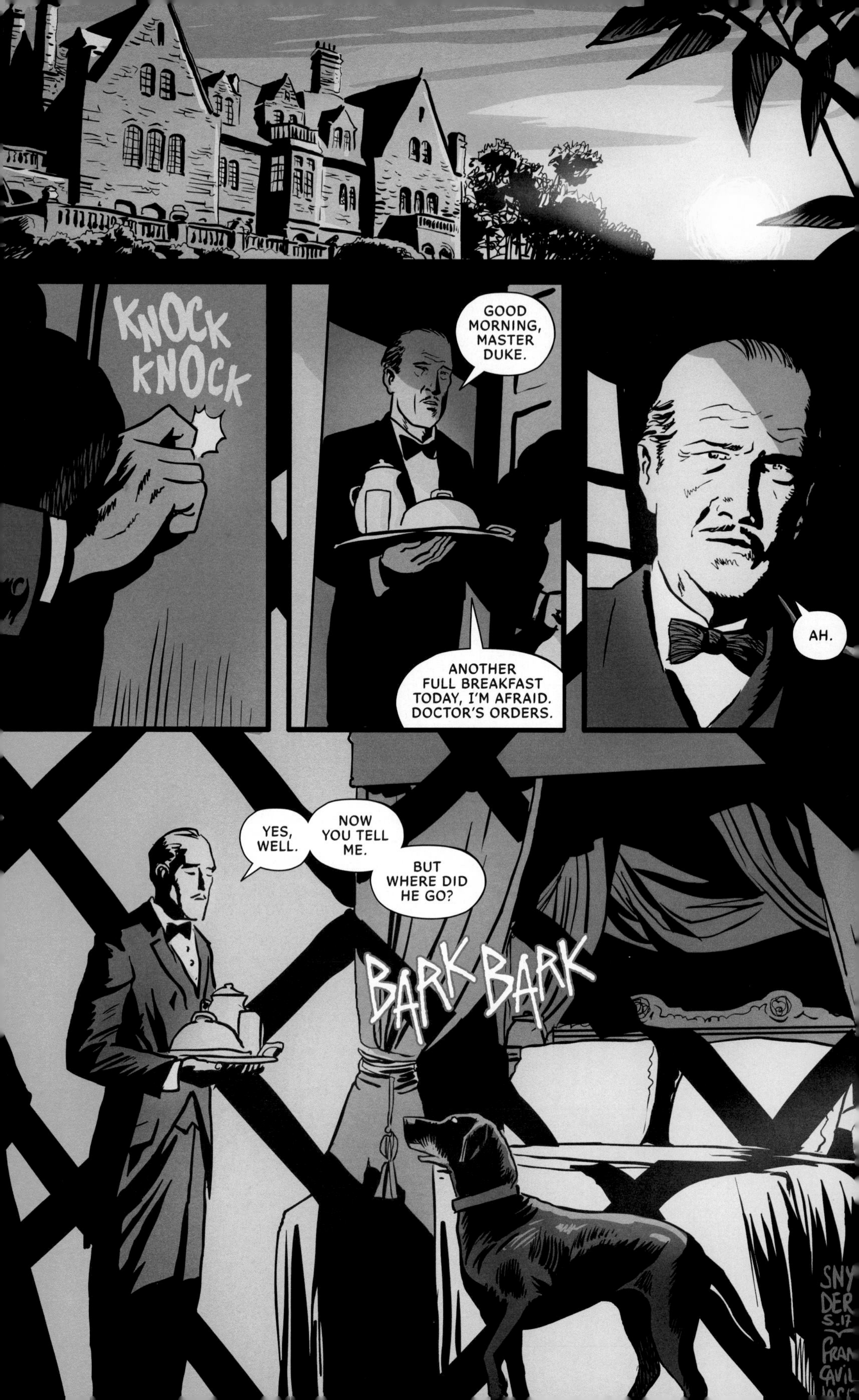
KNOCK KNOCK
GOOD MORNING, MASTER DUKE.
ANOTHER FULL BREAKFAST TODAY, I'M AFRAID. DOCTOR'S ORDERS.
AH.
YES, WELL.
NOW YOU TELL ME.
BUT WHERE DID HE GO?
BARK BARK

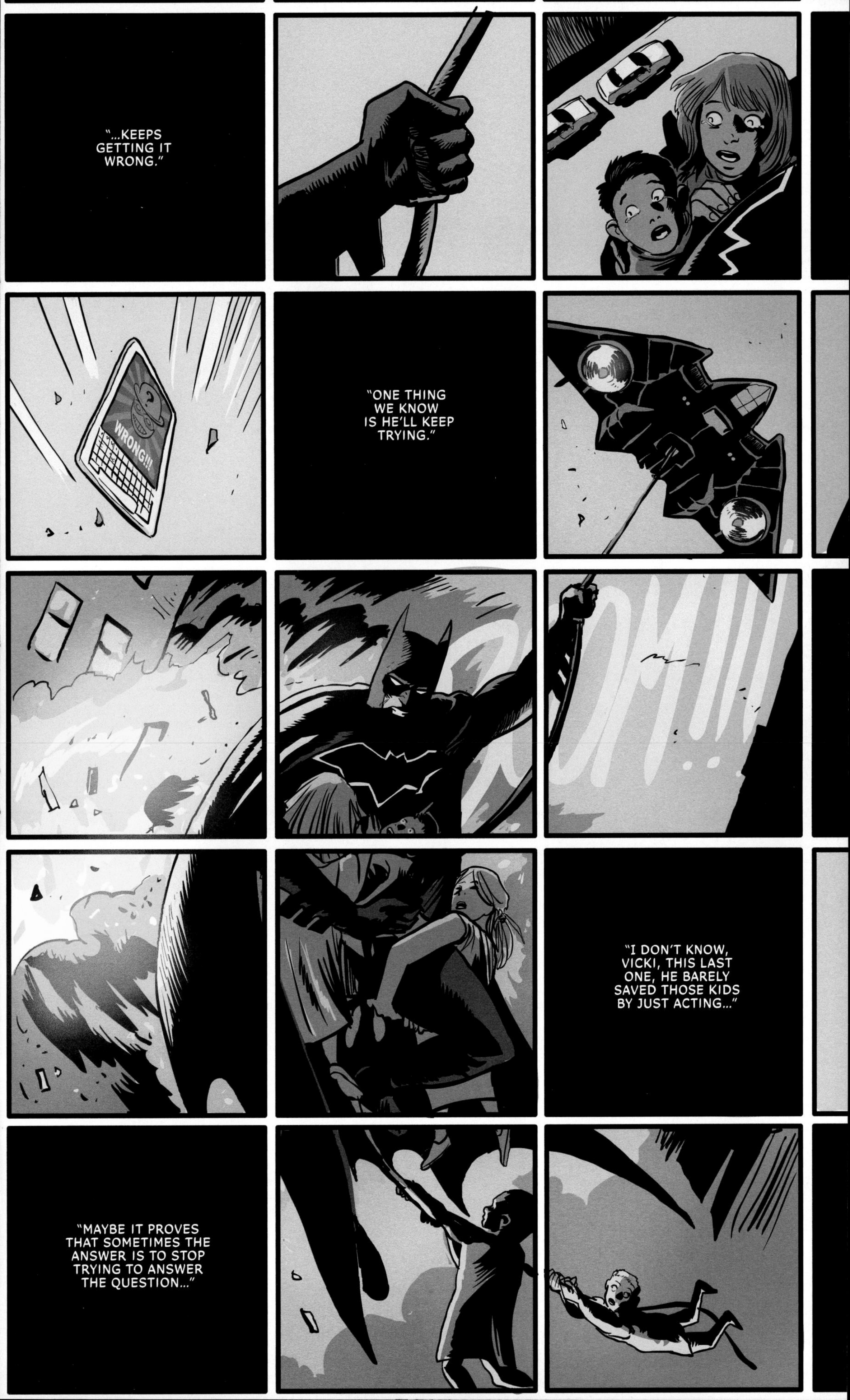
"...KEEPS GETTING IT WRONG."
WRONG!!!
"ONE THING WE KNOW IS HE'LL KEEP TRYING."
"I DON'T KNOW, VICKI, THIS LAST ONE, HE BARELY SAVED THOSE KIDS BY JUST ACTING..."
"MAYBE IT PROVES THAT SOMETIMES THE ANSWER IS TO STOP TRYING TO ANSWER THE QUESTION..."

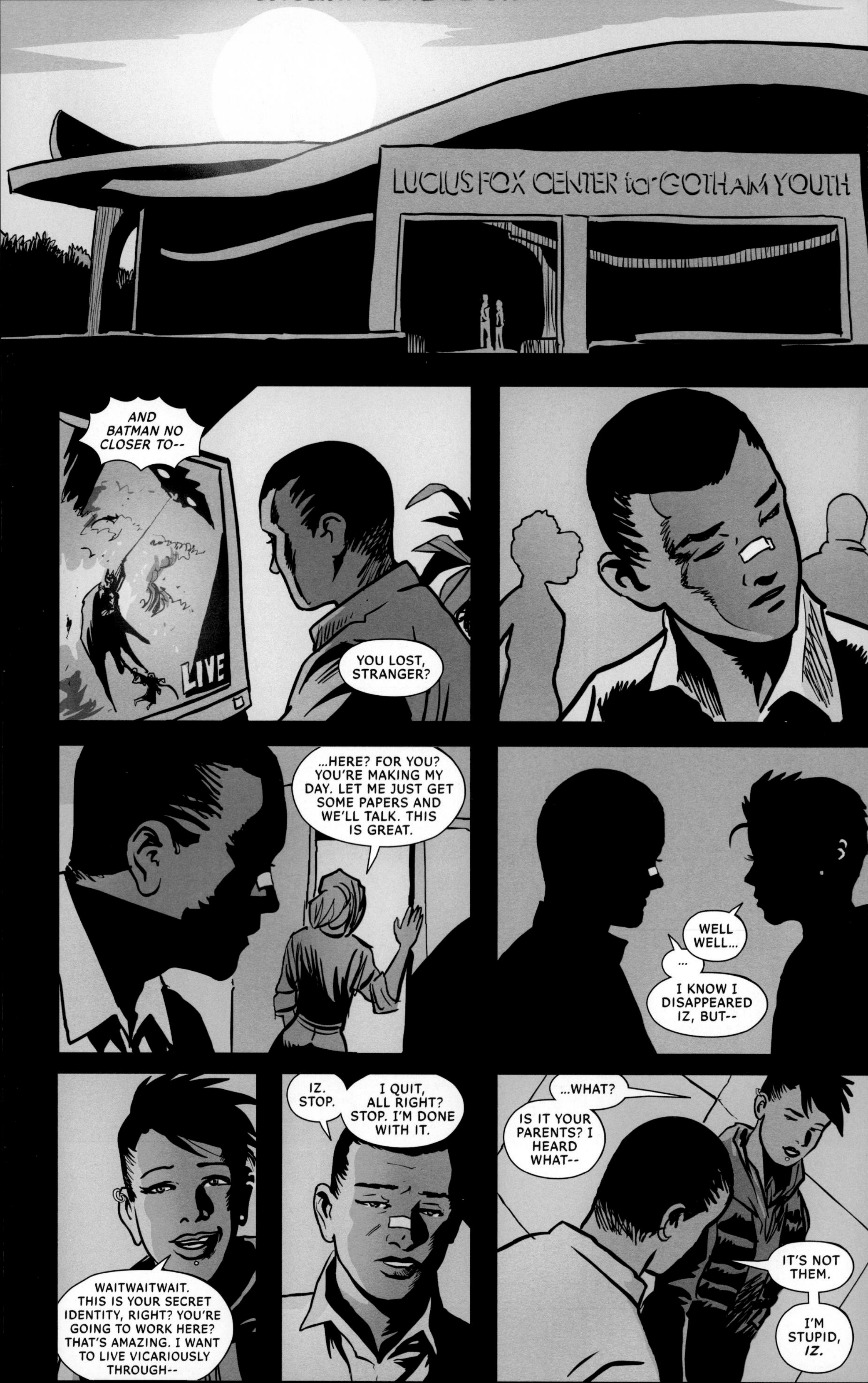
LUCIUS FOX CENTER for GOTHAM YOUTH
AND BATMAN NO CLOSER TO--
LIVE
YOU LOST, STRANGER?
...HERE? FOR YOU? YOU'RE MAKING MY DAY. LET ME JUST GET SOME PAPERS AND WE'LL TALK. THIS IS GREAT.
WELL WELL...
...
I KNOW I DISAPPEARED IZ, BUT--
WAITWAITWAIT. THIS IS YOUR SECRET IDENTITY, RIGHT? YOU'RE GOING TO WORK HERE? THAT'S AMAZING. I WANT TO LIVE VICARIOUSLY THROUGH--
IZ. STOP.
I QUIT, ALL RIGHT? STOP. I'M DONE WITH IT.
...WHAT?
IS IT YOUR PARENTS? I HEARD WHAT--
IT'S NOT THEM.
I'M STUPID, *IZ.*

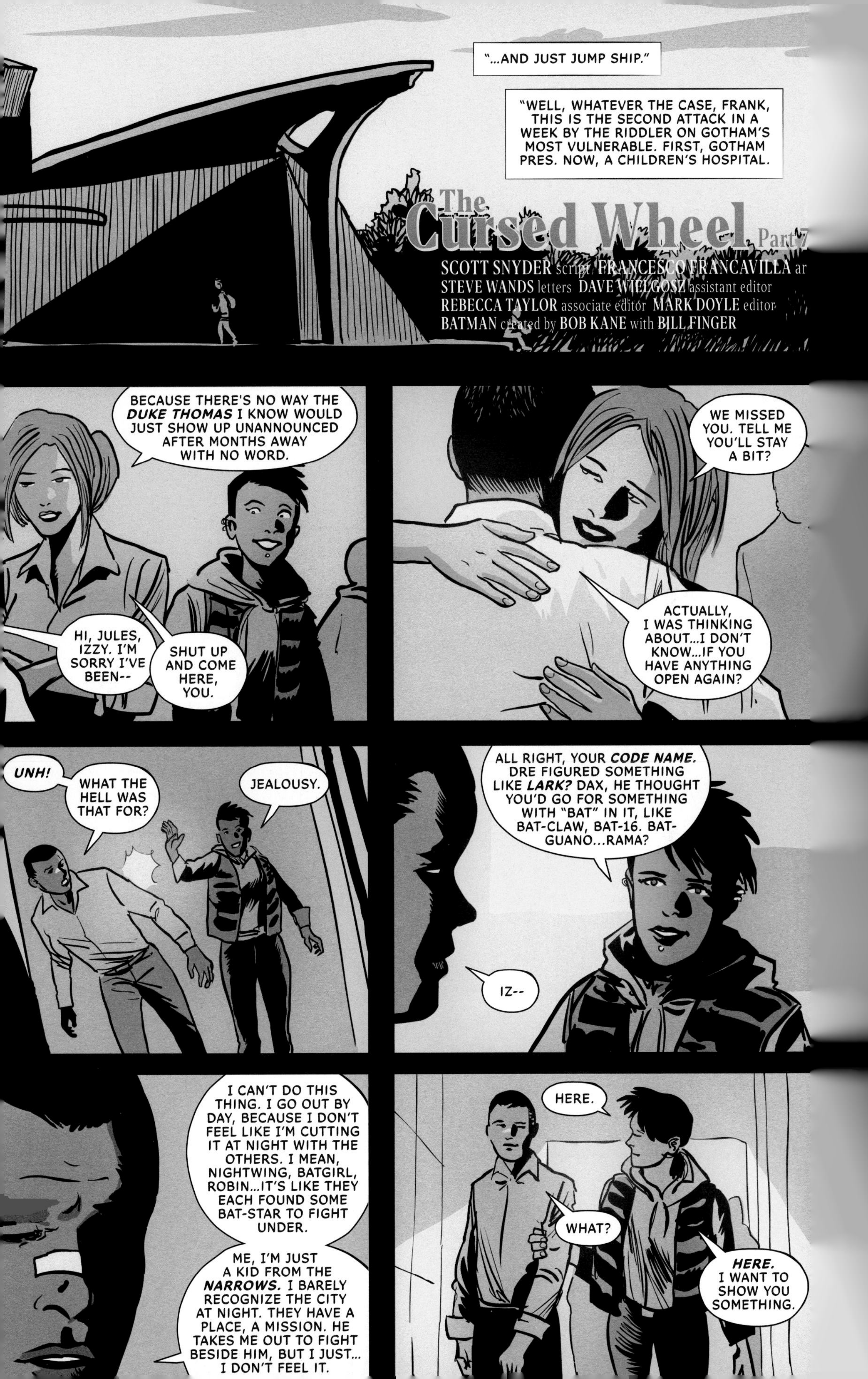
"...AND JUST JUMP SHIP."
"WELL, WHATEVER THE CASE, FRANK, THIS IS THE SECOND ATTACK IN A WEEK BY THE RIDDLER ON GOTHAM'S MOST VULNERABLE. FIRST, GOTHAM PRES. NOW, A CHILDREN'S HOSPITAL.
The Cursed Wheel Part 7
SCOTT SNYDER script FRANCESCO FRANCAVILLA art
STEVE WANDS letters DAVE WIELGOSZ assistant editor
REBECCA TAYLOR associate editor MARK DOYLE editor
BATMAN created by BOB KANE with BILL FINGER
BECAUSE THERE'S NO WAY THE DUKE THOMAS I KNOW WOULD JUST SHOW UP UNANNOUNCED AFTER MONTHS AWAY WITH NO WORD.
HI, JULES, IZZY. I'M SORRY I'VE BEEN--
SHUT UP AND COME HERE, YOU.
WE MISSED YOU. TELL ME YOU'LL STAY A BIT?
ACTUALLY, I WAS THINKING ABOUT...I DON'T KNOW...IF YOU HAVE ANYTHING OPEN AGAIN?
UNH!
WHAT THE HELL WAS THAT FOR?
JEALOUSY.
ALL RIGHT, YOUR CODE NAME. DRE FIGURED SOMETHING LIKE LARK? DAX, HE THOUGHT YOU'D GO FOR SOMETHING WITH "BAT" IN IT, LIKE BAT-CLAW, BAT-16. BAT-GUANO...RAMA?
IZ--
I CAN'T DO THIS THING. I GO OUT BY DAY, BECAUSE I DON'T FEEL LIKE I'M CUTTING IT AT NIGHT WITH THE OTHERS. I MEAN, NIGHTWING, BATGIRL, ROBIN...IT'S LIKE THEY EACH FOUND SOME BAT-STAR TO FIGHT UNDER.
ME, I'M JUST A KID FROM THE NARROWS. I BARELY RECOGNIZE THE CITY AT NIGHT. THEY HAVE A PLACE, A MISSION. HE TAKES ME OUT TO FIGHT BESIDE HIM, BUT I JUST... I DON'T FEEL IT.
HERE.
WHAT?
HERE. I WANT TO SHOW YOU SOMETHING.

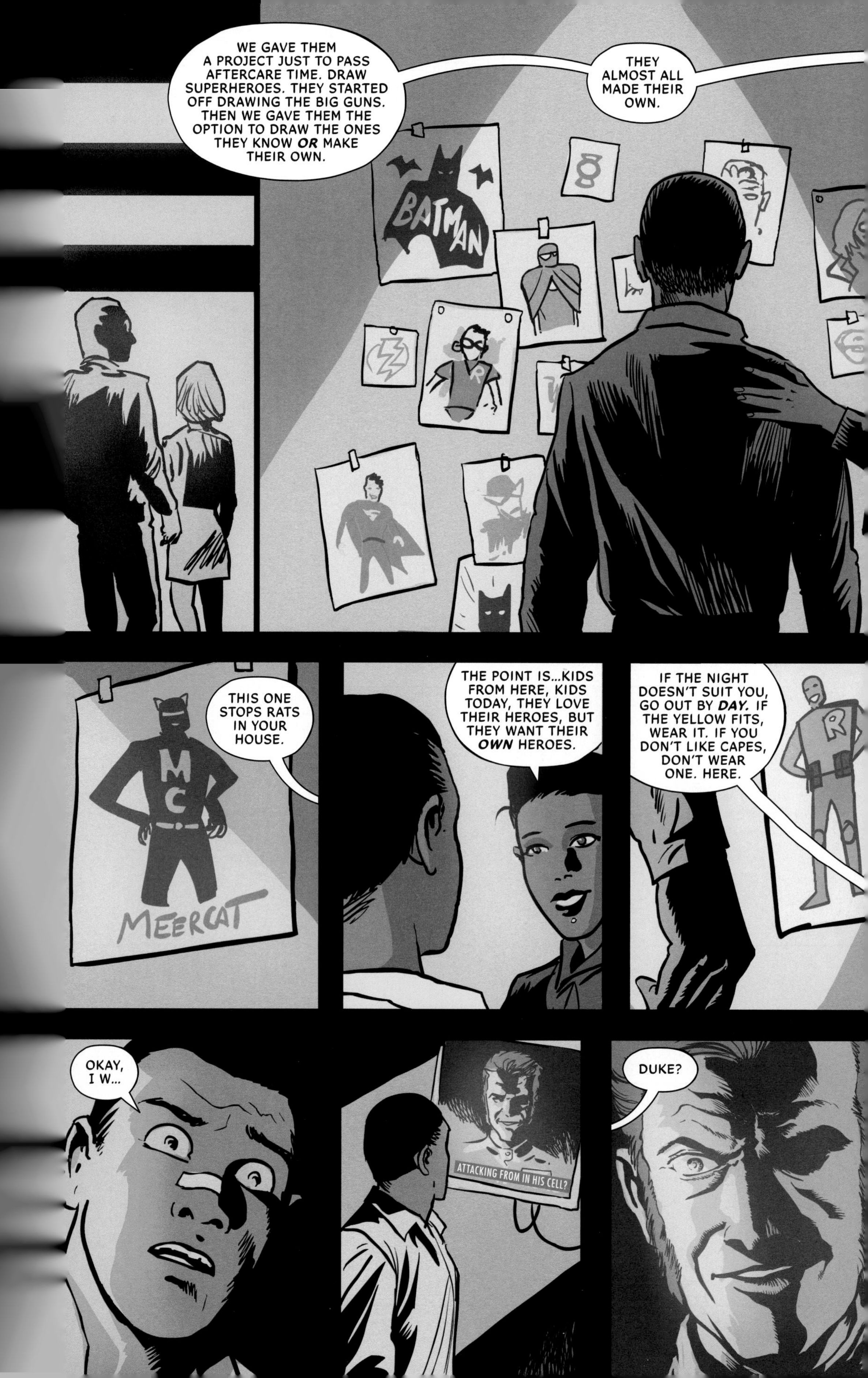
WE GAVE THEM A PROJECT JUST TO PASS AFTERCARE TIME. DRAW SUPERHEROES. THEY STARTED OFF DRAWING THE BIG GUNS. THEN WE GAVE THEM THE OPTION TO DRAW THE ONES THEY KNOW OR MAKE THEIR OWN.
THEY ALMOST ALL MADE THEIR OWN.
BATMAN
THIS ONE STOPS RATS IN YOUR HOUSE.
MC
MEERCAT
THE POINT IS...KIDS FROM HERE, KIDS TODAY, THEY LOVE THEIR HEROES, BUT THEY WANT THEIR OWN HEROES.
IF THE NIGHT DOESN'T SUIT YOU, GO OUT BY DAY. IF THE YELLOW FITS, WEAR IT. IF YOU DON'T LIKE CAPES, DON'T WEAR ONE. HERE.
R
OKAY, I W...
ATTACKING FROM IN HIS CELL?
DUKE?

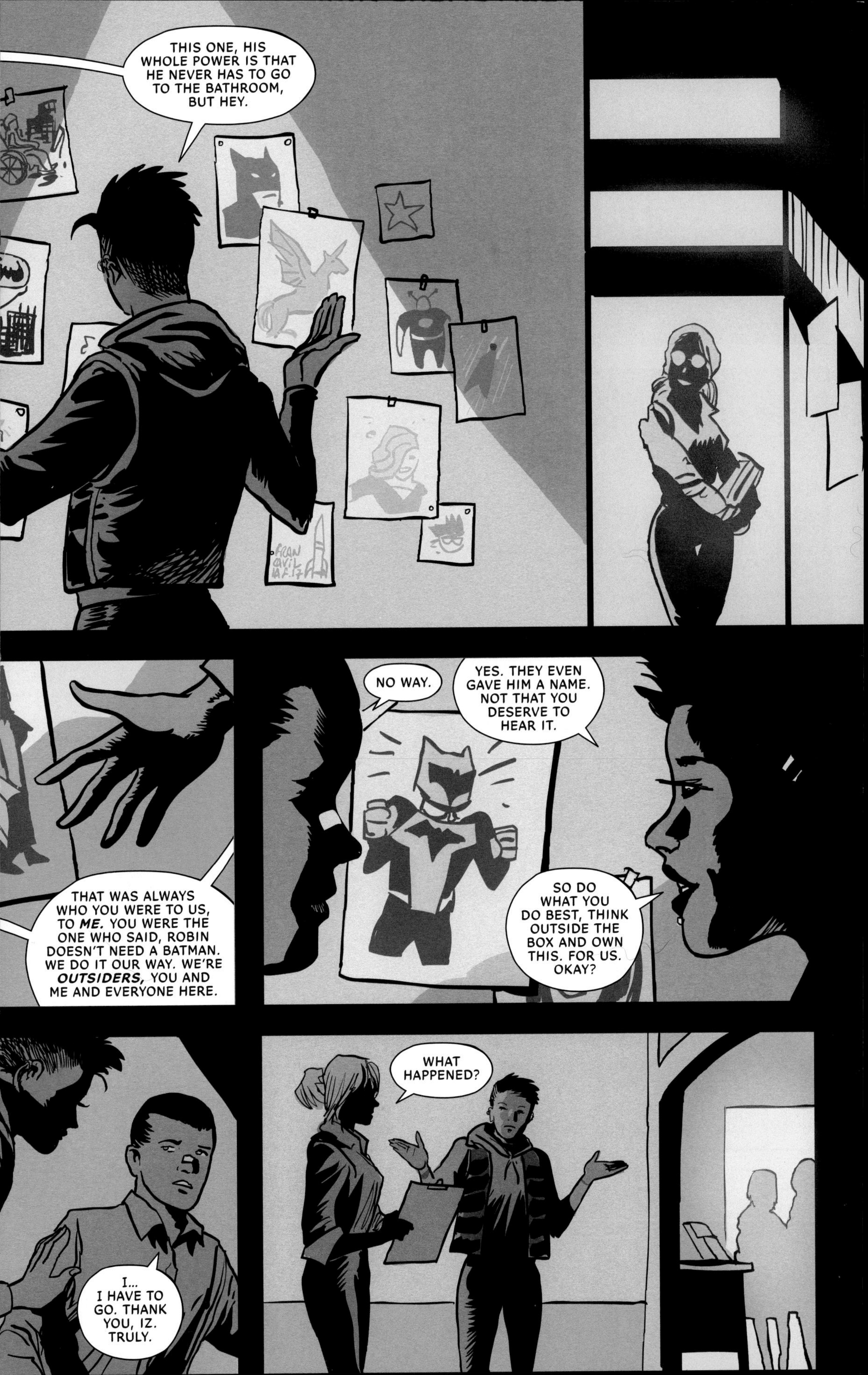
THIS ONE, HIS WHOLE POWER IS THAT HE NEVER HAS TO GO TO THE BATHROOM, BUT HEY.
FRAN GAVIL IAF.17
THAT WAS ALWAYS WHO YOU WERE TO US, TO ME. YOU WERE THE ONE WHO SAID, ROBIN DOESN'T NEED A BATMAN. WE DO IT OUR WAY. WE'RE OUTSIDERS, YOU AND ME AND EVERYONE HERE.
NO WAY.
YES. THEY EVEN GAVE HIM A NAME. NOT THAT YOU DESERVE TO HEAR IT.
SO DO WHAT YOU DO BEST, THINK OUTSIDE THE BOX AND OWN THIS. FOR US. OKAY?
I... I HAVE TO GO. THANK YOU, IZ. TRULY.
WHAT HAPPENED?

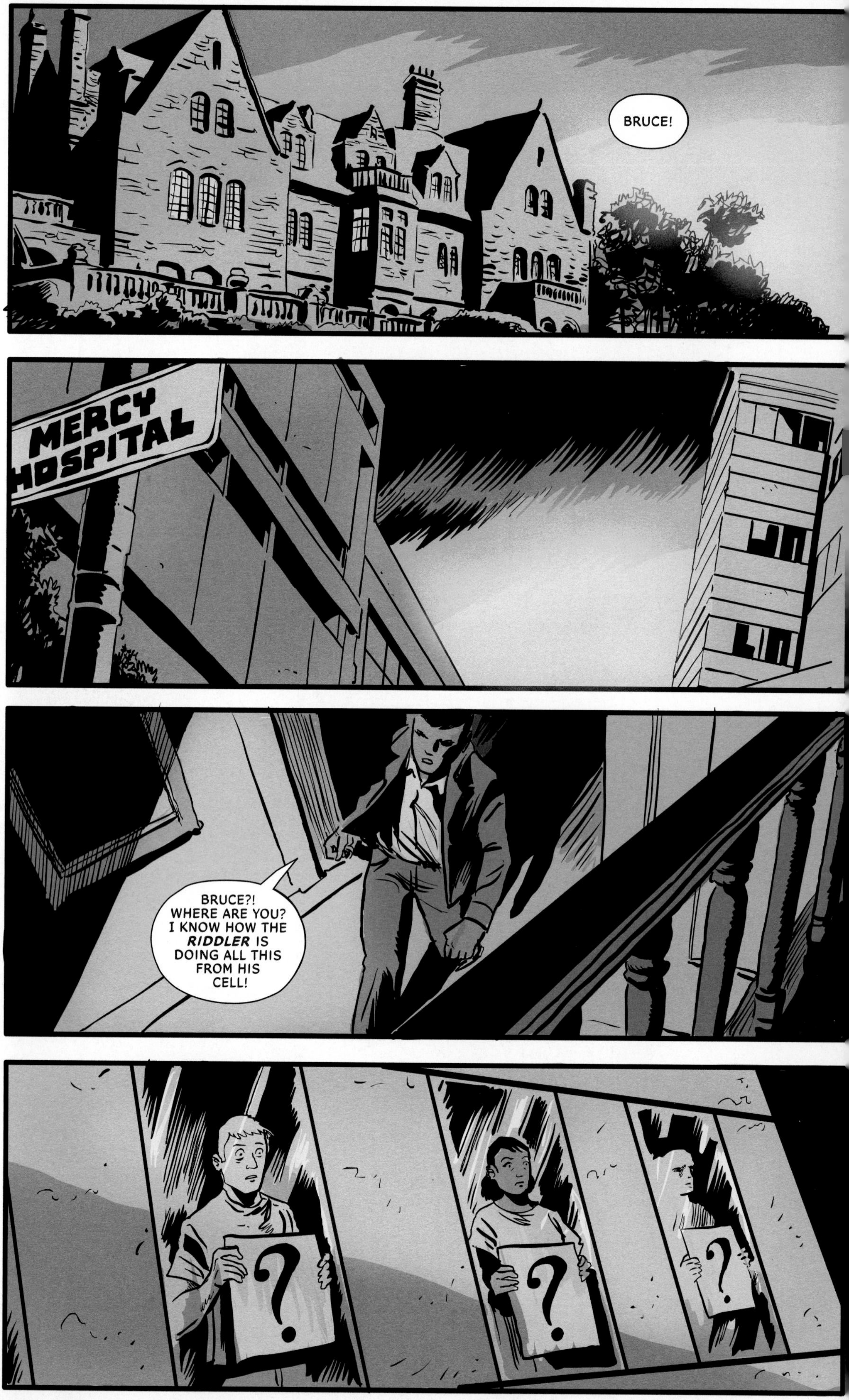
BRUCE!
MERCY HOSPITAL
BRUCE?! WHERE ARE YOU? I KNOW HOW THE *RIDDLER* IS DOING ALL THIS FROM HIS CELL!

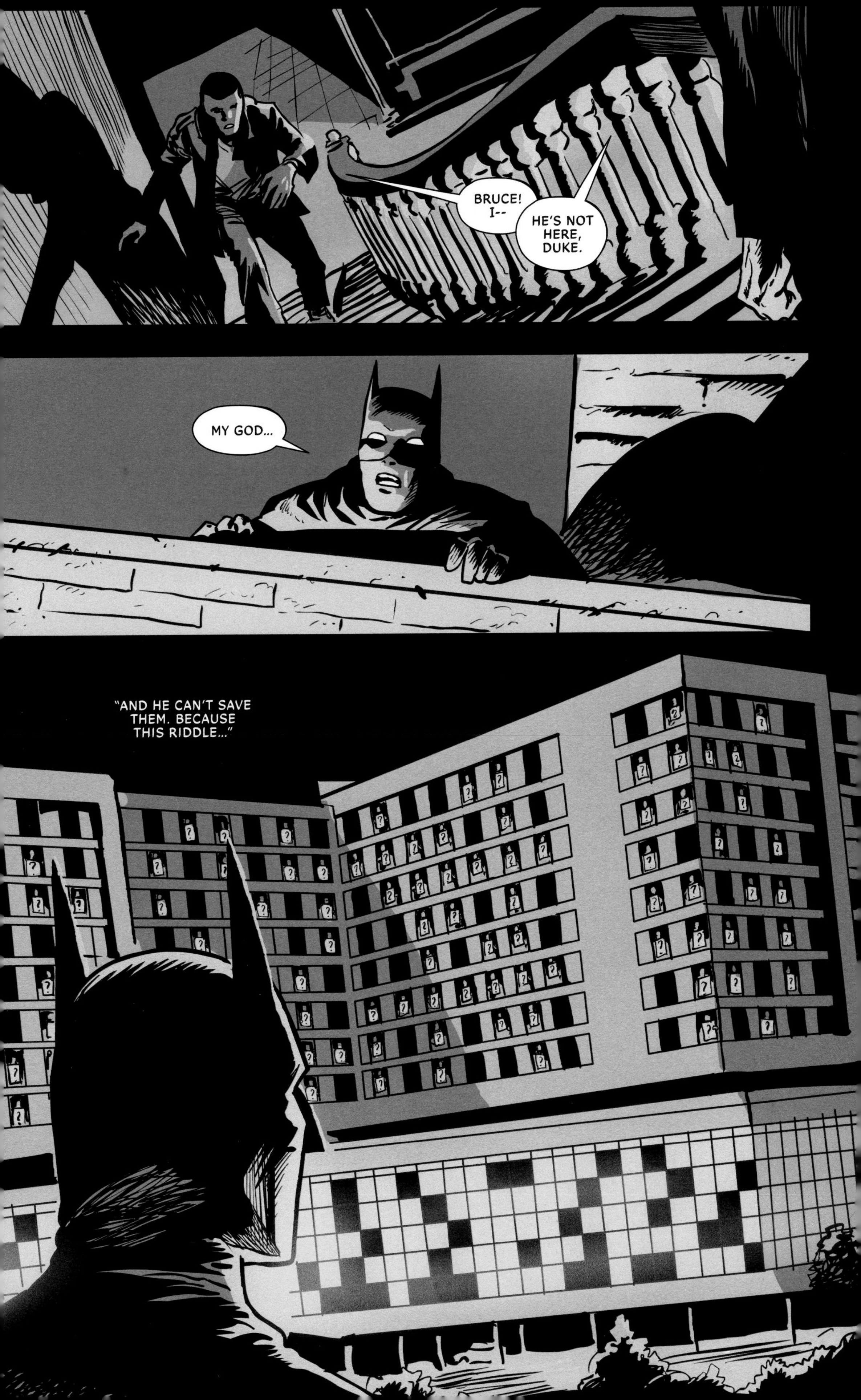
BRUCE! I--
HE'S NOT HERE, DUKE.
MY GOD...
"AND HE CAN'T SAVE THEM. BECAUSE THIS RIDDLE..."

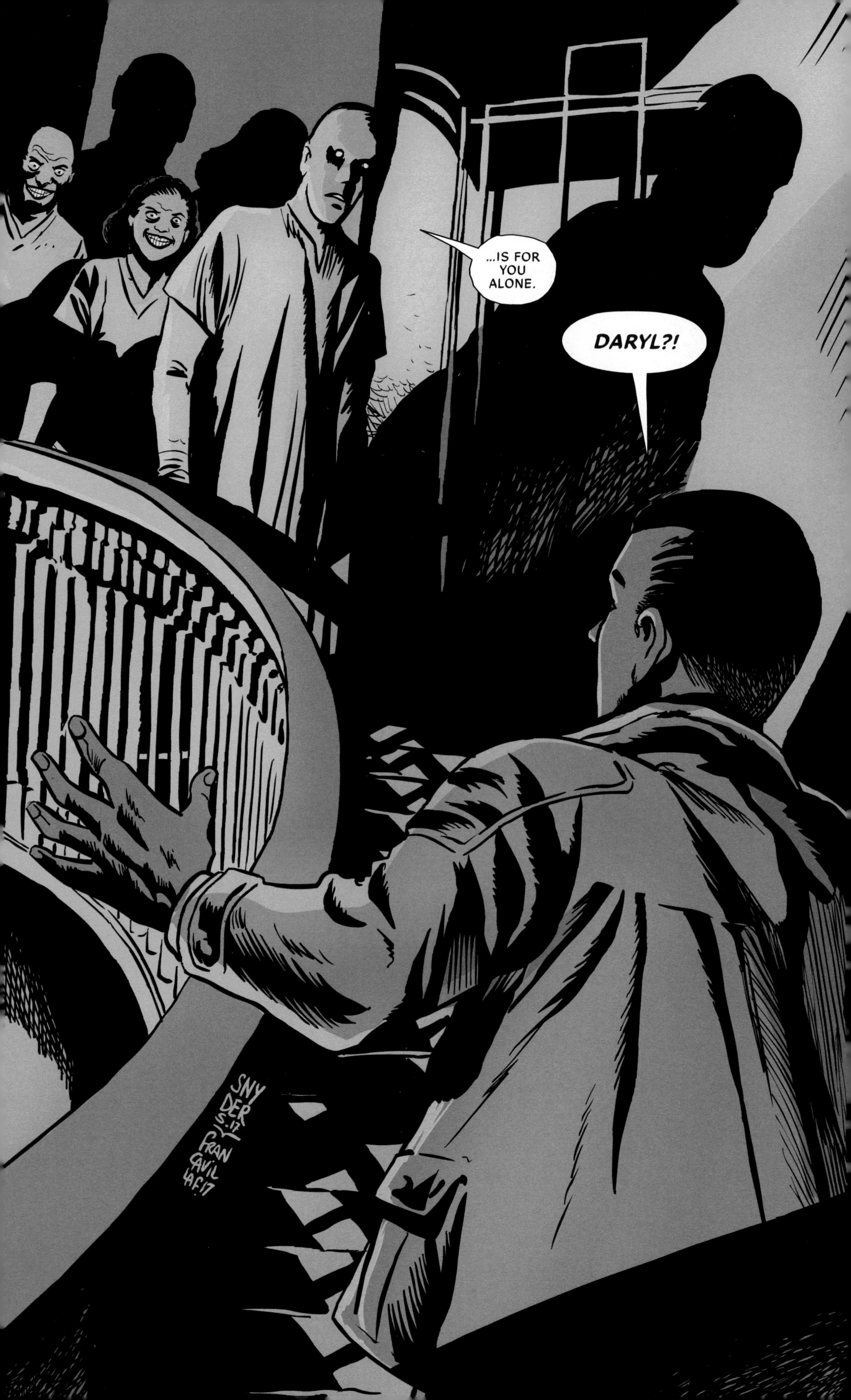
...IS FOR YOU ALONE.
DARYL?!

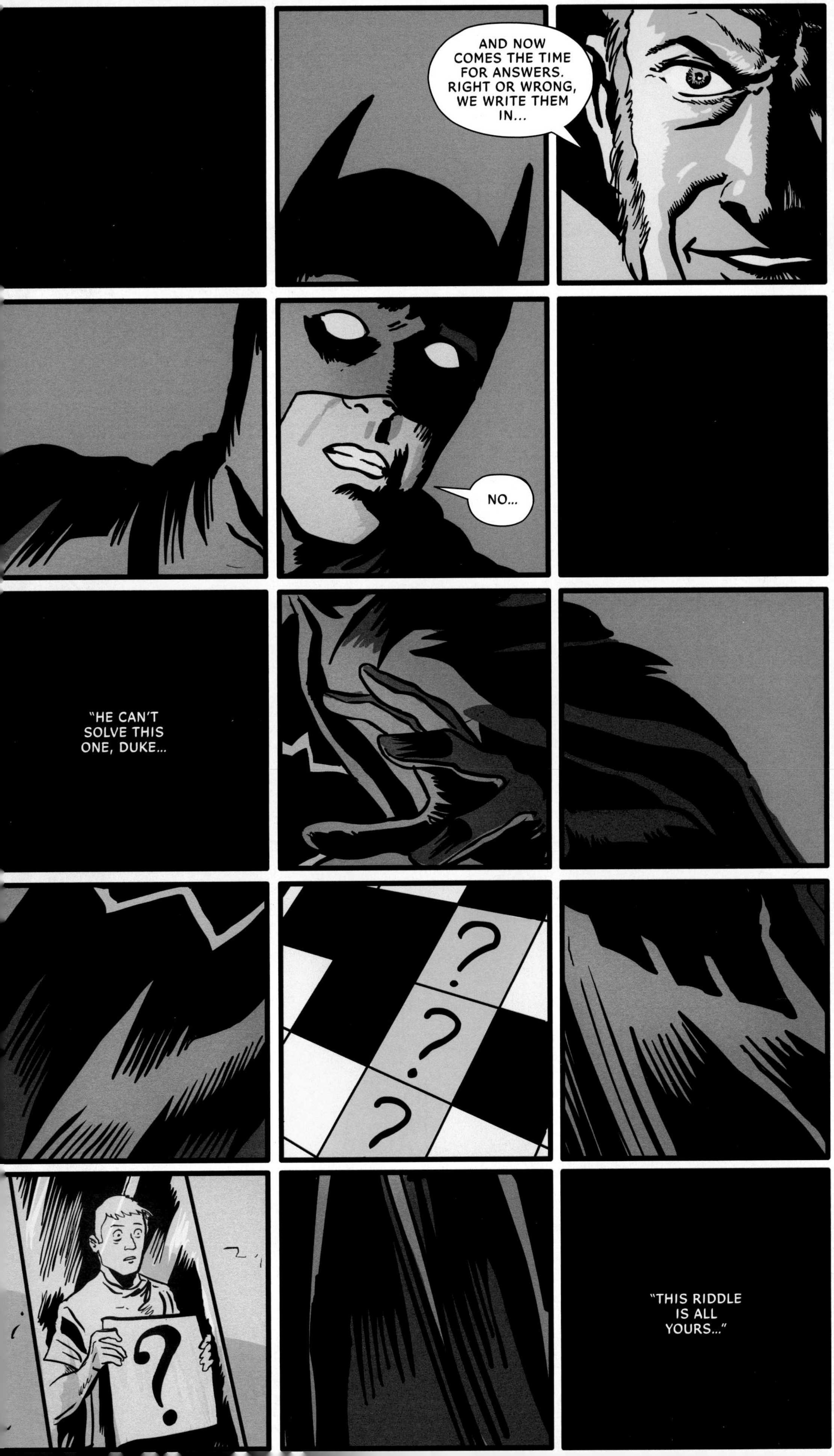
AND NOW COMES THE TIME FOR ANSWERS. RIGHT OR WRONG, WE WRITE THEM IN...
NO...
"HE CAN'T SOLVE THIS ONE, DUKE...
"THIS RIDDLE IS ALL YOURS..."

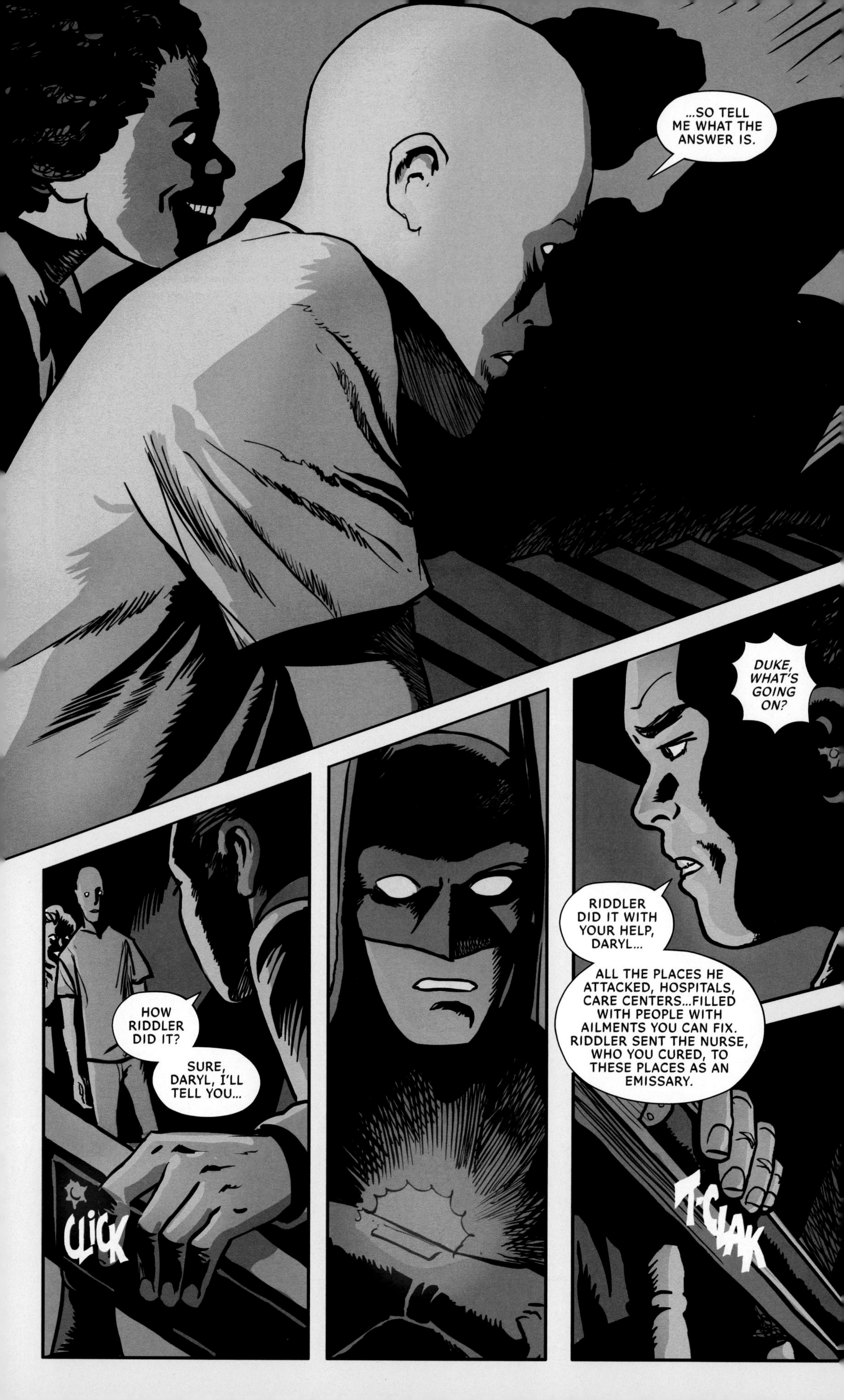
...SO TELL ME WHAT THE ANSWER IS.
DUKE, WHAT'S GOING ON?
HOW RIDDLER DID IT?
SURE, DARYL, I'LL TELL YOU...
CLICK
RIDDLER DID IT WITH YOUR HELP, DARYL...
ALL THE PLACES HE ATTACKED, HOSPITALS, CARE CENTERS...FILLED WITH PEOPLE WITH AILMENTS YOU CAN FIX. RIDDLER SENT THE NURSE, WHO YOU CURED, TO THESE PLACES AS AN EMISSARY.
T-CLAK

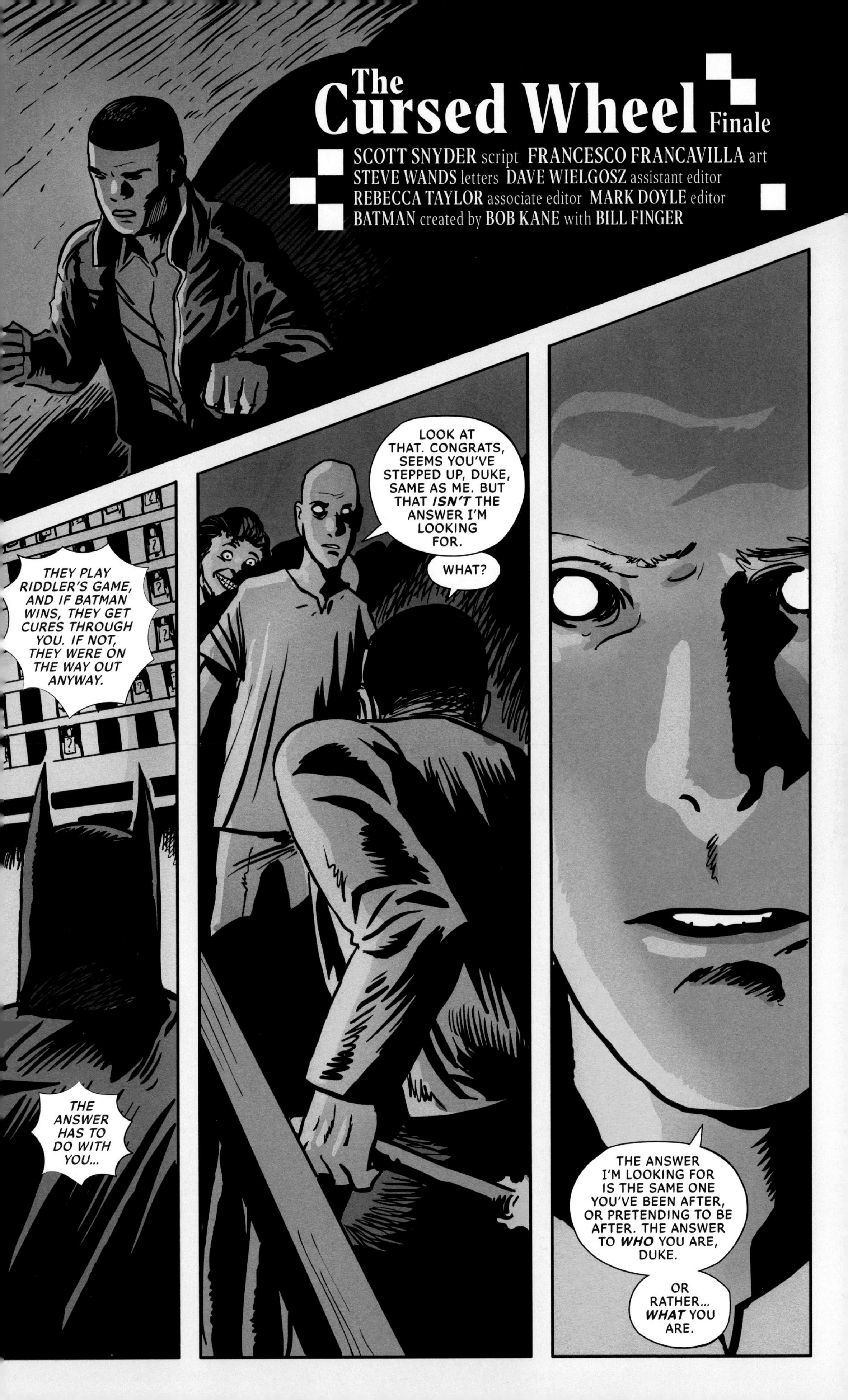
The Cursed Wheel Finale
SCOTT SNYDER script FRANCESCO FRANCAVILLA art
STEVE WANDS letters DAVE WIELGOSZ assistant editor
REBECCA TAYLOR associate editor MARK DOYLE editor
BATMAN created by BOB KANE with BILL FINGER
THEY PLAY RIDDLER'S GAME, AND IF BATMAN WINS, THEY GET CURES THROUGH YOU. IF NOT, THEY WERE ON THE WAY OUT ANYWAY.
THE ANSWER HAS TO DO WITH YOU...
LOOK AT THAT. CONGRATS, SEEMS YOU'VE STEPPED UP, DUKE, SAME AS ME. BUT THAT *ISN'T* THE ANSWER I'M LOOKING FOR.
WHAT?
THE ANSWER I'M LOOKING FOR IS THE SAME ONE YOU'VE BEEN AFTER, OR PRETENDING TO BE AFTER. THE ANSWER TO *WHO* YOU ARE, DUKE.
OR RATHER... *WHAT* YOU ARE.

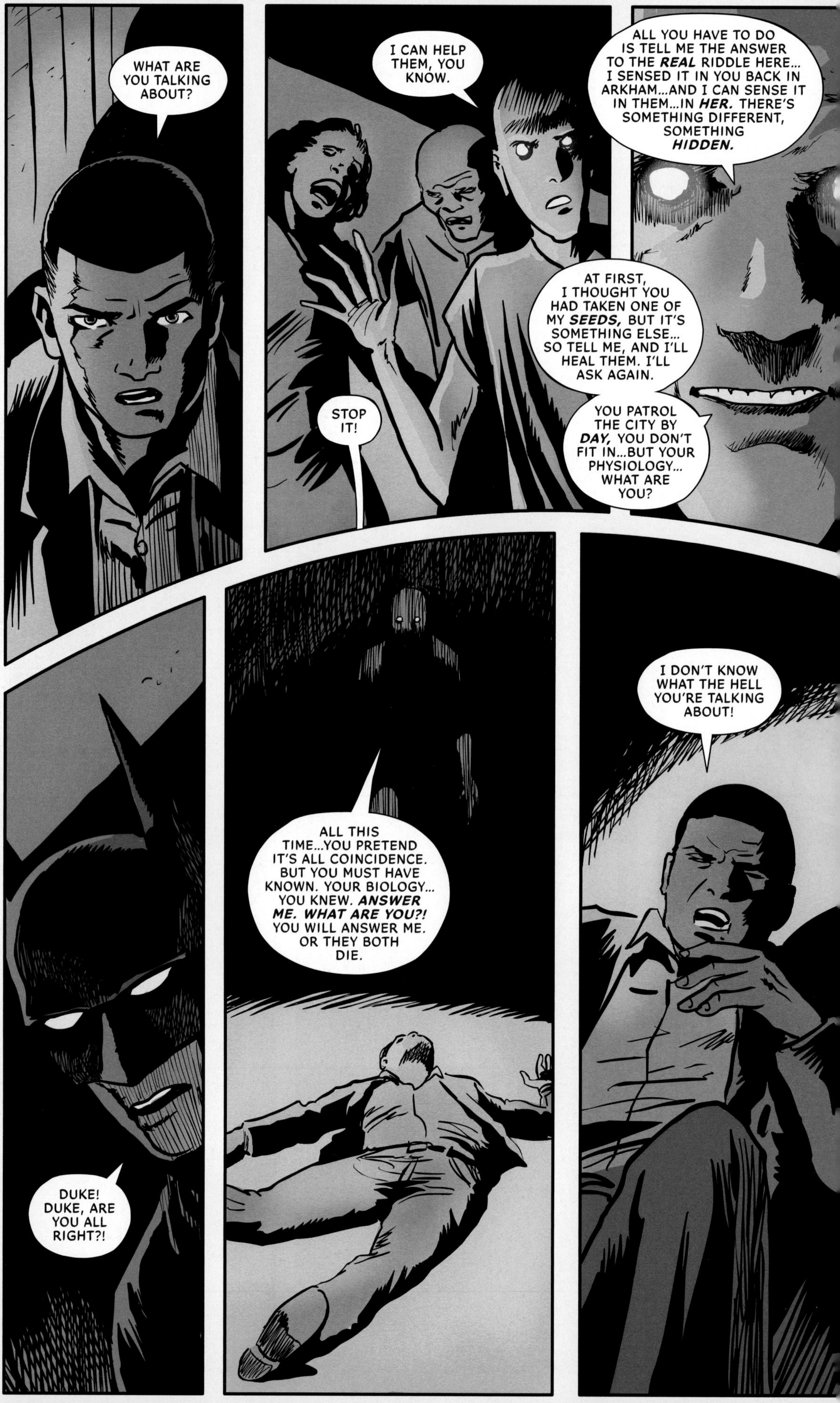
WHAT ARE YOU TALKING ABOUT?
I CAN HELP THEM, YOU KNOW.
STOP IT!
ALL YOU HAVE TO DO IS TELL ME THE ANSWER TO THE REAL RIDDLE HERE... I SENSED IT IN YOU BACK IN ARKHAM...AND I CAN SENSE IT IN THEM...IN HER. THERE'S SOMETHING DIFFERENT, SOMETHING HIDDEN.
AT FIRST, I THOUGHT YOU HAD TAKEN ONE OF MY SEEDS, BUT IT'S SOMETHING ELSE... SO TELL ME, AND I'LL HEAL THEM. I'LL ASK AGAIN.
YOU PATROL THE CITY BY DAY, YOU DON'T FIT IN...BUT YOUR PHYSIOLOGY... WHAT ARE YOU?
DUKE! DUKE, ARE YOU ALL RIGHT?!
ALL THIS TIME...YOU PRETEND IT'S ALL COINCIDENCE. BUT YOU MUST HAVE KNOWN. YOUR BIOLOGY... YOU KNEW. ANSWER ME. WHAT ARE YOU?! YOU WILL ANSWER ME. OR THEY BOTH DIE.
I DON'T KNOW WHAT THE HELL YOU'RE TALKING ABOUT!

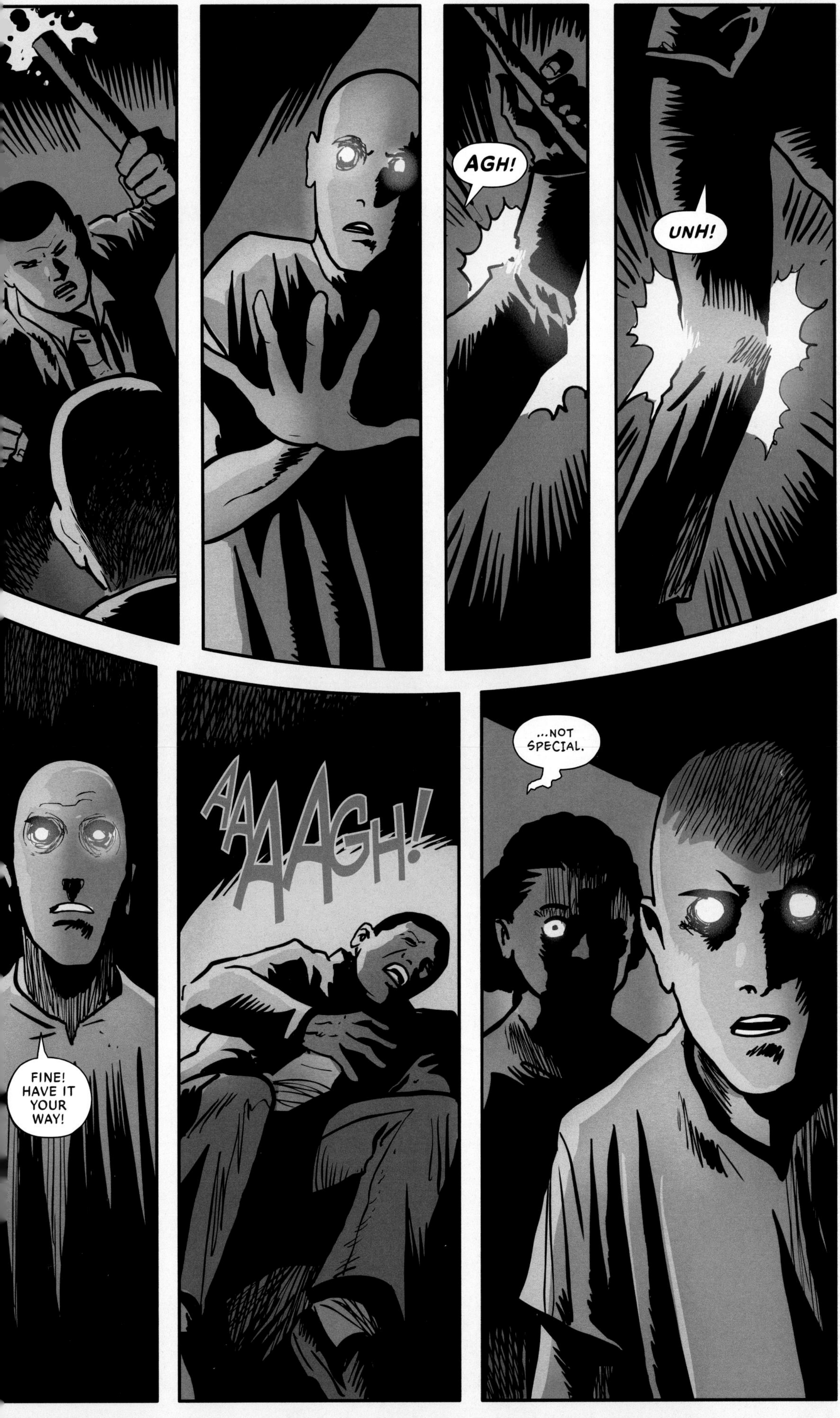
AGH!
UNH!
FINE! HAVE IT YOUR WAY!
AAAAGH!
...NOT SPECIAL.

NOT SPECIAL... NOTHING... NO ONE...

THEN YOU CAN DIE AS A NO ONE. THE PLACEHOLDER YOU ARE. NO ONE'S HERO!

DUKE!

BATMAN, I'M OKAY! IT'S ALL RIGHT.

DARYL WAS THE KEY, DUKE.

NOT... SPECIAL... SPECIAL.

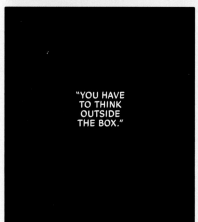

"YOU HAVE TO THINK OUTSIDE THE BOX."

I'LL ASK AGAIN, AND THEN YOU'RE ALL DEAD. WHAT ARE YOU?!

I...

THEN THE ANSWERS...

"...THEY ALL COME FAST."

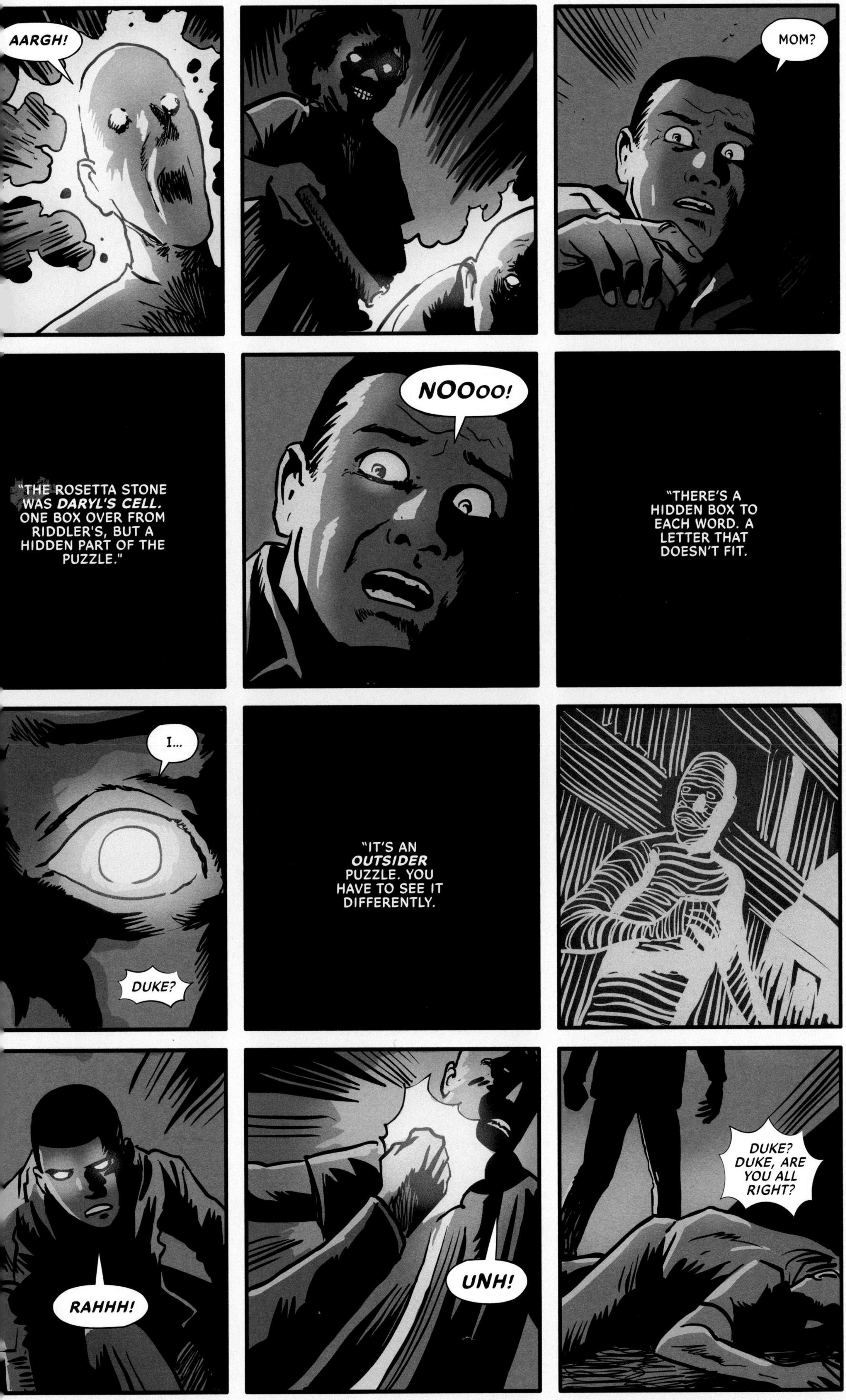
AARGH!
MOM?
"THE ROSETTA STONE WAS DARYL'S CELL. ONE BOX OVER FROM RIDDLER'S, BUT A HIDDEN PART OF THE PUZZLE."
NOOoo!
"THERE'S A HIDDEN BOX TO EACH WORD. A LETTER THAT DOESN'T FIT.
I...
DUKE?
"IT'S AN OUTSIDER PUZZLE. YOU HAVE TO SEE IT DIFFERENTLY.
RAHHH!
UNH!
DUKE? DUKE, ARE YOU ALL RIGHT?

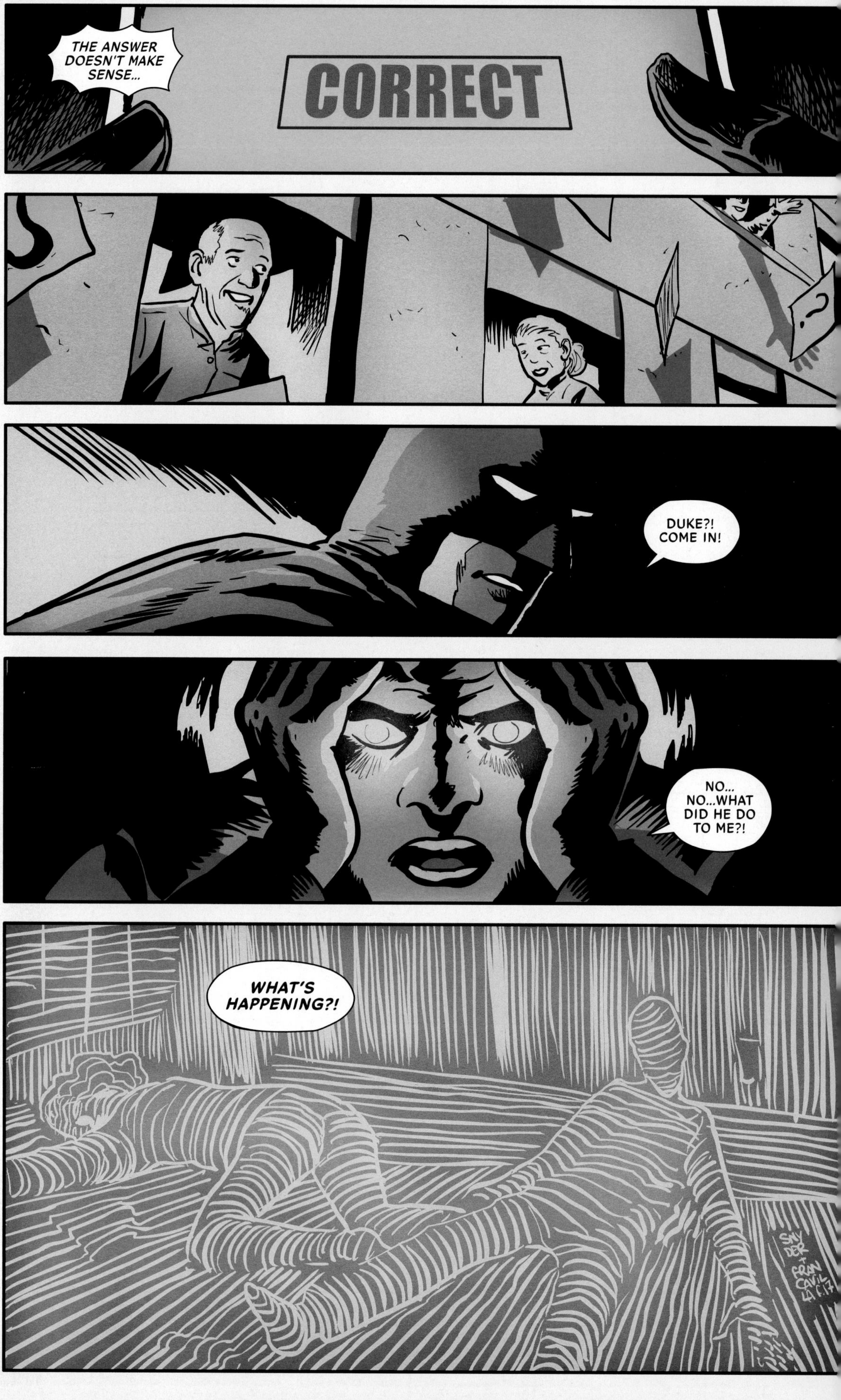
THE ANSWER DOESN'T MAKE SENSE...
CORRECT
DUKE?! COME IN!
NO... NO...WHAT DID HE DO TO ME?!
WHAT'S HAPPENING?!

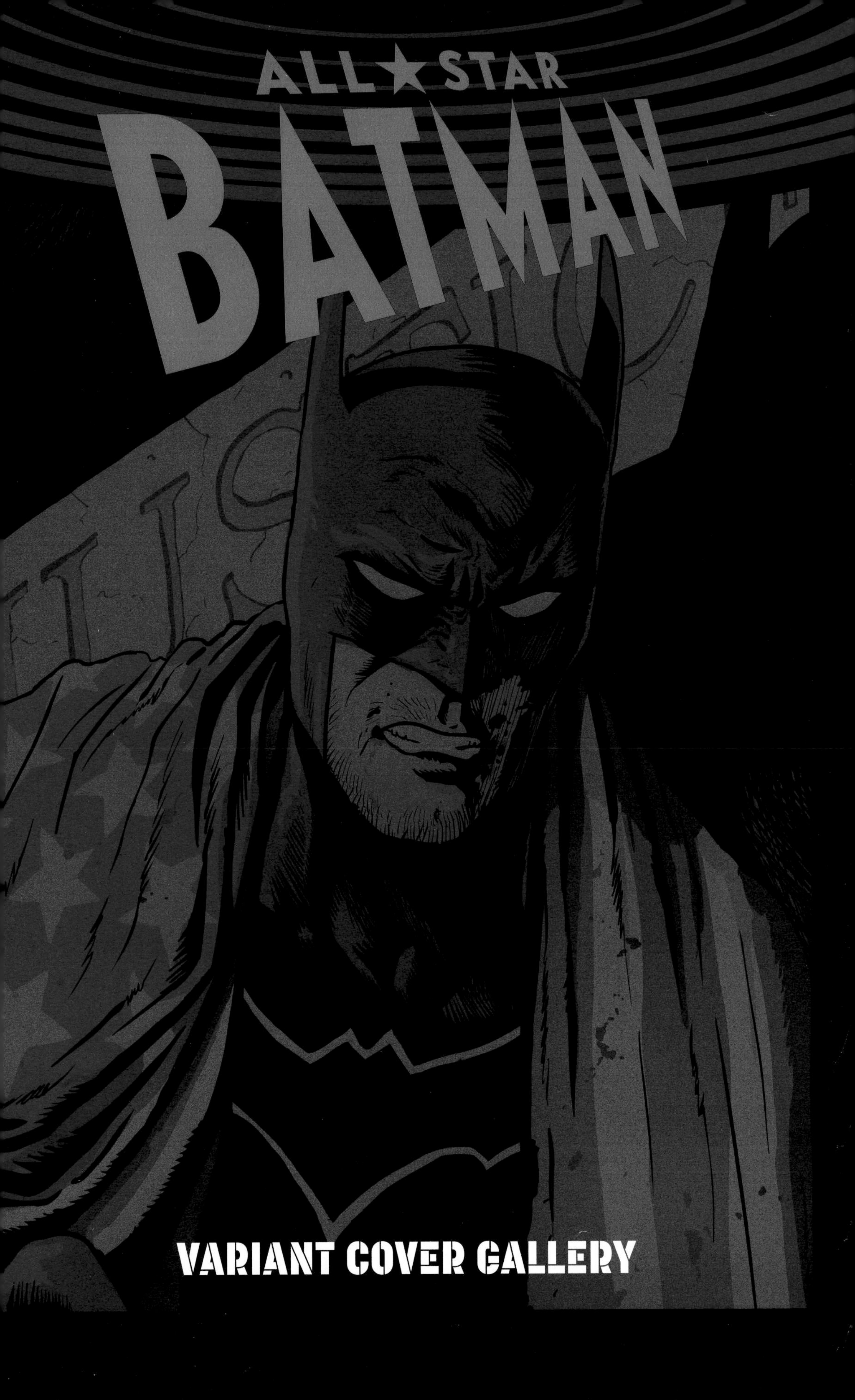
ALL ★ STAR
BATMAN

# VARIANT COVER GALLERY

ALL-STAR BATMAN #6 variant by Jock

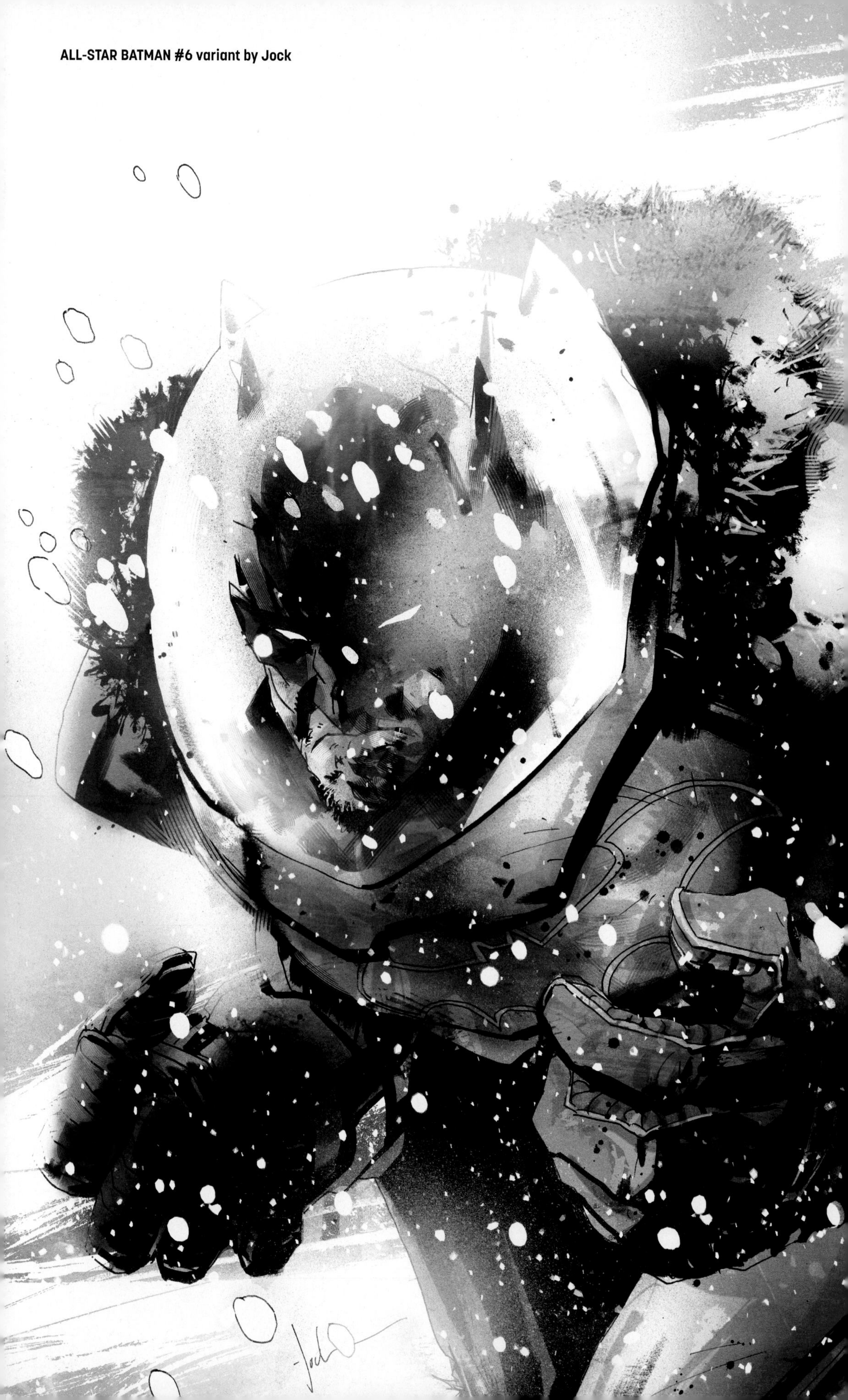

ALL-STAR BATMAN #7
variant by Tula Lotay

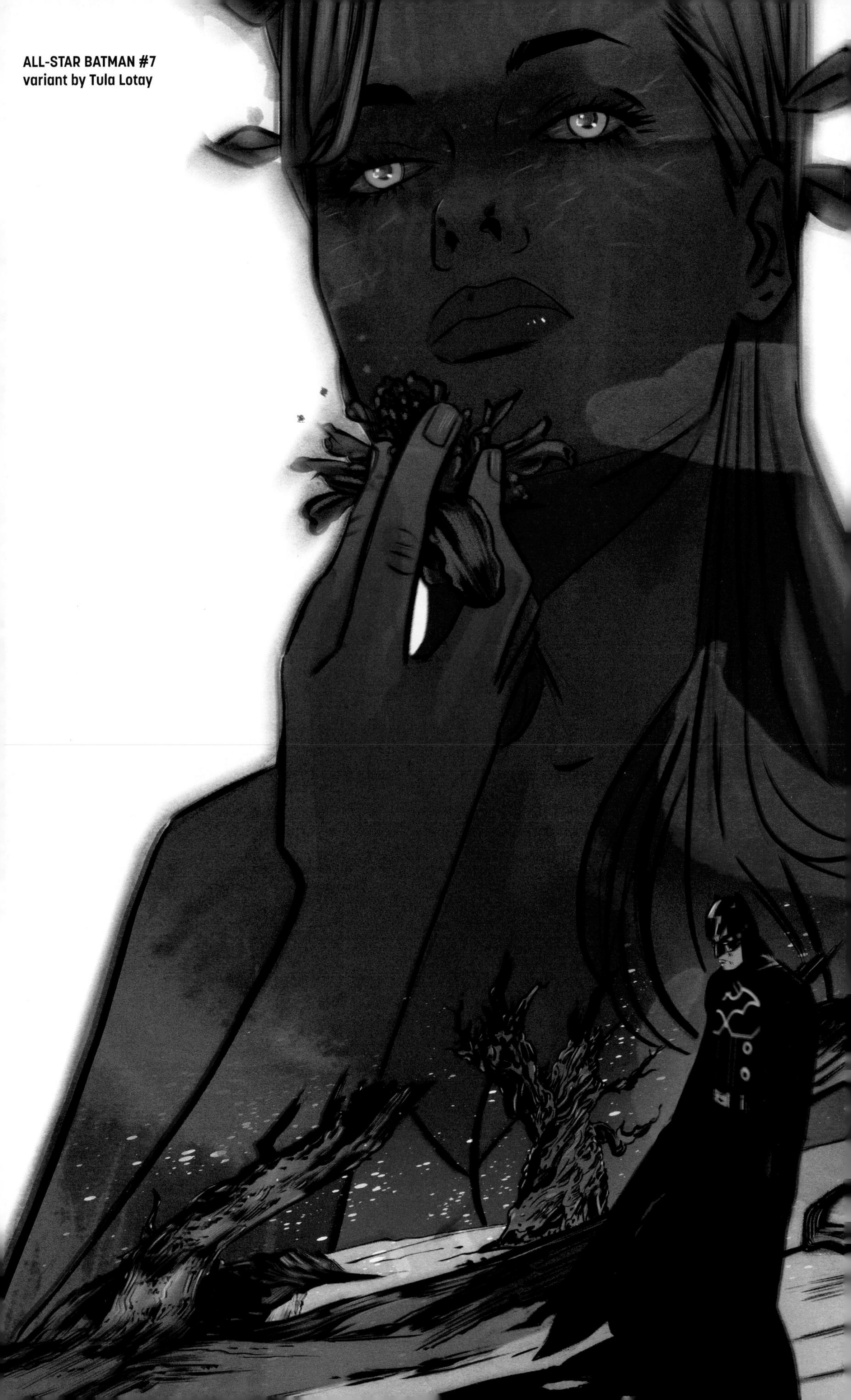

**ALL-STAR BATMAN #8**
**variant by Giuseppe Camuncoli and Dean White**

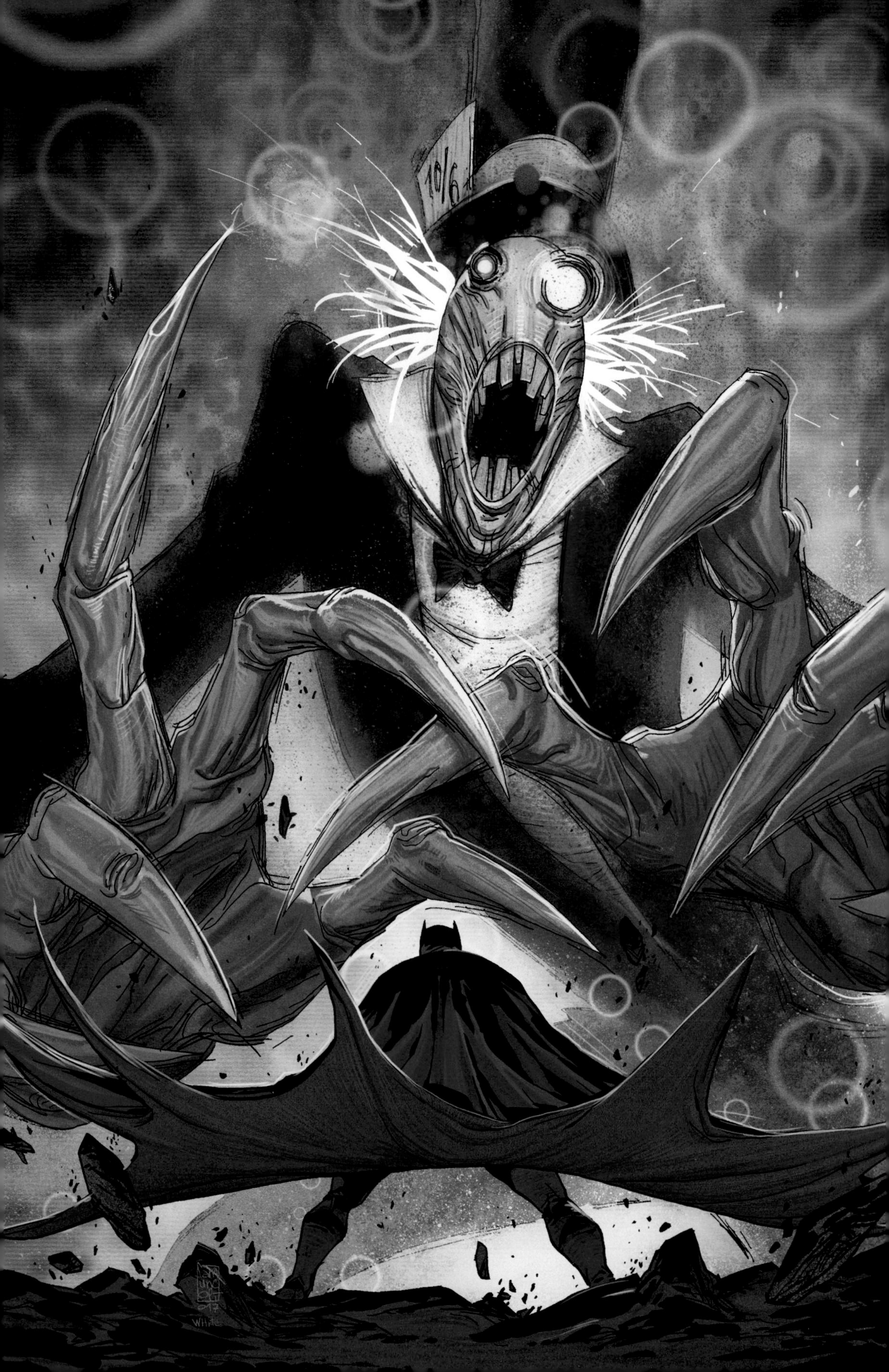
10/6

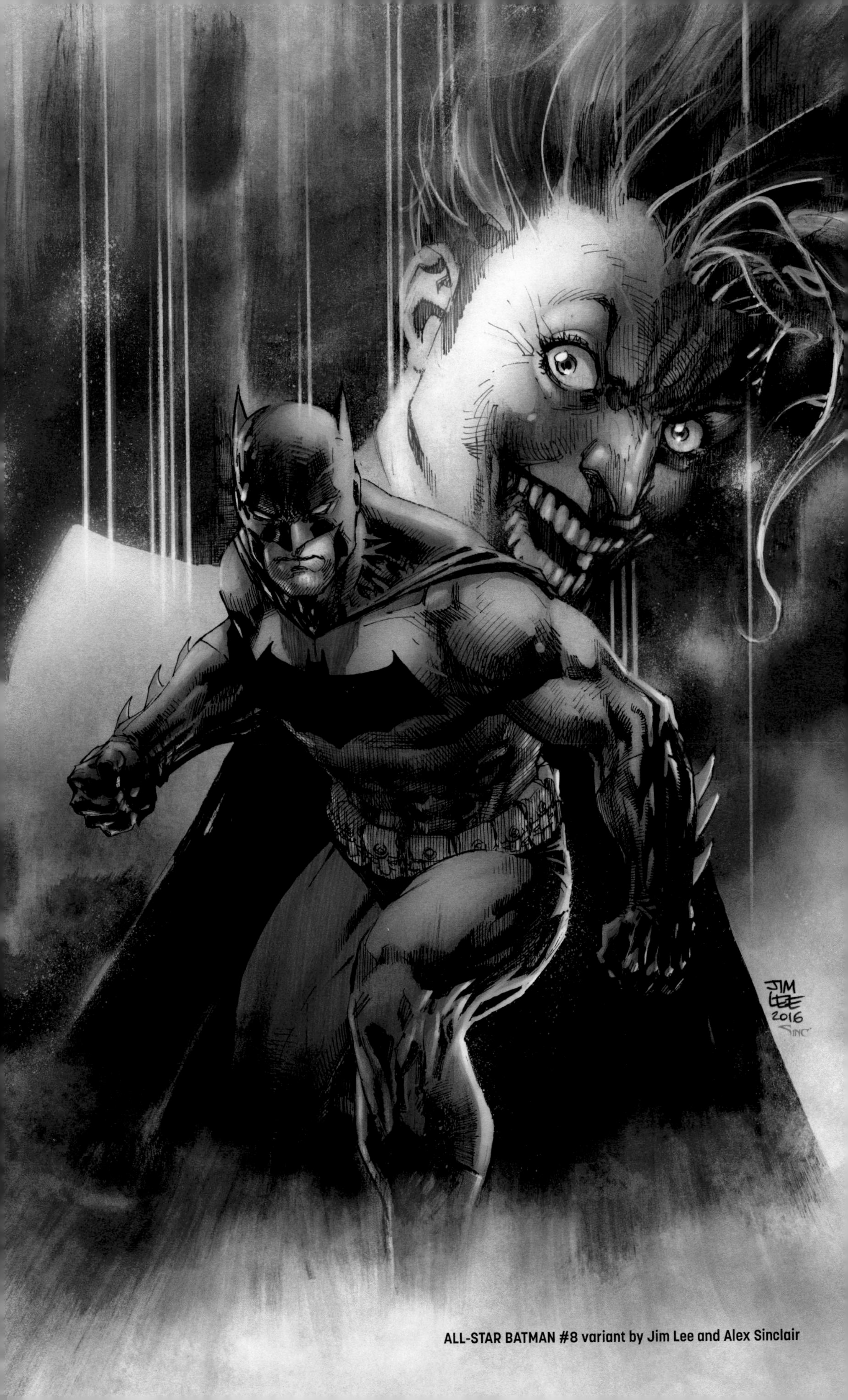
JIM LEE
2016
SINC
ALL-STAR BATMAN #8 variant by Jim Lee and Alex Sinclair

ALL-STAR BATMAN #9 variant by Chris Burnham and Nathan Fairbairn

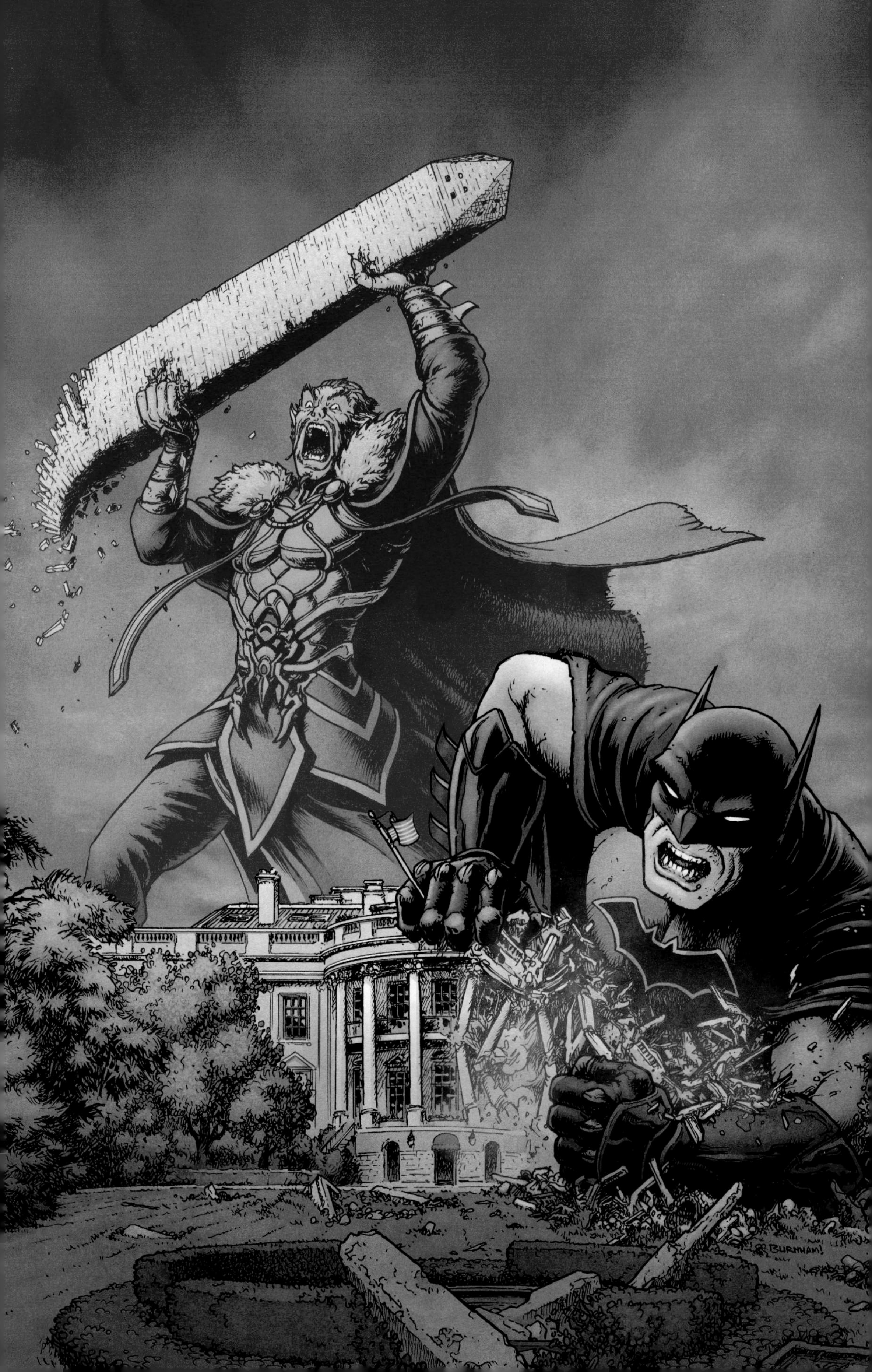
BURNHAM

**ALL-STAR BATMAN #6 variant by Francesco Francavilla**

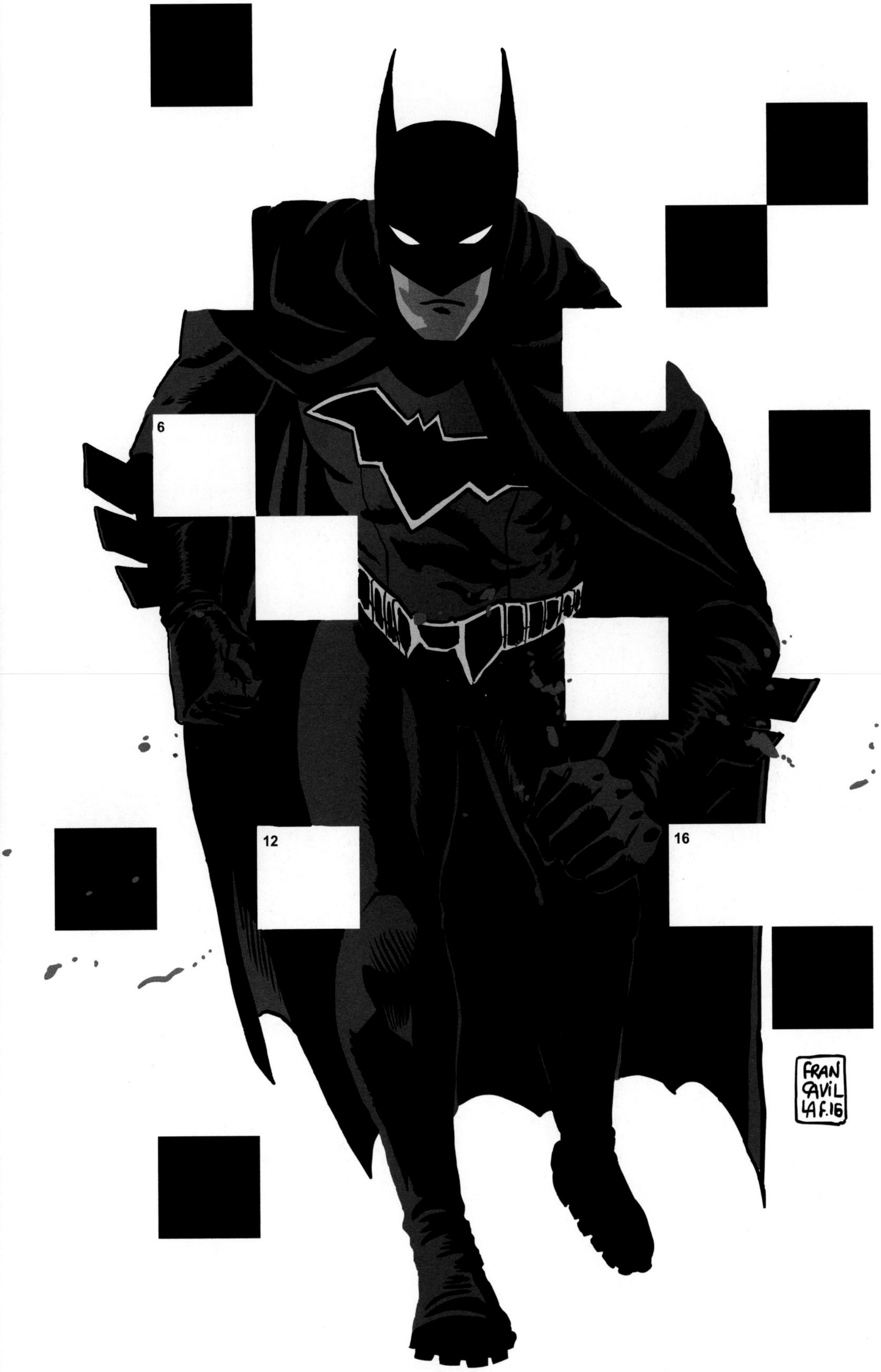
6
12
16
FRAN
CAVIL
LA F.16

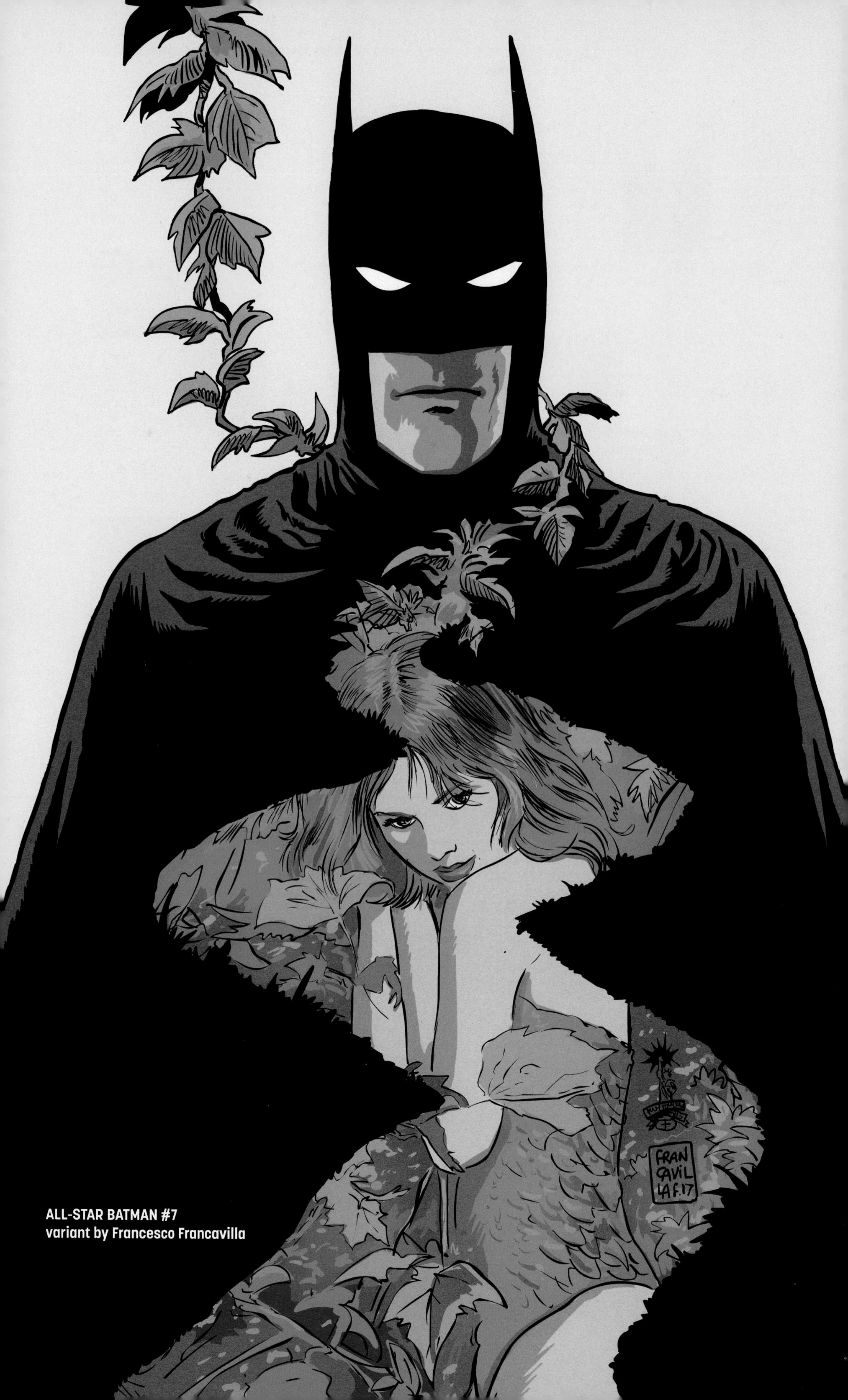
FRAN
CAVIL
LA F.17

ALL-STAR BATMAN #7
variant by Francesco Francavilla

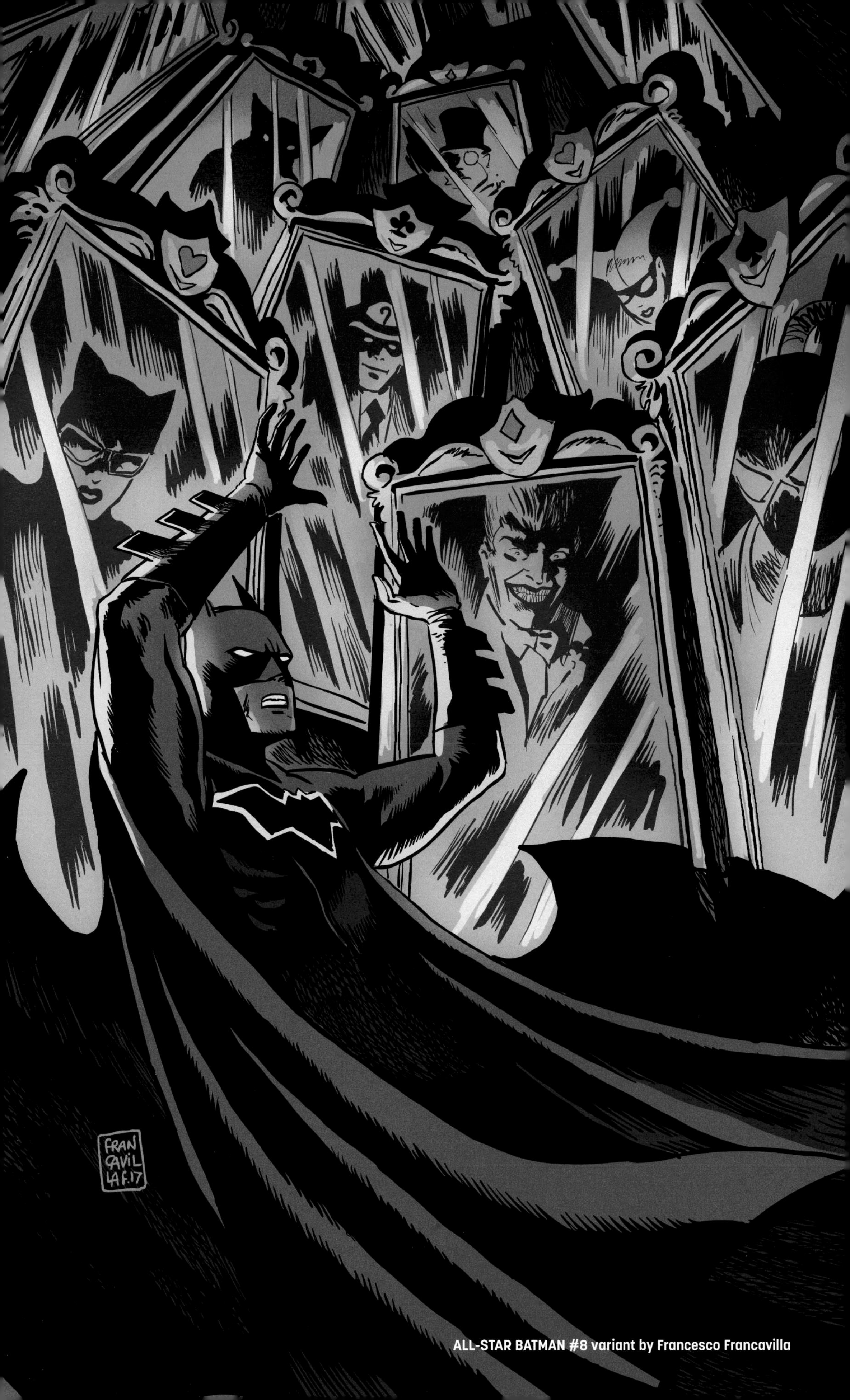
FRAN
CAVIL
LA F.17

**ALL-STAR BATMAN #8 variant by Francesco Francavilla**

ALL-STAR BATMAN #9 variant by Francesco Francavilla

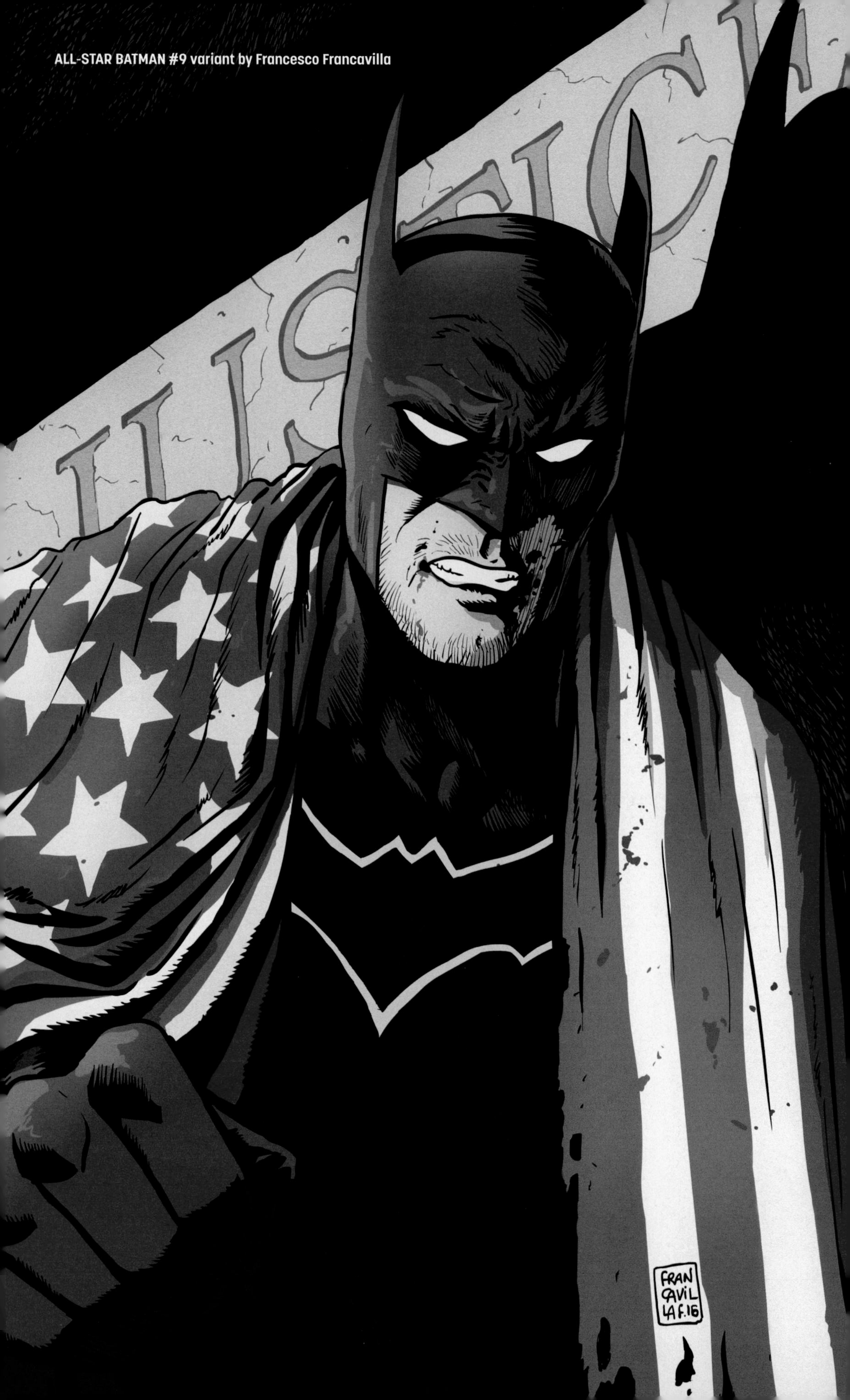
FRAN
CAVIL
LA F.16

"[Writer Scott Snyder] pulls from
he oldest aspects of the Batman
yth, combines it with sinister-
omic elements from the series'
est period, and gives the whole
hing terrific forward-spin."
**ENTERTAINMENT WEEKLY**

THE #1 NEW YORK TIMES BESTSELLER
THE NEW 52!
BATMAN
VOLUME 1
THE COURT OF OWLS
"SNYDER MIGHT BE THE DEFINING BATMAN WRITER OF OUR GENERATION."
— COMPLEX MAGAZINE
SCOTT SNYDER GREG CAPULLO JONATHAN GLAPION


TART AT THE BEGINNING!

# BATMAN

## OL. 1: THE COURT OF OWLS

COTT SNYDER with GREG CAPULLO

THE #1 NEW YORK TIMES BEST-SELLING SERIES
THE NEW 52!
BATMAN
"ONE OF THE BEST TITLES ON THE MARKET."
—THE ONION / AV CLUB
VOLUME 2
THE CITY OF OWLS
SCOTT SNYDER GREG CAPULLO JONATHAN GLAPION JAMES TYNION IV
RAFAEL ALBUQUERQUE JASON FABOK


**BATMAN VOL. 2: THE CITY OF OWLS**

THE NEW YORK TIMES #1 BEST-SELLING SERIES
THE NEW 52!
BATMAN
"THIS IS A BOOK YOU NEED TO READ."
– HUFFINGTON POST
VOLUME 3
DEATH OF THE FAMILY
SCOTT SNYDER GREG CAPULLO JONATHAN GLAPION


**BATMAN VOL. 3: DEATH OF THE FAMILY**

## READ THE ENTIRE EPIC!

BATMAN VOL. 4: ZERO YEAR – SECRET CITY

BATMAN VOL. 5: ZERO YEAR – DARK CITY

BATMAN VOL. 6: GRAVEYARD SHIFT

BATMAN VOL. 7: ENDGAME

BATMAN VOL. 8: SUPERHEAVY

BATMAN VOL. 9: BLOOM

BATMAN VOL. 10: EPILOGUE

Get more DC graphic novels wherever comics and books are sold!

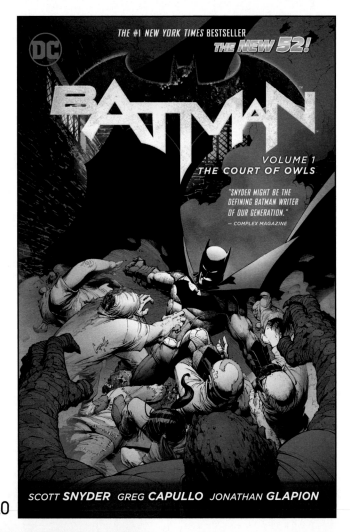

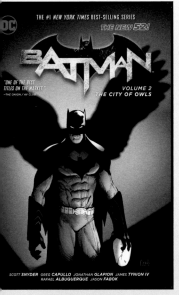

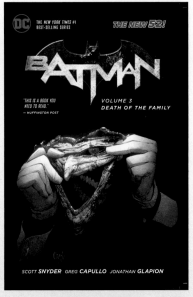

# SCOTT SNYDER
## with JOCK and FRANCESCO FRANCAVILLA

**SUPERMAN: UNCHAINED**
**with JIM LEE and others**

**BATMAN: GATES OF GOTHAM**
**with TREVOR MCCARTHY and others**

**BATMAN: ETERNAL**
**with JASON FABOK and others**